PINCKNEY COMMUNITY
PUBLIC LIBRARY

DISCARDED
Pinckney Community Public Library

Cycle History: Proceedings of the 5th. International Cycle History Conference

Cycle History

Proceedings of the 5th. International Cycle History Conference

**Cambridge, England
September 2–4, 1994**

Edited by Rob van der Plas

Frontispiece photograph from Andrew Ritchie
collection, provided by John Malseed and Rod Safe

**Published by Bicycle Books, Inc., San Francisco
on behalf of the International Cycle History Conference**

Copyright	© with the individual authors, 1995
1st printing	February 1995
Printed	in the United States of America by Thomson-Shore, Dexter, MI
Cover design	Rob van der Plas, based on historic illustrations provided by Andrew Ritchie
Published by	Bicycle Books, Inc. 1282 - 7th Avenue San Francisco, CA 94122 U.S.A. Tel. (415) 665-8214 Fax (415) 753-8572
Availability	Copies of this book available by mail from the publisher at the above address at U.S. $45.00 plus a postage & handling charge of U.S. $3.50 within the U.S. and Canada, elsewhere U.S. $5.00 surface mail, U.S. $12.50 airmail.
Publisher's Commitment	15% of the net proceeds from this publication are earmarked for support of the organizers of the Conference.
Library of Congress Catalogue Card Number	95-75283
ISBN	0-933201-72-9

Table of Contents

1. Thinking About Thinking About Cycles . . . . Russell Mills 11
2. Aspects of a Historical Geography of Technology: A Study of Cycling, 1919–1939 . . . . . . David L. Patton 21
3. Developing a Methodological Approach to the History and Meaning of Velocipedes, Bicycles, and Tricycles . . . . Andrew Ritchie 29
4. The Bicycle—An Exercise in Gendered Design . . . . . Nicholas Oddy 37
5. The Edinburgh Tricycle . . . . Alastair Dodds and Alex Brown 45
6. Diamonds Are Forever: The Socio-Technical Shaping of Bicycle Design . . . . Paul Rosen 51
7. New Tubes for Old . . . . Mike Burrows 59
8. The Bamboo Bicycles of Grundner & Lemisch, Austria . . . . Walter Ulreich 61
9. The Dancing Chain: One Hundred Years of Derailleur Gears . . . . Ron Shepherd 71
10. Touring Bicycle Technical Trials in France, 1901–1950 . . . . Raymond Henry 79
11. Tribology and the Cyclist . . . . Ken James 87
12. Founding of the Dunlop Tyre Company . . . . H. D. Higman 91
13. Colonel Pope and the Founding of the U.S. Bicycle Industry . . . . Albert A. Pope 95
14. The Founding of the Hercules Cycle & Motor Co. Ltd. . . . . Andrew Millward 99
15. Peddling the Bicycle and the Development of Mass Marketing . . . . Ross D. Petty 107
16. A New View of Late 19th-Century Cycle Publicity Posters . . . . Nadine Besse and André Vant . . . 117
17. From Cycling Lanes to Compulsory Bike Path: Bicycle Path Construction in Germany, 1897–1940 . . . . Volker Briese 123
18. Cycling or Roller Skating: The Resistible Rise of Personal Mobility . . . . Hans-Erhard Lessing 129
19. Clubs—Their Part in the Study of Cycle and Cycling History . . . . Les Bowerman 133
20. Malvern Cycling Club, 1883–1912: Social Class, Motivation, and Leisure Use . . . . Roger Alma 139
21. Little and Often—The Records of the Amateur Bicycle Club . . . . Nick Clayton 149
22. T. H. S. Walker—English Cycling Pioneer in Germany . . . . Rüdiger Rabenstein 155
23. The Michaux Memorial Campaign . . . . David V. Herlihy 161
24. The Hoopdriver Recycle . . . . John McVey 171

Other Books from Bicycle Books 175

List of Contributors

Name	Address	Telephone	Position	Remarks
Alma, Roger	11 Hanley Orchard Hanley Swan Worcester WR8 0DS Great Britain	0684-310623		
Besse, Nadine	Musée d'Art et d'Industrie Place Louis Comte 42000 St. Etienne France	773-30485	Curator, Museum of Art and Industry, St. Etienne, France	Paper prepared with André Vant, translated by Roland Sauvaget
Bowerman, Les	Send Manor Ripley, Surrey GU23 6JS Great Britain	483-224-876	Editor of *News & Views* (Veteran Cycle Club); collector	
Briese, Volker	Elser Kirchstr. 39 33106 Paderborn Germany			
Burrows, Mike	11 Basey Road Rackheath Industrial Estate Norwich NR13 6PZ Great Britain	0603-721700	Designer; Principal, Burrows Engineering	
Clayton, Nick	34 Congleton Road Alderley Edge Cheshire SK9 7AS Great Britain	625-582146	Editor of *The Boneshaker*; collector	
Dodds, Alastair	Royal Museum of Scotland Chambers Street Edinburgh EH1 1JF Great Britain	31-2257534	Curator of Road Transport Department of Science, Technology and Working Life	Paper prepared with Alex Brown
Henry, Raymond	124 Chemin de Provence 84320 Entraigues France	906-21308	Member of the Cultural Commission of the FFCT	Paper translated by Roland Sauvaget
Herlihy, David	PO Box 15077 Boston, MA 02215 U.S.A.	617-437-0437	Freelance writer; President of the Lallement Memorial Committee, Boston	
Higman, H. David	Oswestry Transport Museum Oswald Road Oswestry, Shropshire Great Britain	0691-671749		
James, K. W.	Van Road Caerphilly Mid Glamorgan CF8 3ED Great Britain	0222-852700	President, Goldtec Cycle Components Ltd.	
Lessing, Hans-Erhard	Waldparkstrasse 25 68163 Mannheim Germany	621-813-786	Professor, Center for Arts and Materials Technology (ZKM), Karlsruhe	Not personally present; paper read

Name	Address	Telephone	Position	Remarks
McVey, John	19 High Street Whittlebury Northants NN12 8XH Great Britain	0327-857840		
Mills, Russell	Vermont Technical College Randolph Center, VT 05061 U.S.A.	802-728-3391		Keynote Speaker
Millward, Andrew	School of Manuf. Systems Univ. of Central England Perry Barr Birmingham B42 2SU Great Britain	021-3316274		
Oddy, Nicholas	44 Findhorn Place Edinburgh EH9 2NT Great Britain	031-667-5818	Professor of Industrial Design, Teeside Polytechnic	
Patton, David	Department of Geography University of Cambridge Downing Place Cambridge CB2 3EN Great Britain	0223-333399		
Petty, Ross	Babson College Babson Park, MA 02157 U.S.A.	617-235-1200	Associate Professor of Law, Babson College	
Pope, Albert A.	Village Centre, PO Box 468 Stanfordville, NY 12581 U.S.A.	914-868-1188		
Rabenstein, Rüdiger	Hagenkamp 216 48308 Senden Germany	2597-1018	Professor of Sports Studies, Westphälische Wilhelms-Universität, Münster	
Ritchie, Andrew	1617 Oxford Street Berkeley, CA 94709 U.S.A.	510-841-5809		
Rosen, Paul	School of Independent Studies, Lancaster University Lancaster LA1 4YN Great Britain	0524-842700		
Shepherd, Ron	Bicycle Victoria P.O. Box 275 East Melbourne 3002 Australia	613-417-5771		
Ulreich, Walter	Hauptstrasse 35A 2371 Hinterbruehl Austria	2236-23614		

Publisher's Disclaimer

All facts and opinions stated in this work are strictly those of the individual authors. The publisher and editor are not responsible for their accuracy.

Illustrations used, except as stated, are provided by the individual authors, who are responsible for any copyright questions arising from their use in this publication.

Only the contributions received by the publisher before the publication deadline (15 December 1994) have been included in this work.

The sequence in which the contributions are presented here is arbitrarily determined by the editor, consistent with the most logical grouping of related subject matter.

Editor's Preface

The International Cycle History Conference has come of age. The 5th such conference, held 2–4 September 1994 at Emanuel College in Cambridge, of which this volume presents the proceedings, was not only a truly international event; it was exceptionally well attended and presented a wide range of topics. It also demonstrated that history is not dead: several of the contributions dealt with what could be described as history in the making—new technologies and developments that are logical outcomes of preceding historical developments in the past.

The Conference was ably organized by David Patton with the assistance of a dedicated group of people in Cambridge. In addition, much of the support had been provided by the University's Department of Geography and by Emanuel College, where the conference was held and where the participants were housed.

At the concluding plenary session, it became clear that the participants wanted to see these conferences continued on a regular—and preferably annual—basis. In this vein, it was agreed to choose the venues for the next two conferences: South Africa in 1995, and the Netherlands in 1996.

After the volume covering the 1993 conference in Boston, this is the second volume of Proceedings to be published by Bicycle Books, and I would like to express my appreciation for the faith placed in our efforts to provide the best and most accessible Proceedings in book form.

In a volume as diverse as this one, the form and sequence of presentations can be a big factor in determining its usefulness and readability. I have followed essentially the format established for the 1993 conference Proceedings. As for the sequence, I have tried to group the individual contributions into categories of related subjects as much as possible.

Unlike its predecessors, this conference was not planned to have a specific focal theme. When compiling and editing the materials, however, it became apparent that at least two important aspects had emerged in several papers. These were firstly the fact that history is a continuum and is still being made today, and secondly the early emergence of commercialism and advertising. The latter theme provided the inspiration for the dustjacket design and the frontispiece illustration selection for this volume.

Notes on the Dustjacket and Frontispiece Illustration

The illustrations on the front and the flaps of the dustjacket depict the early technique used to produce line illustrations for use in catalogues, when the line engravings were copied—probably traced—from photographs. This group of illustrations shows an interesting modified "boneshaker" design with a pivoted frame.

The main illustration is based on the same photograph that is used for the frontispiece. It depicts an unidentified man (it has been suggested that he may be the early English champion James Moore), with a Phantom bicycle. The photo was taken in a studio (probably the original photo was a carte de visite), against a rural backdrop. The line engraving is from the Phantom catalogue, and shows how early bicycle manufacturers were able to make use of photography in their advertising from the earliest time of the industry.

1. Thinking About Thinking About Cycles

Russell Mills

When David Patton first approached me about giving this talk, I was quite apprehensive. I am a stranger to most of you, and I certainly feel awkward addressing an unfamiliar community in this way. At the same time, I was very excited to have the chance to participate in this conference. There is something very important about bringing together people from industry, from interest groups, and from the academic world. I have been to a few other meetings that try to do this sort of thing, but this one seems quite special. In my time here, I've felt a sense of engagement with the subject matter that seems very unusual.

At the same time, I have felt tensions within the community. We do come from different worlds. I'm sure many of you know the categories better than I do, but one important division is the one between enthusiasts and academicians. We don't share a common methodology—nor am I convinced that we should. But this means that our discussions could easily become fragmented and contentious.

Fortunately, there is one element we all have in common: an interest in bicycles, an enthusiasm, I think I can say, a love, for the machines themselves. It may be that in the machines themselves we may be able to find a touchstone that can keep us centred. And so I would like to talk about some ways of looking at bicycles as material artifacts—a kind of material culture of bicycles. I'll sketch out a few rather basic positions—walking the boundaries, as it were—and then see what sorts of conclusions might be drawn.

In considering bicycles as artifacts, perhaps the most logical way to begin is to focus on the material qualities of the machines: their geometry, the strength of their materials, their efficiency of performance. Among the work that looks at bicycles in this way, my personal favourite is *Bicycling Science* by Frank Whitt and David Wilson.[1] The book is an engaging compilation of scientific research on bicycles and bicycling, presented for a lay audience. Whitt and Wilson look at the physiology of bicycling, the efficiency of bicycle subsystems, and the physical qualities of bicycle materials and components. The book is amply illustrated with graphs and formulas.

It may seem that by adopting an analytical stance based on principles of mechanics, Whitt and Wilson have placed the bicycle outside space, time, and culture—a truly objective analysis. However, I would like to argue that no analysis is really objective. In fact, the very notion of objectivity is a cultural construct. Whitt and Wilson's analysis is both the product and the expression of a particular cultural orientation.[2]

One of the most impressive things about Whitt and Wilson's piece is not the details of their analysis—though it is a virtual gold mine of information—but the very fact that they chose to do the analysis. It is as if, by approaching bicycles in a detailed quantitative manner, the authors are finally taking bicycles seriously. Bicycles are not ordinarily taken seriously in 20th-century industrial culture. Jet planes, locomotives, nuclear reactors, and other machines are taken seriously—but not bicycles. For example, at EPCOT Center, a shrine to technology

---

Synopsis

This paper discusses the study of bicycles as artifacts: a kind of "material culture" of cycling. Bicycles are typically discussed in terms of physical qualities such as efficiency. Recent studies, however, have tended to focus on the social forces that have shaped the design of bicycles. This study focuses on the representational qualities of bicycles and turns its back on the entire question of riding. The mountain bike is seen, not as a new kind of machine, but rather as a representation of a cultural attitude.

(This paper by Russell Mills was presented as the Keynote Address at the Conference.)

located in Florida, General Motors has constructed an exhibit called World of Transportation. The exhibit mainly celebrates the triumph of the automobile. At one point, as a bit of comic relief, the exhibit shows a gentleman who has just crashed his bicycle into a pig pen. I'm afraid this is the way bicycles are usually regarded—as something of a laughing matter. Whitt and Wilson do not laugh—but their stance only seems remarkable in a culture where people usually do laugh at bicycles.

Whitt and Wilson show their seriousness by treating bicycles mathematically. This, too, situates their work culturally. In late 20th-century industrial culture, detailed quantitative analysis is regarded as the most serious form of inquiry—perhaps the only genuinely serious form of inquiry. We are all familiar with the reverential homage that is paid to the latest products of the scientific community—especially when those of us in the humanities contrast it with the vast indifference that seems to greet our own scholarship. Again, this cultural background seems to be an important element in Whitt and Wilson's presentation.

In other ways, too, Whitt and Wilson's analysis is shaped by the culture in which it takes form. In 20th-century industrial culture, we are used to analyzing the parts of a system before looking at how the parts work together, and we find nothing strange about treating a bicycle rider as a metabolic machine. In another culture, people might focus on relationships rather than the behaviour of individual parts.[3] They might find it strange to analyse bicycle riding in terms of work, force, and thermodynamics. So the way Whitt and Wilson approach their subject also locates them in a particular culture.

Finally, even the scientific concepts that Whitt and Wilson draw on in their study can be seen as the products of a particular cultural orientation. According to proponents of what David Bloor has called the "strong programme" in the sociology of science, the very content of scientific knowledge—including logic and mathematics—is the outcome of social processes.[4] According to these sociologists of knowledge, a different social configuration would have produced a different science. This is not a matter of greater and lesser degrees of scientific development, but rather a difference between fundamentally different systems of scientific knowledge. In a different culture, scholars could conduct an equally scientific study of cycles and cycling—but their study would be different because the science they could draw on would be fundamentally different.

In emphasising the cultural specificity of Whitt and Wilson's analysis, I am not suggesting that there is anything wrong with their work. Certainly, Whitt and Wilson do not claim to be presenting an objective, value-free analysis. Rather, I am making a methodological point. The whole idea of a totally "objective" analysis—that is to say, an analysis that treats a bicycle as a distinct and separate entity, using methods that are free of subjectivity and cultural influence—is itself a cultural construct.[5] With that in mind, I would like to look at some ways of thinking about bicycles that explicitly acknowledge the social and cultural elements that lie at the core of the machine.

Perhaps the best known socially-oriented analysis of bicycles was offered by Trevor Pinch and Wiebe Bijker in 1984.[6] Their article, "The Social Construction of Facts and Artifacts," examines the emergence of the modern safety bicycle at the end of the 19th century. This work has been immensely influential, and it is an excellent example of how it is possible to see social relations embedded within a technological artifact.

Pinch and Bijker begin with the notion of "interpretative flexibility."[7] What this means is that any particular physical datum can be interpreted in a variety of ways. For example, consider the large front wheel on a penny farthing bicycle. According to Pinch and Bijker, the height of this wheel meant different things to different social groups. Racers saw it as a way of gaining a mechanical advantage, which allowed the cyclist to go faster. Many women and older riders saw it as a source of instability—a threat to safety. This interpretative flexibility meant that bicycle design was being pushed in different ways by different social groups. To quote Pinch and Bijker:

> Thus there was not one high-wheeler; there was the macho machine, leading to new designs of bicycles with even higher front wheels, and there was the unsafe machine, leading to new designs of bicycles with lower front wheels.[8]

In this instance, the divergent interests of the different social groups led to a divergence in bicycle design. However, it sometimes happens that the interests of several different social groups converge on a single design. In such a case, the convergence of interests produces a stabilisation of the artifact. According to Pinch and Bijker, this happened when pneumatic tires were attached to a low-wheeled safety bicycle. The pneumatic tires solved a vibration problem for riders of safety bicycles at the same time that they allowed the safeties to be ridden faster—faster, in fact, than the high-wheeled designs. Thus, the same design fulfilled the needs of both safety-conscious riders and racers. This convergence of interests led to a stabilisation of bicycle design.[9] Nearly a century later, the safety bicycle is still the standard configuration.

At times, I find myself wondering why Pinch and Bijker's work has been so influential. There is nothing all that startling about the notion that technology is socially constructed. Indeed, as my engineer friends often tell me, it would be very peculiar if technology were not socially constructed. But there is something very significant about the way Pinch and Bijker use the tools of social analysis to account for the specific material form of an artifact. Their method allows us to look at the shape of a bicycle and see not only a certain frame style and a certain wheel size, but also the social interests that are expressed in those design elements. Now that Pinch and Bijker's methods have become well established in the technology studies community, other scholars have begun to build on their findings, developing a more comprehensive and, in some ways, more radical notion of how bicycles—and other machines—have been shaped.

One limitation of the orthodox "Social Construction of Technology" method is that it looks primarily at the processes by which artifacts are stabilised. But other processes are at work as well in the history of bicycle design. As Paul Rosen pointed out in a recent article,[10] mountain bikes are a case where bicycle design diversified rather than stabilised. His paper shows how a number of simultaneous developments, both in industry and in the broader culture, converged to produce the mountain bike and, ultimately, a general pattern of diversification throughout the bicycle industry. Rosen takes into account not only the interests of different bicycle riding communities, but also more general changes in the nature of manufacturing. He shows how even details such as frame angles can be seen as the outcome of a whole range of social processes.

For the most part, Pinch and Bijker discuss bicycles in terms of their riding characteristics: speed, safety, vibration. They also look briefly at aesthetics and moral concerns,[11] but again, the analysis concentrates on what happens when people ride bicycles. Rosen goes somewhat beyond this narrow focus on riding, though the bulk of his treatment is concerned with the development of different designs to accommodate different riding preferences.[12] But I would like to turn my back on the whole question of riding—except as the manner of riding expresses a cultural attitude. I shall argue that in some instances, the success of a bicycle design is only indirectly related to its performance characteristics.

Perhaps the greatest bicycle success story of recent years has been the development of mountain bikes. Not only have mountain bikes been immensely popular, but their introduction seems to have brought about a fundamental change in the trajectory of bicycle development.[13] I would like to discuss the nature of that change, and some of the factors that may have led to it.

First, I would like to suggest that mountain bikes were not all that new and not all that different. Touring bicycles and mountain bkes are both pneumatic- tired safety bicycles.[14] There are many other similarities as well.[15] And yet, mountain bikes were perceived as highly revolutionary machines. Exactly what was it that made mountain bikes seem so different? I would like to argue that mountain bikes were revolutionary, not because they were a new design, but rather because they made an important cultural statement. To understand the nature of that cultural statement, it is necessary to understand how standardised American bicycles had become during the decades following World War II.

Prior to WWII, wide-tired bicycles were the norm in the United States. Indeed, the earliest mountain bikes were based on these pre-war designs.[16] Following the war, American soldiers brought home British bicycles. These bicycles, which were called "English racers," had lighter frames and narrower tires than the traditional balloon-tired models. Very quickly, the narrow-tired designs became the choice of most adult cyclists.[17] Over the next 30 years, narrow tires came to dominate the adult bicycle market in the United States. Wide-tired bicycles were generally regarded as children's toys. By 1970, the so-called "baby boom" generation had reached adulthood, and adult bicycles had become big business. The bicycles had also become highly stabilised. For example, we can take a look at the *Whole Earth Catalog*, a California annual that served as an arbiter of popular taste during the late 1960s and early 1970s. In 1970, the *Catalog* proclaimed that "the touring bicycle configuration is the best by far." They described the touring configuration in the following terms:

> The basic LIGHTWEIGHT TOURING BIKE must have
> drop bars
> centerpull brakes
> derailleur gears (5, 10, 15 speeds)
> narrow leather seat

The article went on to pronounce that "touring cycles also have narrow high-pressure tires for less rolling resistance."[18]

The bicycle described by this "catechism" was recognised throughout the culture of bicycling as the "correct" form. During most of the 1970s, the best bicycle shops displayed only bicycles of this type. Other kinds of bicycles were studiously avoided by serious cyclists. Even the minute details of a bicycle's configuration were expected to conform to the norm.[19] Coaster brakes, mudguards, baskets, and chain cases were all taboo. In some areas, a limited amount of variation was permitted, but there was usually a clear status hierarchy among the variants. For example, Presta valves enjoyed higher status than Schrader valves. Quick release hubs outranked bolt-on hubs. Pedals with toe clips outranked those without. Cotterless cranks were preferred over cottered cranks. Brake lever extenders were considered gauche, as were non-gumwall tires. In other words, the "stabilisation" of the bicycle was pursued with the same zeal as racial purification.

Only against this background of extreme stabilisation is it possible to appreciate the radical nature of the first mountain bikes. As Paul Rosen points out, the new bicycles drew on the resources available to their designers. The frames and wheels were drawn from the material culture—they were "lying around in people's yards."[20] But the new machines also drew on the cultural meanings attached to wide tired bicycles. Rosen suggests, quite accurately, that the clunkers drew on feelings of nostalgia.[21] I would like to suggest that the new machines also drew on more powerful imagery—especially imagery of resistance to authority.

The first mountain bikes were strongly associated with a particular group of people living in Marin County, California.[22] The bicycles expressed many of the values of that social group. Perhaps the most central cultural value was a rejection of conventional norms. This was expressed in a number of ways, including leftist politics, environmentalism, drug use, and a preference for natural foods.[23] The mountain bike embodied this rejection of conventional norms.

Early mountain bikes were an affront to many of the norms of post-war American bicycle design. But those norms were so narrow and rigid that they were easily violated. All it took, basically, was a bicycle with fat tires, upright handlebars, and derailleur gears. And just in case anyone failed to understand the iconoclastic nature of their machines, the riders referred to them as "clunkers."[24]

The suicidal style of riding, too, represented an outrageous departure from the decorum of

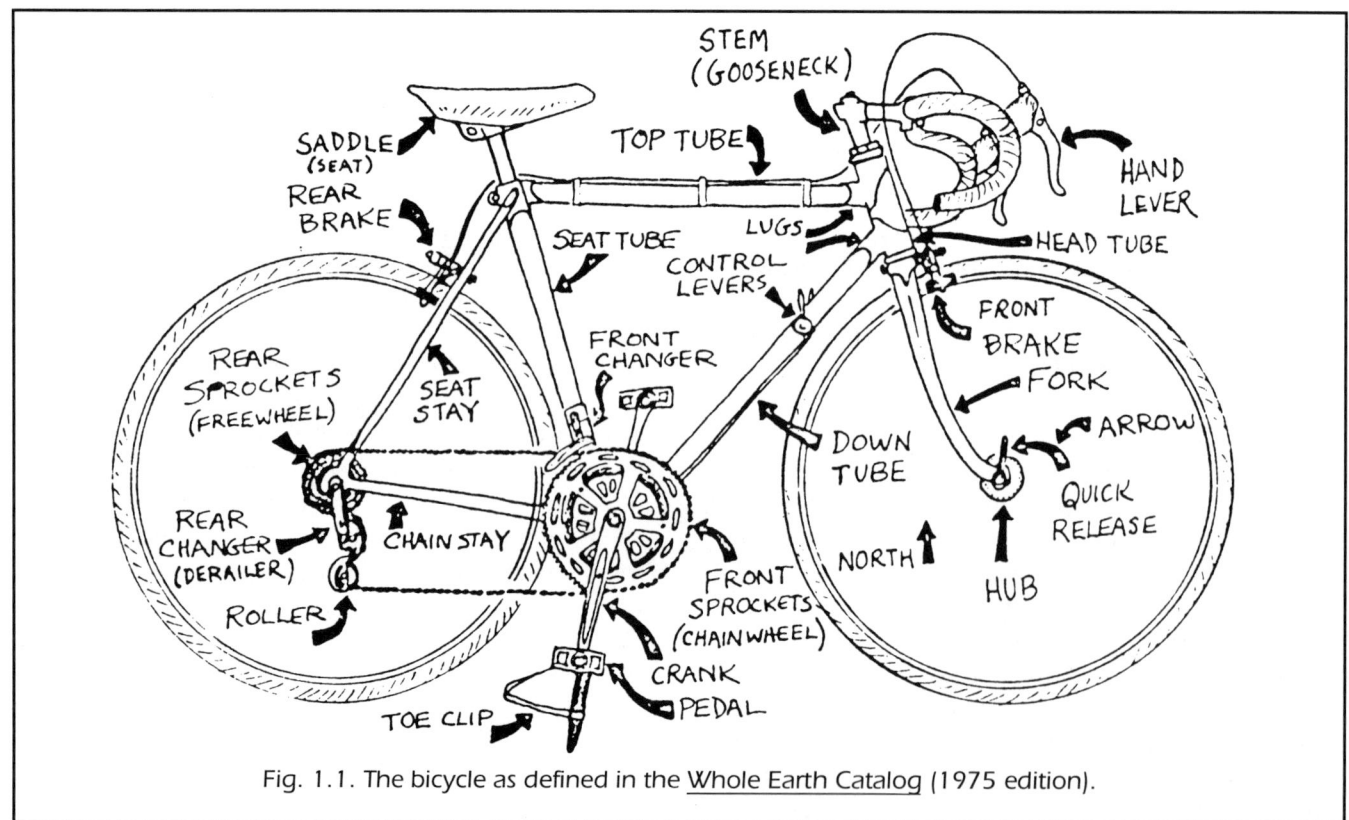

Fig. 1.1. The bicycle as defined in the Whole Earth Catalog (1975 edition).

mainstream cycling. Perhaps the inverted norms of the sport are best illustrated by the instructions given by the starter at the beginning of the 1983 "Repack Revival," a particularly brutal downhill bicycle race:

> If you crash and break a few bones, wait for the first aid crew. Unless you're blocking the good line; if so, then try to drag yourself off to one side. If you see somebody down on the course and bleeding, stop and give help—unless you're on a real good run. Then, shout at the next first aid man.[25]

To further emphasise their unconventionality, the riders called themselves "gonzos" or "crazies."[26]

It should come as no surprise that a wild new bicycle design would be adopted by Marin County hippies.[27] Colin Campbell, in an article on the origin of fashion,[28] suggests that radically new fashions generally originate with Bohemians. One of the central tenets of Bohemianism is the rejection of conventional morality. This means that an innovation is most appealing to Bohemians when it appears to represent an outrageous affront to conventional values.[29] This analysis certainly applies to the development of the mountain bike.

What is not so clear is why the mountain bike should have appealed to the general public. Campbell suggests that in addition to their rejection of conventional values, Bohemians are characterised by a strong idealistic commitment, combined with a strong strain of hedonism.[30] This means that the Bohemian lifestyle offers the utmost in narcissism: pleasure seeking combined with an aura of moral superiority. It is not surprising that Bohemianism appeals to the wider public. To be sure, most ordinary citizens do not actually adopt a Bohemian life style, but they can vicariously participate by adopting the fashions that originate in Bohemian culture.[31]

The lifestyle of the Marin County riders and builders certainly fits Campbell's description of Bohemianism, and the spread of the mountain bike to the general public followed the course outlined by Campbell. Most ordinary cyclists do not emulate the suicidal riding styles of the Marin County extremists; indeed, it is generally believed that the vast majority of mountain bikes are ridden only on pavement.[32] What seems to be happening is a kind of imaginary emulation—one in which, by simply possessing a mountain bike, an ordinary rider participates in the same culture as the Gonzos without ever needing to leave the pavement.[33]

But the case of the mountain bike represents something more significant than a story of a new machine succeeding in the marketplace. It brought about a tidal shift from stabilisation to diversification in bicycle design.[34] In many ways, this shift resembles the shift from classicism to romanticism that occurs periodically in the world of art.[35]

One of the hallmarks of classicism is a belief in universal truths. Deviation from these universal principles is seen as an ethical and intellectual failure.[36] Uniqueness and variety are seen not as expressions of creativity, but as threats to stability.[37] Another characteristic of classicism is a distrust of personal feelings. Universal truths are discovered, not through the emotions, but through the use of reason.[38] The goal of classicism is a fusion of reason, morality, and aesthetics, focusing on universal, unchanging themes.[39]

During the classical period of the 18th century, British and European poetry tended to focus around a few eternal themes. Rather than drawing their subject matter from their own individual experience, poets wrote "imitations" of classical authors.[40] Individualism and enthusiasm were rejected in favor of a "universal" standard of decorum.[41] Standard verse forms emerged: in England, the heroic couplet; in France, the Alexandrine couplet.

Similar goals and practices can be seen in the bicycle culture of the early 1970s. The *Whole Earth Catalog* was not alone in promoting the idea of a universal bicycle. The whole apparatus of bicycle culture—shops, trade journals, advertising, fixit books—celebrated the standard bicycle configuration as a triumph of rationalism. Authors praised its unparalleled efficiency and utility.[42] Riders who preferred nonstandard features were seen as uninformed, and the proponents of the standard form lost no time in seeking to educate them. At one point, I tried to buy a decent bicycle with upright handlebars, and I thought the shop owner was going to call the bicycle police. He explained the many advantages of drop bars as if he were speaking to a four-year-old, and when I mentioned my neck problem, he suggested that perhaps bicycling was the wrong form of exercise for me.

Like many cultural doctrines, classicism contains the seeds of its own destruction. By emphasising stability and coherence, classicism tends to suppress variety and individuality.[43] With its emphasis on reason and its distrust of emotion, classicism turns its back on a large portion of human experience.[44] And by insisting on a single standard of judgment, classicism often comes to be identified with authoritarianism.[45]

Romanticism is the cultural counterpoint to classicism. Romantics attribute the stability and coherence of classicism to a lack of imagination. Where classicism focuses on reason, romanticism emphasises the emotions.[46] And where classicism insists on universal standards of morality and aesthetics, romanticism is identified with unconventionality and resistance to authority.[47]

During the Romantic period of the late 18th and early 19th centuries, reason was replaced by inspiration as the source of "true poetry." According to Keats, "if Poetry comes not as naturally as the Leaves to a tree it had better not come at all."[48] Poets rejected the notion of universal themes, focusing instead on individual experience.[49] Romantic artists glorified the French revolution and praised unconventional morality, even going so far as to represent incest as a legitimate expression of human love.[50] Heroic couplets were rejected as dull and confining, and poets experimented with new verse forms.

Similarly, with the emergence of mountain bikes, the quest for an ideal bicycle design yielded to a search for variety and individuality. By 1986, the editors of the *Whole Earth Catalog* had become converts to romanticism. Here's what they said about bicycle design:

> Long stagnated by a tradition of being traditional, bicycle designers and makers have awakened at last. The results are encouraging: new ideas are being tried, excellent steeds can now be had for a reasonable price, and bikes in general have become more competent. About time.[51]

Once again, the *Whole Earth Catalog* openly expresses a cultural attitude that pervades the bicycling community. Today, much of the bicycle trade press shows little interest in traditional designs. They save their most glamorous photography and their gushiest prose for designs that can be described as "revolutionary." And while in 1970, riders were expected to adapt themselves to the standard configuration, today cyclists can choose from a bewildering variety of frame shapes, handlebars, suspensions, brakes, and gearing systems.

I should point out that this doesn't have all that much to do with people riding down mountains. Certainly, a small subset of mountain bike owners do ride their bicycles that way—just as a tiny fraction of road bicycle owners ride their bicycles in a way that necessitates lycra clothing, streamlined helmets, and aero bars. But for most riders, the functionality of a mountain bike—or a road bicycle—is never fully exercised. Its capabilities remain merely "virtual capabilities"—much like the capability of some high-priced stereo equipment to reproduce sounds that cannot be heard by the human ear. But those virtual capabilities have great cultural importance, and people are often willing to pay a substantial premium for them.

What I am suggesting, then, is that the particular design of a mountain bike—or a road bicycle, or an automobile, a nuclear reactor, or a jet plane—is shaped not only by its capability to perform certain

Fig. 1.2. Mountain bike adapted for urban use (from Bicycle Books collection).

functions, but also by its ability to embody important cultural meanings. Furthermore, I am willing to argue that when there is a conflict between functionality and cultural significance, functionality is likely to take the back seat.

Now that I have yanked the bicycles out from under their riders and insisted on reading them rather than riding them, I would like to return to safer territory and make a few general observations about bicycles—and especially about bicycle scholarship.

As I mentioned at the beginning of this talk, I am pleased by the diversity of perspectives represented at this conference. I would like to think that when a group of people from different backgrounds get together, the resulting discourse will be responsible and mutually intelligible. But I am not sure that this will automatically happen. Sometimes it seems to me that scholarly disciplines have become so self-contained that they are virtually immune to corrective influence from outside.[52] As an escapee from the field of literary criticism, I have certainly witnessed this firsthand. Without going into too much detail, I'll simply say that in my earlier life, I have encountered some very bizarre interpretations of literary works—and that the commentary of outsiders was not generally welcomed by the community of literary critics. I'm sure many of you have experienced similar things in your own communities.

This immunity to corrective influence is not limited to academic disciplines. In a whole range of situations, when evidence comes into conflict with a theory, our response is to maintain the theory and reject the evidence. This tendency is especially pronounced when the evidence is put forward by those who do not share our scholarly or political perspective. An extreme example is today's neo-Nazis, who do not seem to be embarrassed by the Holocaust. Indeed, rather than trying to account for the Holocaust, they tend to deny it altogether.

If we do have this almost unlimited capacity for self-deception, then the mere presence of people from different disciplines is not likely to make our discourse any more responsible. But I would like to argue that when we introduce physical artifacts, the picture changes.

In our relations with the physical world, there appear to be limits to the range of interpretations that can be sustained.[53] For instance, I may believe that a bicycle is the ideal commuting vehicle. But when I have to ride my bicycle to work over muddy roads in the rain, my interpretation begins to fall apart. Similarly, the Marin County cyclists overinterpreted their bicycles when they first started riding them on the fire trails of Mount Tamalpais. Their interpretation became difficult to sustain when the bicycles themselves fell apart.

When our theories encounter resistance from the physical world—in this case, from the bicycles themselves—we have two choices. We can alter our theories—I can elect to ride my bicycle to work only on sunny days—or we can alter the physical world—as the California riders altered their bicycles. But we cannot simply keep repeating our theories more loudly and citing more authorities in support of our interpretations.

I believe that by focusing on artifacts—in this case bicycles—we can ultimately overcome the insularity of our various perspectives and achieve genuine interdisciplinary insights. For instance, David Patton is a cultural geographer (at least I think that's what he is), and I most certainly am not. Several years ago, I heard him give a talk about bicycles as the product of a global manufacturing system. To illustrate his point, he brought in one of his own bicycles and showed us where each of the parts came from. Now if a cultural geographer helps me understand something about bicycles, then bicycles have also helped me understand something about cultural geography. This is interdisciplinary inquiry in its best sense.

In my mind, the great promise of a conference such as this one is that we are all connecting with each other through the bicycles: by talking about them, asking questions about them, and commenting on each other's interpretations. And if, as I have suggested, the bicycles themselves have the capacity to resist interpretive excess, then our discourse will remain within bounds as long as it is grounded in the machines themselves.

The announcement for this conference posed the question, "Where are the bicycles?" Well, they seem to be all around us—not only in the conference displays, but everywhere in the city of Cambridge. I'm happy to see that the bicycles are here, and I am sure that they are as present in our thoughts as they are in our surroundings. Let us keep one analytical eye on the machines themselves, even as we seek to engage one another in more rarefied critical territory.

Notes

1. Frank Rowland Whitt and David Gordon Wilson, *Bicycling Science: Ergonomics and Mechanics* (Cambridge, Mass: MIT Press, 1974).

2. This notion of "objectivity" as a cultural construct is common to a whole range of critical disciplines. One of the earliest treatments is Wayne Booth's study, *The Rhetoric of Fiction* (Chicago: University of Chicago Press, 1961). Other important treatments include Paul Feyerabend, *Against Method* (London: New Left Books, 1975) and David Bloor, *Knowledge and Social Imagery* (London: Routledge and Kegan Paul, 1976).

3. Even within the western tradition, alternative views have been proposed. For example, David Bohm (*Wholeness and the Implicate Order* [London: Routledge and Kegan Paul, 1980]) has argued for a concept of physics based on wholism rather than analysis by parts, and Rupert Sheldrake (*The Presence of the Past: Morphic Resonance and the Habits of Nature* [New York: Vintage, 1988]) claims that causation is non-local and that the universe as a whole "learns by experience." But views such as these are not common, and they are generally viewed as being outside the mainstream of the western tradition.

4. David Bloor, op. cit.

5. The science studies literature contains a large number of studies that undermine the notion of "value-free" inquiry. In *The Social and Economic Roots of Newton's Principia* (New York: H. Fertig, 1991), Boris Hessen argues that Newton's *Principia* embodied the economic interests of the British ruling classes. Sociologist Robert Merton claims that the conduct of science is based on the social norms of impersonality, cooperation, disinterestedness, and skepticism. For a summary of his views, see *The Sociology of Science: Theoretical and Empirical Investigations*, ed. Norman W. Storer (Chicago: University of Chicago Press, 1973). Ian Mitroff found, contrary to Merton's claims, that scientific practice was characterized by deep personal involvement, intense competition, and attachment to one's own theories. See "Norms and Counter-Norms in a Select Group of the Apollo Moon Scientists: A Case Study of the Ambivalence of Scientists," *American Sociological Review*, 39 (1974), 579–595. Feminist scholars argue that science expresses the values of a masculinist society. See Evelyn Fox Keller, *Reflections on Gender and Science* (New Haven, Conn.: Yale University Press, 1985) and Sandra Harding, *The Science Question in Feminism* (Ithaca, N.Y.: Cornell University Press, 1986). It is fair to say that within the science studies community, the notion of an "objective, value-free" inquiry is generally regarded with a great deal of suspicion.

6. Trevor J. Pinch and Wiebe E. Bijker, "The Social Construction of Facts and Artifacts; or How the Sociology of Science and The Sociology of Technology Might Benefit Each Other," *Social Studies of Science* 14 (1984), 399–441, updated and reprinted in Wiebe E. Bijker, Thomas P. Hughes, and Trevor J. Pinch (eds.), *The Social Construction of Technological Systems: New Directions in the Sociology and History of Technology* (Cambridge, Mass.: MIT Press, 1987), pp. 17–50. Page references are to the MIT Press version.

7. Ibid., pp. 40–42.

8. Ibid., p. 44.

9. Ibid., pp. 45–46.

10. Paul Rosen, "The Social Construction of Mountain Bikes: Technology and Postmodernity in the Cycle Industry," *Social Studies of Science*, 23 (1993), 479–513.

11. Pinch and Bijker, op. cit., pp. 35–36, 44–45.

12. Rosen, op. cit. See especially pp. 489–493.

13. Cf. Rosen, op. cit., pp. 493, 504–506.

14. Oddly, Rosen claims that mountain bikes "differ from the safety bicycles that Pinch and Bijker discuss," because:

    > they have smaller wheels and fatter tires, flat handlebars, gear shifters on the handlebars rather than on the frame, and a higher bottom bracket, cantilever brakes, and at least fifteen gears. (Rosen, op. cit., pp. 485–486).

    As my subsequent analysis will make clear, these features distinguish mountain bicycles from touring bicycles; however, both fit Pinch and Bijker's description of a safety bicycle as "a low-wheeled bicycle with rear chain drive, diamond frame, and air tires" (Pinch and Bijker, op. cit., p. 39).

15. For example, both mountain bikes and touring bicycles have derailleur gears and lack mudguards and chain cases.

16. Joe Breeze's first custom-built mountain bike frames were based on the Schwinn *Excelsior*, a fat-tired

design that was first produced in the 1930s. Breeze's sketches are reproduced in David Patton, "A Natural History of Mountain Bikes" (Master's degree thesis, Troy, N.Y.: Rensselaer Polytechnic Institute, 1991).

17. The U.S. bicycle industry tried to repel this "British invasion," in part by publishing pamphlets extolling the merits of traditional broad-tired designs, e.g., John Auerbach, "Crisis in the American Bike Industry" (New York: Bicycle Institute of America, 1954).

18. *Whole Earth Catalog*, Spring 1970, p. 111.

19. The material in this paragraph is based on my personal observations, confirmed by several informants within the American cycling culture. Some of those informants are current or past shop owners.

20. Rosen, op. cit., pp. 486–487.

21. Ibid., pp. 487, 499.

22. Charles Kelly, "Clunkers Among the Hills," *Bicycling*, Jan./Feb. 1979, pp. 40–42.

23. Much of my information about this community comes from David Patton, who has interviewed members of the community and reviewed early copies of their newsletters. His Master's thesis (see Note 16) is a rich source of information about mountain bicycles and mountain bicycling.

24. Kelly, "Clunkers Among the Hills."

25. Frank Berto, "Repack Revisited," *Bicycling*, March 1984, pp. 20–21.

26. Charles R. Kelly, "The Vanguard: ATB's and their Dedicated, Imaginative Band of California Builders," *Bicycling*, March 1985, p. 129.

27. This group has been referred to as "hard core hippie bike bums" (Richard Grant, foreword to Charles Kelly and Nick Crane, *Richard's Mountain Bike Book* [London: Pan, 1990], p. 21). However, Andrew Ritchie suggests that it might be more appropriate to describe them as "counter-culture" figures.

28. Colin Campbell, "The Desire for the New: Its Nature and Social Location as Presented in Theories of Fashion and Modern Consumerism," in Roger Silverstone and Eric Hirsch, eds., *Consuming Technologies* (London: Routledge & Kegan Paul, 1992), pp. 48–64.

29. Ibid., p. 59.

30. Ibid., pp. 59–60.

31. Ibid., p. 60.

32. This is an article of faith in the cycling community, but there seems little empirical support for it. Rosen claims (op. cit., pp. 500–501) that "most mountain bikes are used primarily on city streets rather than on wilderness trails," but he offers no source for this claim. A review in *Bicycling* magazine claims that "almost 80% [of all fat-tired bicycles] never leave the pavement" (*Bicycling*, March 1989, p. 92), but it is not clear where this figure comes from. Andrew Ritchie has suggested to me that many mountain bike riders spend most of their time on the pavement but take their cycles off the pavement once in a while. An operator of cycling tours told me that his tours are confined to pavement, but he provides mountain bikes for riders who do not bring their own machines. His logic is that the mountain bikes are more likely to withstand abuse and thus are more suitable for renting out to inexperienced cyclists.

33. Cf. Campbell, op. cit., pp. 60–61.

34. Cf. Rosen, op. cit., p. 504–506.

35. Classicism and romanticism have been the subject of innumerable treatments over the years. The basic distinction is generally credited to Goethe and Schiller. An excellent and concise treatment of the subject is Walter Jackson Bate, *From Classic to Romantic: Premises of Taste in Eighteenth Century England* (Cambridge, Mass.: Harvard University Press, 1946). In the following discussion, I shall draw heavily on Bate's presentation.

36. Bate, op. cit., pp. 18–23.

37. Ibid., pp. 11–12.

38. Ibid., pp. 23–24.

39. Ibid., p. 7.

40. For English readers, perhaps the most familiar of these are Pope's "Imitations of Horace." French poets of the classical period practiced a different kind of "imitation," writing tragedies in the classical manner, based on stories from Greek mythology.

41. Bate, op. cit., pp. 14–15.

42. For an example of this kind of rhetoric, see Richard Ballantine, *Richard's Bicycle Book* (New York: Ballantine, 1972), pp. 11–15.

43. Bate, op. cit., pp. 27–31.

44. Ibid., pp. 40–41.

45. Ibid., p. 41.

46. Ibid., pp. 93–94.

47. For a thorough discussion of this theme, see Irving Babbitt, *Rousseau and Romanticism* (New York: Meridian, 1955).

48. John Keats, Letter to John Taylor, 27 February 1818, in *John Keats, Selected Poems and Letters*, ed. Douglas Bush (Cambridge, Mass.: Riverside Press, 1959), p. 67.

49. Bate, op. cit., p. 131.

50. See Mario Praz, *The Romantic Agony* (Cleveland, Ohio: World Publishing, 1933), pp. 109–110.

51. *The Essential Whole Earth Catalog* (Garden City, N.Y.: Doubleday, 1986), p. 264.

52. Thomas Kuhn claims that different scientific paradigms are "incommensurable" *(The Structure of Scientific Revolutions*, 2nd. Ed. [Chicago: University of Chicago Press, 1970], p. 112). If this is true of different orientations within a single discipline, it is even more so of different disciplines.

53. Cf. Andrew Pickering's concept of *situated resistance*. The concept is developed in Pickering's article, "Living in the Material World: On Realism and Experimental Practice," in David Gooding, Trevor J. Pinch, and Simon Schaffer, eds., *The Uses of Experiment: Studies in the Natural Sciences* (Cambridge: Cambridge University Press, 1989).

David L. Patton

2. Aspects of a Historical Geography of Technology: A Study of Cycling, 1919–1939

In this paper I argue for the need to pay attention to the ways in which technology and geography become fused. The basic point is extremely simple. A person in Cambridge, say, may think of London as "an hour away." But this sense of distance takes for granted great networks of motorways and automobiles, railroads and locomotives, and the human activity of planning, building, and maintaining them. Distance has become a thoroughly techno-geographic concept.

I suggest a method for disentangling the knot, illustrating the argument with examples drawn from my current work on cycling and cyclists in inter-war Britain. The plan of the paper is briefly to provide a working definition of the subject, describe my approach to the study of cycling, offer some findings from that study, and discuss further research.

Geography has been defined as: "The study of the earth's surface as the space within which the human population lives."[1] And however we define technology, we seem to be surrounded by it. We can make the general observation: "Technology is more than just machines. It is a pervasive, complex system whose cultural, social, political, and intellectual elements are manifest in virtually every aspect of our lives."[2] If we ask a philosopher for a more rigorous definition, we find that: "technologies…mean practical implementations of intelligence."[3] A geographically informed study of technology, then, takes as its subject those "areas and spaces where the human population lives with and through pervasive, complex, practical implementations of intelligence."[4]

In what follows I consider cycling to be such a practical implementation of intelligence, and inquire into how the population of inter-war Britain lived with and through bicycles. The interest in cycles is premised on their curious status in the modern industrial world, at once mechanically excellent and socially marginal. The choice of the inter-war years is due to a supposed stagnation of cycle design at a time of explosive growth in motoring and other consumer technologies.[5]

Enthusiast Literature

My research method involves approaching the union of technology and geography through the reading of enthusiast literature. I follow Daniel Miller, Ruth Schwartz Cowan, and others who seek to redress the historical bias favoring production studies of technology, and who recognize that the material culture of life in place is in part constructed through technological consumption.[6] I am interested not only in the initial diffusion of technologies, but also in what happens "downstream" as they are put to everyday use. I am interested in techno-geographic change on the scale of the "annihilation of time and distance" brought about by the railroad.[7]

I have studied 21 years of *Cycling* magazine, the single most comprehensive English-language source for information on the culture of cycling. Both consumers and producers of cycling technology

---

Synopsis

This paper presents a case study in the geographic study of technology based on a systematic reading of the specialty newspaper *Cycling* for the years 1919–1939. The following themes are examined: *Cycling* as a business; discrimination against cyclists; cycling as self-expression; generation and gender stereotypes; and lightweight bicycles as a technical fix. It is argued that this array of issues points to an incoherent response to change. In turn, that incoherence appears to have been due to a tension between the opposing demands of tradition and technological progress.

looked to this newspaper/magazine for information about people and places in the sport and pastime, about bicycles and cycle equipment, and for confirmation of and/or reassurance about their social position.[8]

Five Themes

For this paper I have chosen five themes from *Cycling* as especially significant. The selection is somewhat arbitrary, but each is part of the complex geographical and technological elaboration of cycling.

1. The Business

First, it must be recognized that *Cycling* was itself a business enterprise, a successful pioneer specialty journal. It was the first newspaper published by, and was still, throughout the period, a valuable part of the portfolio of Temple Press, its parent company.[9] *Cycling* thrived during much of the period, showing increases in circulation, average issue size, percent of total pages devoted to advertising, and, in all likelihood, revenue and profit (see Figs. 2.1 and 2.2).[10, 11] These are indicators that the magazine succeeded overall in balancing the interests of its readers, advertisers, writers, and owners. *Cycling* defined and controlled a "consumption junction" in Cowan's terms, that place where micro and macro influences intersect, where individual consumption choices meet industrial production decisions.[12]

2. Discrimination

Running through the pages of *Cycling* is a consistent theme of discrimination, of being the underdog. Although cyclists were extremely numerous, they alternately felt ignored, misunderstood, threatened, and victimized.[13] These sentiments were aired frequently in features about accident investigation, taxation, road and land use planning, countryside preservation, and legislation for safety.

There was a long-running battle, for example, over the requirement that cyclists carry rear lights at night to make them more visible to passing motorists. Cyclists opposed the idea vehemently, on grounds ranging from inconvenience to injustice. The whole issue of sharing the road with motor vehicles was extremely controversial. Some cyclists felt they were literally being run off the roads, and accident figures reached scandalous levels.[14] One secondary account claims that in the 1920s "Road safety was the most contentious issue of the decade."[15] Readers were of the opinion that "The sole cause of the terrifying fatalities on our roads to-day is the indiscriminate speed of the motor-propelled vehicle."[16] Cars caused noise and pollution, and went hand-in-hand with indiscriminate land speculation and development. "You cannot know [nature] intimately seated in a car or charabanc travelling along a tarmac road."[17]

3. Self-Expression

The activity of cycling in all its facets provided people with a means of finding and expressing their self-identity. In a 1934 letter-writing feature, readers

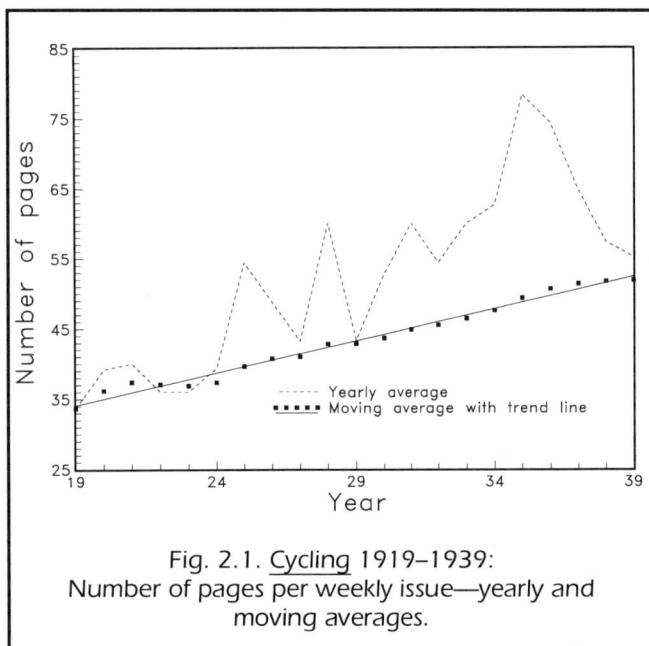

Fig. 2.1. Cycling 1919–1939: Number of pages per weekly issue—yearly and moving averages.

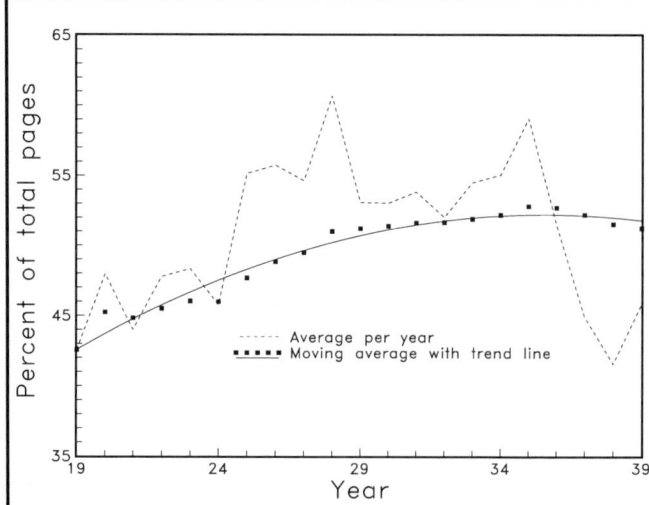

Fig. 2.2. Cycling 1919–1939: Advertising content as percentage of total pages—average per year, moving average, and trend line (see Note 11).

gave their own reasons "why I am a cyclist." There the bicycle is praised as "the means to see nature," and cycling is "the great game without which life would be terribly empty." It "enables me to cover more ground than walking, while I can see and hear more than when motoring," "it is the finest sport and exercise for man, woman and child," "it gives exercise and economy, and is a hobby with no retiring age."[18] Cyclists differentiated themselves from each other and from non-cyclists through distinctive fashions in clothing and bicycles, brand loyalties, favored holiday destinations, and sub-cultural labeling. A "speed man" and a "potterer," for example, had very different styles of riding. Cyclists seem to have felt the need, and had the means, to find individuality in the crowd. Urban residents with cycles were able to reach the countryside on a regular basis, and this set them apart from their contemporaries.[19]

One of the principal ways in which cyclists expressed themselves was through voluntary association in cycle clubs. In 1934, there were nearly 400 Greater London cycle clubs, and 1,200 in Britain as a whole.[20] The majority of these were district or neighborhood clubs, but many were based on shared interests other than cycling. Thus we find the Eligible Ladies' C.C., the Blackburn Squires Catholic C.C., the Burton Working Men's C.C., the London Fire Brigade C.C., the Vegetarian C. and A.C., and many more.[21]

I have charted the London clubs against the contemporary network of Class I roads[22] (Fig. 2.3). Several points are worth noting about this map. First, the club locations do not simply reflect population. Inner east London, for example, in the area of Whitechapel, was extremely densely populated, but had no clubs. Neither do the clubs plot simply as an index of rising or of middle income. Whitechapel was a poor district whose residents might not have been able to afford the time and expense for sociable cycling, but a number of clubs were located in wealthy districts such as Chelsea. There were fewer in the very wealthiest areas such as Mayfair, and none at all in St. John's Wood, but there were at least two clubs in fashionable Knightsbridge. The number of clubs located in central London, with its crowded living conditions, deserves further study. And the cluster near Willesden, for example, might be explained by the prime cycle touring districts to its west and northwest rather than by population or income factors. It seems clear that future work will require multiple explanations to account for the distribution of London cycle clubs.[23]

4. Generation and Gender

In spite of the forms of self-expression noted above, *Cycling* reported and fostered stereotypes of generation and gender. The generations were divided

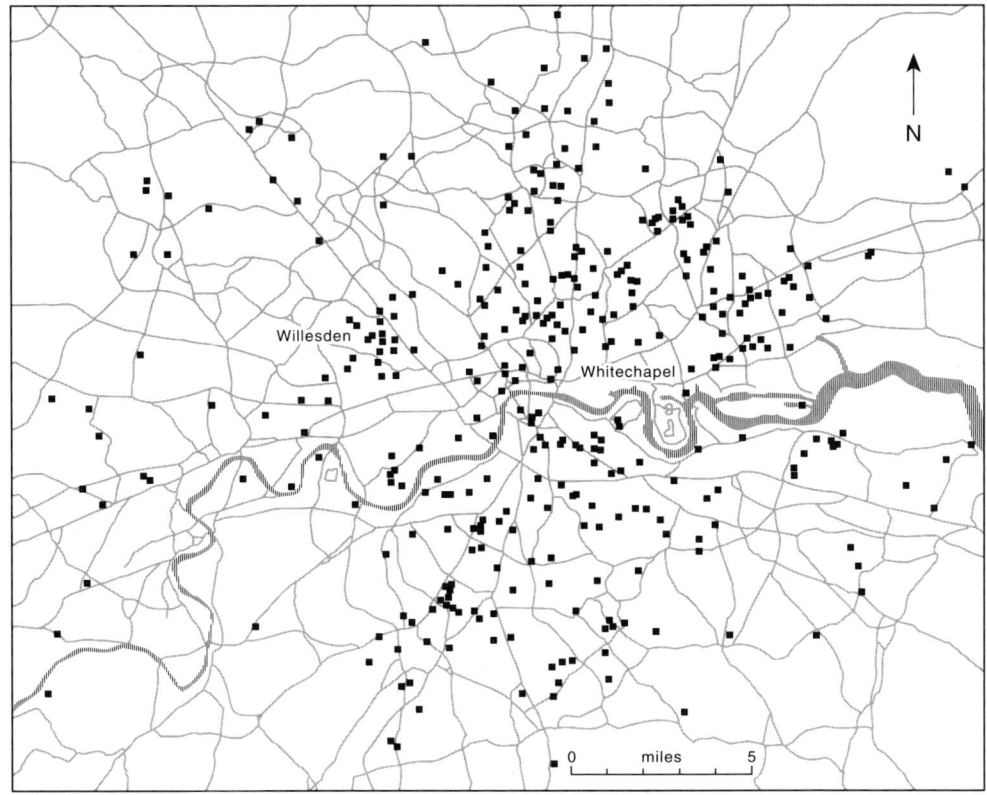

Fig. 2.3. Cycling clubs of Greater London, 1934, with Class I road network (Cycling Manual, 1934; Ordnance Survey).

between youth and age, novice and veteran, and the division was reinforced in advertising and editorial content. G. H. Stancer, for example, a weekly columnist, Secretary of the Cyclists' Touring Club, and a proud member of cycling's old guard, related a brush he had with a driver who forced him off the road. "Had I not been fortified in nerve and mind and muscle by 50 years of varied road experience, what might have happened?"[24] Age distinctions show up not only in anecdotes, but also in clothing and mechanical fashions, standards of public behavior and citizenship, and levels of interest in nature and the opposite sex. Sometimes *Cycling* drew attention to a generation gap when there was evidence that it did not exist. Readers were asked for their opinions on new government safety proposals in 1938, and they reiterated the usual opposition to rear lights. *Cycling* claimed that "These are the considered opinions of a generation of cyclists entirely different from those who fought rear lights more than 10 years ago."[25]

Cycling was also extremely gendered. Women appear in advertisements, in special features aimed at them and at families, in photos of club runs and dinners, and in celebrity endorsements, but there were no women on the editorial staff of *Cycling*. Only one regular feature writer and the occasional letter writer were female. Women partners were sought after for companionship, but patronized on medical, technical, and moral grounds. They were proposed as ideal club mates who would bring decorum to their office, but were caricatured in stereotypical fashion in humor features.[26] There were some prominent women members of the Cyclists' Touring Club, the largest national cycling organization, and a few clubs catered for women, but only 13 women appear as club secretaries in the 1934 list of 1,200 cycle clubs. Toward the end of the period several record-setting women riders achieved prominence, and some moved into promotional positions with manufacturers, and occasionally wrote for *Cycling*, but overall the reporting was of a white, male activity.[27]

5. The Technical Fix

Throughout the period *Cycling* advocated a new kind of lightweight bicycle, amounting to what we would now call a technical fix.[28] Readers, writers, and advertisers endorsed new bicycles as a remedy for a perceived decline in, or a challenge to, their sport and pastime. The traditional roadster bicycle was often portrayed in images of sobriety, reliability, comfort, resistance to change, and maturity. The new style lightweights, by contrast, were associated with ideas of technical progress, fun, speed, athleticism, change, modernity, and youth.[29] They were meant to popularize cycling, which in turn would help hold the tide against the myriad changes being wrought by motoring.[30] *Cycling*, as the standard bearer of the sport and pastime, heavily promoted this re-definition of cycling, hoping the excitement would be contagious.

Conclusions and Further Work

Enthusiast literature preserves the record of consumption junctions, which are prime sites for investigating the union of geography and technology. The record cannot explain, or even expose, all the cultural elements of an activity, but it can help refine hypotheses, and eliminate others. On one hand, it would be difficult to support the proposition that cyclists of the 1920s and 1930s were political radicals if no mention of radical cyclists ever appeared in the pages of the principal record of the activity.[31] On the other hand, even this brief look at inter-war *Cycling* has provided guidance on how to proceed with more assurance into the investigation of techno-geography.

- ☐ *Cycling* was a national periodical with a strong London bias. Nearly one-third of all the cycle clubs in the country were based within 10 miles of the printing plant, providing a captive audience, and making *Cycling* a de facto in-house organ for London cycling.[32] It remains to be seen how well provincial cyclists were served by this metropolitan paper.

- ☐ Cyclists discriminated among themselves on the basis of income, age, gender, technical aptitude, and other qualities. At the same time, they felt discriminated against, via society's enthusiasm for motoring. To investigate this further, I plan to work on the records of London road accidents. How and to what degree was some loss of life found or made socially acceptable as the price of progress? Who were the victims of road accidents, where did they live and work?

- ☐ Self-expression among cyclists contributed to and reflected the urban mosaic, at least in London. No single factor accounts for the number and distribution of cycle clubs there. It would be pertinent to ask what combination of factors was responsible.

- ☐ *Cycling* reinforced notions of gendered and generational space. Neither racing nor solo touring were generally accepted activities for women, for example, and although lightweight bikes were promoted for young riders, there were many messages that older gents should be happy with more traditional mounts.

- ☐ *Cycling* reported on a technological lifestyle at a time of great social and cultural change. In the enthusiasm for improved bicycles the outlines of a technological fix are apparent. One wonders if cyclists might have gained a new social contract more directly through political activity.

The specific evidence presented in this paper can be reorganized as a pair of observations. First, the response in *Cycling* to changing conditions of the sport and pastime seems incoherent to us. It cannot be denied that everyday conditions on the road changed for cyclists, as motor vehicle registration figures alone indicate.[33] Nevertheless, a reader today is surprised that cyclists did not react more strongly to these changes. The contemporary responses ranged across a spectrum from no response, to polemical journalism, technical improvements, appeals to the King, and tips on how to avoid roads with heavy traffic.

Second, this incoherence can be traced to the tension between the twin demands of tradition and technological progress, common to each of the themes examined here. Cyclists were, by all accounts, proud of their traditions, both as pioneers of the road, and as Britons.[34] Villages, ancient castles, cathedrals, and earthworks feature prominently as touring destinations. At the same time, the bicycles of the 1920s and 1930s were sophisticated products of modern industry, British bicycles were among the best in the world, and the freedom that cycling afforded citizens was exhilarating. What cyclists of the day failed to notice was that the very machines which brought them so much enjoyment, and even the vintage cycles of the late 19th century, were products of an industrial economic system transforming forever the traditional village-centered rural life they held dear. The more they promoted, and longed for, "scientifically-built bicycles," the further away that life receded.[35]

Temple Press was itself caught on the horns of this dilemma, as an innovative publisher that sold images of Olde England in the pages of *Cycling*. They began with a single cycling newspaper, but by the mid-1930s published two popular auto magazines, *MotorCycling*, a stable of specialized trade and industry journals, and *The Aeroplane*.[36] The firm was technologically progressive and professionally managed. To power their presses, which were advanced German models, they installed one of the first Diesel engines in Britain. They commissioned market surveys from the British Tabulating Machine Company, which grew into the computer giant ICL.[37] For all the opinion and passion expressed in its pages, *Cycling* was, at one level, a small, nostalgic cog in a larger machine. It is important to ask what boardroom decisions shaped the editorial policies of *Cycling*, to what degree it was a compromised authority, and whether the loyalty of its readers was misplaced.

Others might attribute the tensions in inter-war cycling culture to different causes. *Cycling*'s compromises could be just another case of an institution adjusting to cultural modernism, for example. But that argument would need to be illustrated with the kind of evidence I have used here. Any cultural phenomenon as significant as the transition to modernism must register in the substance of people's lives. This paper has sought to clarify, in a straightforward way, how and where technological culture reaches and is shaped by real people in real places. It is in surprising documents like the weekly magazine of the sport and pastime of cycling that we can find un-self-conscious discussion of the making of techno-geography.

Notes

1. R. J. Johnston, senior ed., *Dictionary of Human Geography*, London: Blackwell, 2nd ed., 1986, 175.

2. Albert H. Teich, ed., *Technology and Man's Future*, 3rd ed., New York: St. Martin's Press, 1981, 1.

3. Frederick Ferré, *Philosophy of Technology*, Englewood Cliffs, NJ: Prentice Hall, 1988, 26.

4. On the concept of living "through" technologies, see: Marshall McLuhan, *Understanding Media: The Extensions of Man*, London: Routledge and Kegan

Paul, 1964, 90: "It is a persistent theme of this book that all technologies are extensions of our physical and nervous systems to increase power and speed."

5. The numbers of motor vehicles of all types in Great Britain increased from 331,000 in 1919 to 3,149,000 in 1939, a relative increase of 851%. The number of private motor cars experienced a relative increase of 1749% in the same period. Source: B. R. Mitchell, *British Historical Statistics*, Cambridge: Cambridge University Press, 1988, 557–58.

6. On technologies as ways of life see: Langdon Winner, "The Political Philosophy of Alternative Technology," in Teich, op. cit., 369–85. On material culture and consumption, see: Daniel Miller, *Material Culture and Mass Consumption*, Oxford: Blackwell, 1987; and Ruth Schwartz Cowan, "The Consumption Junction: A Proposal for Research Strategies in the Sociology of Technology," in Wiebe Bijker, Thomas Hughes, and Trevor Pinch, eds., *The Social Construction of Technological Systems*, Cambridge, MA: MIT Press, 1986, 261–80. See also: Roger Silverstone and Eric Hirsch, eds., *Consuming Technologies*, London: Routledge, 1992; Colin Campbell, *The Romantic Ethic and the Spirit of Modern Consumerism*, Oxford: Blackwell, 1987; and Mary Douglas and Baron Isherwood, *The World of Goods: Towards an Anthropology of Consumption*, London: Allen Lane, 1978.

7. Wolfgang Schivelbusch, *The Railway Journey: The Industrialization of Time and Space in the 19th Century*, Berkeley, CA: University of California Press, 1986, 33 ff.

8. My reading of *Cycling* was based on a systematic sample of every tenth issue from the years 1919–1939.

9. A useful, if extremely flattering, in-house history of Temple Press exists. See: Arthur C. Armstrong, *Bouverie Street to Bowling Green Lane: Fifty-five Years of Specialised Publishing*, London: Hodder and Stoughton, 1946.

10. Circulation figures are given irregularly on the cover of *Cycling*. A figure of 55,000 was claimed as of 31 March 1933. The number grew in 1934 from 60,000 in February to 75,000 in July. The high figure I recorded was "circulation exceeds 80,000 weekly" on 12 February 1936. The statement on revenue and profit is speculative, but Armstrong says "The venture was self-supporting from the start." Ibid., 28.

11. Fig. 2.1 shows an increasing average issue size throughout the study period. The dashed line traces the year-by-year changes in the average size (n) of issues sampled. Square dots plot issue size as a moving average as of each year (after 1919). The solid line is a best-fitting, in this case linear, curve showing the growth trend of the moving average. (For 1919, n=33.67 pages per issue. For the period as a whole, 1919–1939, n=51.87 pages per issue.) Fig. 2.2 reports advertising (revenue-generating) content (n) as a percentage of total pages. The dashed line connects year-by-year averages from the sample. Square dots show advertising content as a moving average percentage as of each year (after 1919), and the solid line is the best-fitting, in this case parabolic, curve tracing the trend in advertising as a percent of total contents. (For 1919, n=42.57% advertising. For the period as a whole, 1919–1939, n=51.25% advertising.) Two possible explanations are available for the observed decline in advertising and page totals after 1935. A competing paper, *The Bicycle*, entered the market in February 1936, and might be responsible. Or, advertisers and readers may have retreated from *Cycling* in anticipation of hard times. For statistical help I consulted: Jane Miller, *Statistics for Advanced Level*, 2nd ed., Cambridge: Cambridge University Press, 1989, 25–27.

12. I have taken liberties with Cowan's concept. In a strict interpretation, the artifact in question here is the newspaper *Cycling*, and the consumption junction moves to the newsstand. Cowan, op. cit., 262–63.

13. There is some official justification for this feeling. In one MOT report, the council states on page 5: "…it is the duty of the driver of any mechanically-propelled vehicle so to drive at any time that he can pull up within the limits of his vision." But on page 10 they say: "We cannot take the view that the duty is solely upon the following vehicle to remove the risk of collision with the rear of a cycle or other vehicle…" See: Ministry of Transport, Transport Advisory Council, *Report on Accidents to Cyclists*, London: HMSO, 1938. As regards the number of cyclists on the road, in the national traffic census of August 1935, an average of 3.1 million cyclists per day were counted at 4,830 recording stations. The report states: "Perhaps the most significant feature which emerges from an examination of the data afforded by the Census is the increase in the use of pedal cycles…. It will be seen that the totals at these points…[represent] an increase in the four years of 95 per cent." Ministry of Transport, Road Traffic Census, 1935: Report Including Tables and Statistics of Traffic, London: HMSO, 1936, 6.

14. In 1930, 7,305 persons were killed in road accidents in Great Britain. The annual toll rose to a high of 9,169 in 1941. Compare this with 2,694 for all fatal industrial accidents in 1939. Also note the 3,814 road deaths in 1993, with greatly increased volumes of traffic and 32 million British drivers. See: Ministry of Transport, *Preliminary Report on Fatal Road Accidents which Occurred During the Six Months ended 30th June, 1933*, London: HMSO, 1933, 4; and *Annual Abstract of Statistics, 1935–46*, London: HMSO, 1948. 1993 Department of Transport figures reported in Cambridge *Evening News*, Friday, 20 May 1994, 1. Driver registration figure from BBC Radio, 9 August 1994.

15. Mick Hamer, *Wheels within Wheels: A Study of the Road Lobby*, London: Routledge & Kegan Paul, 1987, 31.

16. In a letter from A. T. Nash, *Cycling*, 27 July 1938, 130. The Ministry of Transport did not take such a direct position, but did report: "We are greatly impressed with the seriousness of the problem of accidents in which cyclists are involved." They noted that between 1928 and 1935 there had been a 103% increase in fatalities to cyclists, and a 149% increase in injuries (from 691 to 1,400 and from 27,680 to 69,052 respectively). Source: Ministry of Transport, *Report on Accidents to Cyclists*, op. cit., 4.

17. In a letter from E. G. Duck, *Cycling*, 21 December 1934. Temple Press seems to have accepted rather than initiated this de facto division between mechanically-propelled and muscle-powered road travel. During the early inter-war years, their weekly *MotorCycling* was heavily promoted in the pages of *Cycling*. They recommended it "To every cyclist who has motorcycling ambitions." *Cycling*, 29 October 1926, A30. As far as I can tell, no ads for *Motor Cycling* appeared in *Cycling* between late 1930 and the end of my survey in 1939.

18. *Cycling*, 21 December 1934, 678–79.

19. In a poll of reader opinion, touring in Britain ranked as the most popular phase of cycling. *Cycling*, 9 November 1938, 673.

20. Source: *Cycling Manual*, 1934. Cycling's annual list was extensive, but not exhaustive. Branches of the Clarion Cycling Clubs, for example, were not reported.

21. Ibid.

22. The *Cycling Manual* gives the home addresses of club secretaries. These were located as precisely as possible using street atlases, then plotted against Class I roads on map sheets covering Greater London. Ordnance Survey, *New popular one-inch map series*, 1:63,360, various dates of publication, 1930–1948.

23. I plan next to correlate locations on this map with data from a comprehensive study of 1929 in which a team of researchers made a street-by-street survey of London social conditions. See: Sir Hubert Llewellyn-Smith, Director, *The New Survey of London Life and Labour*, London: London School of Economics and Political Science, 1930–35, 9 vols., including maps.

24. *Cycling*, 23 August 1939, 260.

25. *Cycling*, 27 July 1938, 130.

26. See: "Should Women Race?," *Cycling*, 24 November 1921, 387; "Eve and the Club," *Cycling*, 15 April 1932, 398; page of A. J. Charles cartoons on women as race officials, *Cycling*, 1 August 1930, 125.

27. See, for example: Letter from Jessie Springall, "Women and Road Sport," *Cycling*, 12 January 1938, 50; Billie Dovey, "Cycling Women Can Help," *Cycling*, 27 September 1939, 378–79; and the entire issue "Special Number for the Woman Cyclist," *Cycling*, 15 June 1938.

28. A technical fix is an inappropriate, narrow technical solution to problems with a significant social content. The technical fix can go wrong by underestimating the social dimensions of an existing problem, or by inadvertently causing new social or environmental ones.

29. W. M. Robinson, "Wayfarer," was perhaps the most tireless promoter of lightweight cycles. In his weekly column he regularly rhapsodized about the benefits of "as little bicycle as possible." Details of the specifications vary, but he insisted on "small frames, low brackets, small wheels, light tyres, and low gears" as opposed to "25-in. and 26-in. frames, with big wheels, heavy and dead tyres, sit-up-and-beg handlebars, and brakework of the Forth Bridge type." See "Little and Good," *Bicycling News and Motor Review*, 4 November 1936; "The Future of Cycling," *Cycling*, 27 June 1924, 526.

30. Not all writers in *Cycling* recommended the same types of lightweight cycles for all riders. "Videlex," for example, advised "ease, not speed." See: "Foolish Bicycle Fashions," *Cycling*, 8 August 1930, 143–44. The overall debate, however, illustrates to what a remarkable degree cyclists of the day were concerned

31. Of course such appearances could be actively suppressed. For example, there were overtly political cycling organizations, most prominently the Clarion clubs, whose 50 branches advocated a brand of socialism. It is curious that *Cycling* reports some of their events, but does not include the Clarion clubs in its annual club listing.

32. Unfortunately, no distribution record or subscriber list survives.

33. This is to ignore for the time being other waves of social change such as economic depression, massive unemployment, and industrial relocation.

34. On cyclists' role in road improvement, see: Reginald Wellbye, "How the New Roads Came," *Cycling*, 7 January 1927, 8–9; and J. T. Lightwood, *The Cyclists' Touring Club, Being the Romance of Fifty Years' Cycling*, London: The Club, 1928. This seems to be one area of parallel international development. For the American case, see: Philip P. Mason, "The League of American Wheelmen and the Good Roads Movement, 1880–1905," unpublished Ph.D. dissertation, University of Michigan, 1957.

35. The earliest use of this phrase I found in my survey is: *Cycling*, 30 October 1919, A7.

36. Armstrong, op. cit., 165.

37. *Cycling*, 9 November 1938, 673. On British Tabulating Machine Co., see: Martin Campbell-Kelly, *ICL: A Business and Technical History*, Oxford: Clarendon Press, 1989.

with the technical details of their bicycles at a time when cycle design was supposedly frozen.

Andrew Ritchie

3. Developing a Methodological Approach to the History and Meaning of Velocipedes, Bicycles, and Tricycles

This paper is in part a response to Nicholas Oddy's paper, "Non-Technological Factors in Early Cycle Design," given at the 4th International Cycle History Conference and published in *Cycle History, Proceedings of the 4th International Cycle History Conference*, and in *The Wheelmen*, May 1994.

Let me begin by quoting an opinion from the middle of the 19th century which impresses me as relevant to the discussion about history, "invention," and methodology which is currently going on among historians of technology and cycle historians. Joseph Newton spoke to the London Association of Foremen Engineers in November 1865 about his perceptions of the development of technology in his time, and his speech was reported in *English Mechanic*:

> In affecting those vast onward strides in every branch of mechanical industry which have been made in England since the dawning of the present century, it is easy to discover the fact that the impetus has been derived not alone from the action of the few, but the combined influence of the many. I venture to say that there is scarcely an invention of an engineering nature in practical use at present which owes its existence to any one man. It is possible that the idea of a contrivance for accomplishing a certain purpose may have been the production of one fertile brain, but in its realisation, in the perfecting of details, in the surmounting of practical difficulties, in short in the working out of the scheme, ninety-nine times in the hundred, the inventor is indebted to others for suggestions, and even more tangible assistance....[1]

Technological progress in the first half of the 19th century, thought Newton, had been achieved by the efforts of people who built on the achievements of their predecessors, and of the cooperation and collaboration between them all. Progress was made, he maintained, not by isolated individuals, but by the concerted application of groups of collaborators. It is a thought to bear in mind as this discussion about bicycle history proceeds.

The search for appropriate methodology in researching and writing the history of the bicycle benefits greatly from remembering that history consists of the overlapping and interacting of people and actions in many different fields of human activity, and that thought and action follow each other, interact, fertilize, contradict, and stimulate each other frequently within a logical, chronological framework.

The most interesting thing about Nicholas Oddy's sometimes puzzling paper, "Non-Technological Factors in Early Cycle Design," is that it undertakes to examine and question, in the light of recently advanced theories about the development of technology, the usually unconscious and assumed methodology which underlies attempts to chart the history of the bicycle. It begins to ask what exactly we mean when we talk about "the history" of the bicycle, and how we can explain the many puzzling and uneven aspects in the complex story of bicycle history.

Oddy explores ideas introduced by Trevor Pinch and Wiebe Bijker in their well-known paper "The Social Construction of Facts and Artifacts,"[2] and his

---

Synopsis

Historians should be aware of both technological and social aspects of the bicycle. In the quest for a greater understanding of historical events and the bicycle's impact and significance, it is crucial to examine the frequently unconscious and assumed methodology which underlies historical inquiry.

argument, echoing Pinch and Bijker, may be summarized like this. Most cycle histories construct "a linear chronological framework with technological development as its key determinant." Such an approach is not universally applicable, and a more "socially constructed approach," a "non-technological viewpoint," is a potentially useful way of reconsidering previously held assumptions. If we re-examine many of the familiar aspects of cycle design history from a "non-technologically centered" viewpoint, it is evident that "major problems in plain technological developmental interpretation could be resolved by seriously considering the 'social construction' of design forms."

Mr. Oddy considers the documentation of the Kirkpatrick MacMillan velocipede and its descendant by McCall, and the rise of the front-driven velocipede. He concludes that "the time has come where a major reassessment of cycling history is required," suggesting that this will be most successfully carried out by the application of the "socially constructed approach" which he is outlining.

This rejoinder to some of Mr. Oddy's ideas attempts to ask a number of pertinent questions, to examine in detail some of Mr. Oddy's assertions, and to offer some of my own conclusions.

I pose two interrelated basic questions about his thesis. First, what precisely is the weakness of the "linear chronological framework" of technological development which he criticizes? Secondly, what exactly does he mean by the "socially constructed approach" which he suggests might be better? These two questions are inter-related because, of course, the history of technology is already intrinsically and inescapably the history of a "socially constructed" activity.

I argue here that the "linear technological framework" which he criticizes has a strong, historical logic, and that it should not be dismissed too easily as a convenient methodological framework. But I agree with him that it is necessary to identify "non-technological" forces which drive forward the process of technological change, and argue that this is not a new idea and that I think there is a great deal of "socially constructed" material which is already well integrated into cycle histories. Some important aspects of bicycle history, in fact, occur with only the most marginal relationship to change or development in the machine itself, for example, social and club life, or the liberation of women in the 1890s, and of course, the daily commute for millions of Chinese and Indian cyclists.

I suggest that we should look most fruitfully (but not exclusively) at user/customer reactions, and the economics of the industry and the marketplace (including professional racing) for new sources of "socially constructed" illumination of the process of technological change. And I conclude by suggesting that what we need as a methodological guideline for continuing our research is a framework grounded in conventional historical approaches, which includes a willingness to intensify our receptivity to "social" issues, but that this does not really amount to an introduction of "new" methods as a substitute for "old." Intensive, old-fashioned research, intelligent conclusions drawn from accurately analyzed source material, and good communications between researchers like ourselves are definitely good methodology.

Allow me to quote from a familiar classic of cycling literature, the Badminton *Cycling*, 1889 edition, in which journalist and bureaucrat George Lacy Hillier, in looking back over a mere 20 years of cycling history, addresses some of the same issues Mr. Oddy raises. He is writing right at the dawn of the safety bicycle:

> England may be looked upon as the home of cycling; the national habit of organisation which our countrymen possess in an eminent degree, and the national love for every form of strong personal exertion, combine to make it a pursuit in every way adapted to the taste of our people....
>
> In the streets of our great cities and in highways and byways throughout the land, carriages, swift and serviceable, propelled by the power of human muscles alone, have become common. The sight of a traveller of either sex, seated on a light machine, and proceeding with considerable rapidity and apparently but little exertion, is so usual that the wayfarer hardly turns his head to look at the accustomed sight. Yet it is but a very short time ago that the passage of a cyclist was wont to produce an exhibition of considerable excitement, and sometimes even demonstrations of hostility.
>
> It is however not only as a means of locomotion that the cycle has produced a change in this and many foreign countries. The manufacture of these carriages has caused a considerable trade to come into existence, and a new and very exciting mode of racing has been added to the sports of the world. The historian of cycling has therefore something to say of it as a trade, as a sport, and as a pastime: beyond this, again, there is something to be said as to the social

organisation to which it has given rise, and the not inconsiderable industry to which the requirements of the cycling public give employment outside the limits of the cycle-builder's factory.[3]

Lacy Hillier remarks on the rapidity and universality of the bicycle revolution, and its wide-ranging economic and social impact. And Hillier, the grandfather of cycling historians, is right: as historians, we cannot ignore any of the social contexts within which cycling has an impact, and which in their turn affect the design and technology of the machine itself. The history of cycling, as Lacy Hillier suggests, should be considered in at least four separate but interconnected contexts—as transport ("a means of locomotion"), as a trade and industry, as a sport, and as a pastime.

Taking my clue from Lacy Hillier, I would like to examine briefly these four areas. In each of the four areas it will, I hope, be possible to demonstrate how both chronology and "social" factors play a crucial part in the evolution of bicycle history.

1. Cycling As Transport

Mr. Oddy is at his weakest in writing about this issue. Historians are wrong to treat the bicycle as a serious means of transport, he says. "The concept that the design development of cycles revolved around providing a serious means of transport suits the 'functionalist' nature of old-fashioned history of technology and serves those histories based on precedent, but it avoids addressing what perceptions of cycles really were at the time of their currency, and how those perceptions might account for the strangely broken history of the technological development of the cycle."

Mr. Oddy thinks that "one of the key factors of cycling history is the cycle's uselessness in practical terms," that 19th-century cyclists were mistaken in their belief that cycling was a serious means of transport, and that "at no time in the 19th century does any cycle offer a substantial advantage over other available forms of transport." "Even at the close of the century," he argues, "practical applications were minimal."

Mr. Oddy struggles to develop a coherent point of view on this issue, but never succeeds. He sees the early evolution of the bicycle as an on-again, off-again affair, a series of failures. The hobbyhorse was a useless novelty; Kirkpatrick MacMillan's velocipede was "an effective means of transport" but it could not rival the railways, and therefore did not make any headway.

Focusing attention on the reporter's comment at the end of the famous article in the *Glasgow Argus*, 1842, "This invention will not supercede the railways," Mr. Oddy asks us to approve of his selection of this comment (as opposed to the more commonly quoted passages) as an example of using a "non-technologically oriented approach," and expresses the opinion that it is "probably the most telling statement of attitudes towards machines such as MacMillan's in the mid-century," whereas commonsense indicates that this comment is almost certainly a tongue-in-cheek editorial aside.[4]

I'm not really sure what Mr. Oddy is trying to convince us of here. Of course the bicycle was never, except for very short distances, a rival of the railway. But if there is one thing that emerges with utmost certainty from close textual readings of 19th-century cycling history, it is that the velocipede and then the bicycle were a useful means of personal transport, and were generally regarded as such by those who used them. The reason that the bicycle was useful was that it was faster than walking and cheaper than a horse or a bus (or train for short distances). That was precisely its advantage over other means of transport. As Sir Albert Rollit, M.P., put it at the opening of the 1892 Stanley Show, "The cycle is the poor man's horse and the rich man's hobby."[5]

Hundreds of passages, all of which I cannot possibly quote, make this abundantly clear, and they start to occur with great frequency even in the prehistory of the bicycle.

> Sir—I manufactured a velocipede to carry three persons when I was in Scotland. It was made in a fortnight. I enjoyed the pleasure of driving it for a month....You have no idea how much labour and money it saved in that time. The distance we travelled with it would have cost us for riding at the rate of 14 shillings per day for 19 days.[6]

> ...It must be borne in mind that the fittest use of the Bicycle is not to treat it as a toy...but to use it as a vehicle, as an ordinary means of transit from one place to another, over roads rougher or smoother as the case may be....Even postmen are now assiduously practising with the object of accelerating their movements in country districts innocent of railways."[7]

> ...in the pursuit of business cycling is of great value. In many parts of the country labourers are able to live at a considerable distance from their work, and

mechanics are to be seen in considerable numbers with their tool-bags slung at their backs riding home at the end of their day's labour....In Coventry, which may be looked upon as the peculiar home of cycling, it is fast becoming the custom for workmen to go home on their bicycles during the dinner-hour (lunch-time).

As a vehicle for business purposes the tricycle has even a larger future before it than the bicycle. It will carry a considerable quantity of luggage, and can be drawn up to the side of the street and left unprotected until the owner returns. The number of shopkeepers who employ the carrier tricycle for the purposes of distributing their parcels, or circulating daily supplies to their customers, is steadily increasing. The milkman, the newsvendor, the butcher, send an active lad on their daily rounds.[8]

The goal of cheap personal mobility (not necessarily without a considerable initial investment, of course) is perhaps more than any other the social force which has driven forward the evolution of the bicycle and the process of change in cycle technology. From the concern of a small minority in the early days, it became a mass concern by the 1890s, when millions of bicycles were manufactured, and is still today, perhaps more than ever before, a vital form of transportation.

Why are there so many bicycles in Oxford and Cambridge or Davis, California? Why are there millions of bicycles in India and China? Why do I ride my bicycle into town to do my daily errands? The answers are simple: it's quick, it's cheap, it's independent, and it's convenient.

2. Cycling As a Trade

It is in looking at the bicycle industry, at the actual production of the machine itself that, I would suggest, we see most clearly the strong, persuasive validity of the "linear chronological development" which Oddy criticizes, and how this technological development is always modified by "social" issues. What we as historians need to examine, once the bicycle has moved out of the blacksmith's shops of the amateur mechanics in about 1867–68, is the organization and economics of industrial mass production, and the necessity to sell a product.

The production of the boneshaker, in Britain and France, as the foundation of the bicycle industry, presents a fascinating opportunity, as yet not fully undertaken, to study the growth of a large, modern, consumer industry out of the fragmentary, scattered workshops of isolated craftsmen.

A contemporary French illustration of the Compagnie Parisienne des Vélocipèdes in 1869 shows that the bicycle industry was big from the beginning, and it never gets any smaller. From that point on, we are dealing with many different kinds, models, designs of machines, mass-produced annually to fulfill the demands of a consumer market, machines which had to be designed on the drawing board, estimated, have materials ordered, be metal welded, brazed, filed, drilled, threaded, plated,

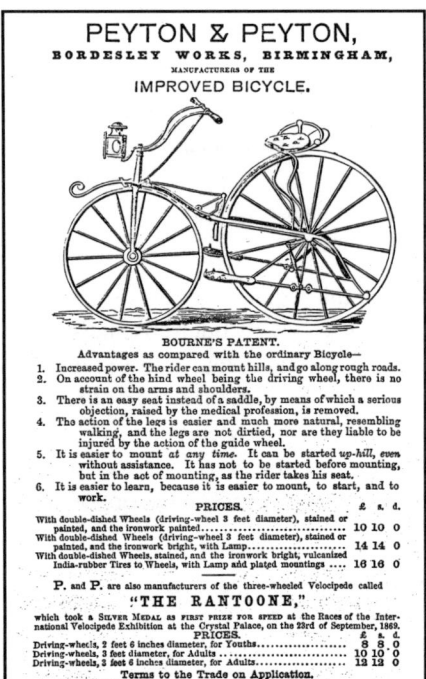

Fig. 3.1. Peyton and Peyton's "Improved Bicycle," advertisement included in Wheels and Woes, "Words of Warning to Would-be Velocipedists, by a Light Dragoon," London, 1870.

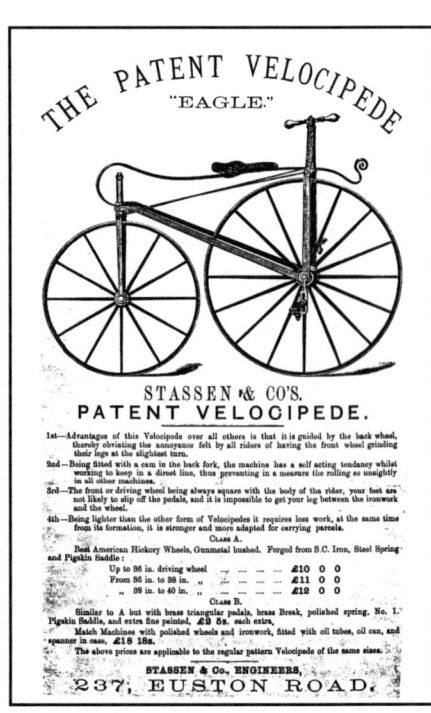

Fig. 3.2. Advertisement for the Eagle Patent Velocipede, illustrated in Nick Clayton's Early Bicycles, Shire Publications, 1985.

painted, and assembled—and then advertised and distributed.

All the time, the customer had to be considered. What had he bought last year, and what would he be likely to buy next? The annual balance sheets cast an iron logic over the proceedings. This can be seen at work from a close reading of texts written by those closest to the design process, the manufacturers' catalogues and advertisements in cycling papers. These examples show the constant desire for change and improvement and innovation, for a better, lighter, faster, more efficient, more advanced machine.

But the underlying drive behind this process of change is not of course for technological change per se, but for change in response to a perceived practical need, which always has a "social" cause. And it is this constantly changing practical need which, I would submit, most frequently drives forward the evolution of the bicycle. It is, after all, a machine which is used, tinkered with, ridden to victory upon, crashed from, suffered upon by living, breathing human beings.

Let's look at two examples, where we see manufacturers trying to provide answers to practical problems of the front-driven boneshaker.

Peyton and Peyton's fascinating "Improved Bicycle" seems to look both forward and back—back to velocipede design, and forward to the rear-driven bicycle. The manufacturers offer a well-articulated list of "advantages as compared with the ordinary bicycle: it has power, there is no strain on the arms because it is rear-driven, the front wheel does not rub on the inside of the legs, and it has a seat instead of a saddle, which removes 'a serious objection raised by the medical profession.'" There are no customer testimonials.

Stassen's "Eagle" velocipede is advertised with similar conviction. Its main selling point is that it is steered by the back wheel "thereby obviating the annoyance felt by all riders of having the front wheel grinding their legs at the slightest turn," the alleged advantage being that the front wheel is always square to the body of the rider (Figs 3.1 and 3.2).

Both of these designs were tackling real problems and providing logical solutions to them. We would be absolutely justified in assuming that some aspects of the design advantages suggested in these two machines would have been incorporated into future designs soon after, but that did not happen. Both of these machines were failures and disappeared. Why? Why did the high-wheel bicycle win the battle of evolution in the early 1870s?

My answer to the question is based partly in my experience as a rider. My own feeling is that a larger front wheel (giving a bigger gear) provided flexibility, the fly-wheel effect that the jerky rear-driver did not have; that it accelerated smoothly and efficiently; and that there was an interaction between pedalling and steering which a skillful rider, high above his work, could master.

The fact that the larger front-driven bicycle was chosen by racing cyclists and was successful in racing also had a huge impact on determining it as the machine of choice for the next 15 years. Safety did not become the issue until much later, when it became one of the "social" forces which quickly drove the technologically-dominant "ordinary" to its grave.

In both of these examples quoted above, technological change is embraced by makers in their search for a more acceptable, more efficient machine to put onto the market. The manufacturers hope they will be able to put their ideas into production in competition with other machines in the process of design evolution. Everybody is looking at what everybody else is doing, especially since the first shows had already begun by 1869. But design "logic" is not necessarily what works best in practice, or meets favor with the user.

Later, through the 1880s and 1890s, shows become more and more important in the process of design evolution and accelerate the exchange of information. The market drove technological development forward. Hard decisions had to be made about each year's models, and this factor is repeated year after year, the cyclical heartbeat of the industry. Demand, profit, and success, the commercial logic of mass production in the marketplace, are the driving forces behind technological change. Fashion, of course, may also play a part in the vagaries of change, and aesthetics may become incorporated into the logic of production.

3. Cycling As a Sport

Lacy Hillier again, in 1891:

> We venture to credit the comparatively small section of racing men with being the cause of the rapid improvement which has been made in bicycles and tricycles. Possibly the manufacturers would tell us that the racing men gave them more trouble, and were more difficult to please, than any other section of their customers, and doubtless this would be quite true; but it

is particularly this fact which has brought about a desire on the part of the manufacturers to meet these particular gentlemen, and in that endeavour they have vastly improved the machines they manufacture, not only for the small class of racing men, but also for the much larger body of general riders.[9]

A rapidly developing sport like cycling never stands still, its advance is constant; the records of today are but the average performances of tomorrow....Machines are being invented, developed, remodelled, day by day; the apparently perfect contrivance is but the crude germ of some startling development....[10]

The importance of racing has, I feel, been drastically underestimated, often treated as an afterthought, in bicycle design evolution, whereas it has in many respects been absolutely central.

Racing proves which machine, and which design of machine, is better than the others at achieving speed under given conditions (road or track, for instance). That has always been one of its purposes. Racing was crucial from the moment that rival boneshaker manufacturers competed for customers, and there was professional racing right from the very beginnings of the sport in 1868, contrary to the common assumption that amateurism necessarily precedes professionalism.

Probably racing accelerated the evolution of the boneshaker into the fine, light, beautifully constructed (and dangerous) high-wheeler, as Andrew Millward points out in his excellent paper, "The Genesis of the British Cycle Industry."[11] The front-driven boneshaker was fluid, easily driven forward, and it responded to acceleration in the naturalness of rotary motion. Contemporary lever-driven velocipedes were jerky and would not accelerate easily.

Racing on the track and on the road was tremendously important for manufacturers throughout the 1880s and 1890s, indeed the chasing after records and advertising victories was already a crucial part of their marketing strategy at this time.

The bicycle manufacturer is in business to succeed—he wants his own machine to be a winner. A rider chosen by a maker to ride his machine in competition for prizes became a de facto professional. Amateur riders not so supported disliked the professionals' perceived advantages, and this conflict caused no end of problems in the sport.

The testing of new ideas in racing has always been an intrinsic aspect of the evolution of cycle design. The pneumatic tire, the derailleur gear, cotterless cranks, clipless pedals...all were tested and proved in races.

The current state of racing shows a fascinating and still unfolding dichotomy as far as design is concerned, with the manufacturers concerned to generate and market fashion vying with the very real concerns of competitive cyclists. Yet we would misunderstand the situation completely if we did not remind ourselves that machines evolve in different ways for very different purposes.

In the last few years we have witnessed momentous events in racing. Lemond beat Fignon in the 1988 Tour de France by an unprecedented 8 sec. margin because he used radical technology—aero bars. Now we have Boardman and Obree using radical new designs to break track records under highly controlled conditions, just as the motor-paced

Fig. 3.3. From Le Monde Illustré, 21 Nov. 1868.

Fig. 3.4. "Costume original des dames au concours de vélocipèdes, à Bordeaux," from Le Monde Illustré, 21 Nov. 1868.

riders of the 1890s did. We have radical aero-ization of road bikes for relatively flat time trials, but in the hills these bikes are not favored, and for the hard business of the road, the good old road bike stays practically the same, with the recent changes being confined to clipless pedals and integral brake and derailleur levers. Miguel Indurain's road bike of 1994 is not much changed in overall design from Fausto Coppi's of 1950.

The bicycle has been and still is constantly evolving in an almost bewildering series of permutations. Certainly we must include racing as a powerful agent of change when we evaluate appropriate research methodology.

4. Cycling As a Pastime

I will be brief here. That cycling in the late 19th century was a pastime which reached out to touch people's lives, and had a considerable social force is shown by the following statistics from The Hub, 24 July 1897. In 1897, there were 1,869 cycling clubs in Britain, of which 295 were in London, 55 in Birmingham, and 45 in Liverpool. Together they had about 100,000 members. The C.T.C. had 40,000 members. The Catford C.C. had 428 members, the London County C. and A. C. had 400, the Tottenham Wheelers, 200.

Cycling as a pastime was primarily a social activity. It impacted the evolution of bicycle technology with demands for comfort, durability, and safety. Pneumatic tires made cycling on public roads thinkable for the masses. Cycling as pastime merged with cycling as transport. Cycling as pastime created a mass of smaller economic activities—dealing with clothes, hotels, and accessories.

Conclusion

The question "What do we mean by history?" is what Mr. Oddy is in reality asking throughout his article. And the questions we must also add here, which are closely linked to discussion of methodology, are: "What kinds of sources are available to us to tell our story? What do these sources tell us? What use exactly are we going to make of these sources?" And, finally, "How are we going to interpret the information we get from our sources, and what larger inferences, deductions and conclusions are we entitled to make from them?"

Here, in this context, we should pause for a moment to remind ourselves how lucky we are to have, in the 150 years of the bicycle's history, such a rich and diverse complex of objects (bicycles themselves), photographs, illustrations, and written materials upon which to draw. Primary written materials include general and specialist newspapers and magazines, books and annuals, novels, guides, sales catalogs, patent files, personal memoirs, race programs, maps, and other items—materials which run the whole gamut of activity in the industry, the sport, the pastime, and in transportation.

The newspaper literature is rich and plentiful. There is a lot of information waiting to be discovered. Perhaps one aspect of methodology needs to be adaptability, the ability to make sense of many different kinds of evidence—having the "nose" to know where to look next.

Pictures, too, are important sources of evidence, and are not frequently analyzed as source material. In general, in researching bicycle history, we encounter 4 or 5 categories of pictures: photographs, line engravings, manufacturers' or advertising sketches, and poster art, but by far the most common are photographs, and news and advertising line engravings. We need to look at the context in which a picture was created, as well as its contents, to make sense of it.

Consider the two well-known engravings showing velocipede racing (Figs. 3.3 and 3.4).Can we take them as photographically close to reality? From about 1850 to 1890, magazines such as the *Illustrated London News* and *Le Monde Illustré* often copied photographs as a source for line engravings, and knowing this helps us to understand that these illustrations are probably close to reality. They show women's racing and indoor racing, and they tell us

Fig. 3.5. Female cyclist, carte de visite by Parisian photographer Reutlinger, from Munby Collection, Cambridge University Library, England.

that as a spectacle, racing was already intensely popular. It is fair to conclude that we are looking at professional entertainers—someone is making a good deal of money here.

The solitary lady rider in Fig. 3.5 poses a different problem. Certainly we know that she is French, and we can get solid information about her machine. But to know anything reliable about her, who she is, and what she is doing, is a little more difficult. Is this a photograph of a professional velocipede racer, one of the ladies depicted in Fig. 3? Perhaps, yes, but she might also be a circus performer. Knowing that Reutlinger was a Parisian photographer who specialized in photographing actors and actresses confirms that we are making the right conclusion in labeling her an entertainer, and this also tells us a good deal about the origins of women's cycling in France—but we still do not know the specific context of this photograph. We have to look carefully and weigh the evidence—we cannot just make assumptions about such a photo.

A well-rounded, meaningful effort to interpret bicycle history should attempt to make use of all the relevant source material, weighing and balancing it perceptively, and relating different areas together so that the relationships illuminate and are as much as possible truthful to the evidence of history. The goal of the historian is to show the "truth" of a situation or complex of situations, and ensure that it will be amply and elegantly demonstrated by the evidence.

In the end, this discussion of methodology should be useful in helping to clarify what is and what is not historically "true." It should help to define terms, to define what we mean by evidence, and how we interpret historical evidence. In other words, it should give us a better chance of constructing some kind of order around the "truth," a skeleton upon which to hang the flesh.

I don't really think we need a reassessment of cycle history, or a change in the methodology used to approach it, so much as an intensification and deepening of our research. Shifts in emphasis can certainly be valuable, and the re-examination of established assumptions crucial. There is a great deal of fascinating material still to be uncovered. The documentation is extraordinary, and goes back right to the very beginnings of the velocipede's existence. We are not dealing with fossils lying deep in the ground, but with bold, well-preserved skeletons just waiting on the surface to be discovered.

New discoveries and conclusions are most likely to come from good old-fashioned archival digging, good communications between researchers, and intelligent interpretations of reliable data backed by a broad knowledge of the field than from the application of a sketchily defined "new" methodology. "Chronological" and "social" approaches are equally likely to yield historical insight. The "linear chronological framework" of technological development can be a very useful guide as long as it is always remembered that it is people and their economic and social relationships that inevitably push technology forward.

Emerging technology is, after all, inevitably a "social" activity.

Notes

1. *English Mechanic*, 1 Dec. 1865.
2. Trevor Pinch and Wiebe Bijker, "The Social Construction of Facts and Artifacts: Or How the Sociology of Science and the Sociology of Technology Might Benefit Each Other," in *The Social Construction of Technological Systems* (New Directions in the Sociology and History of Technology, edited by W. Bijker, T. Hughes and T. Pinch), 1984.
3. Viscount Bury and G. Lacy Hillier, *Cycling*, The Badminton Library, London, 1889 Edition; Introduction, pp. 2–3.
4. The passage in question, which has until recently been generally accepted as an account of MacMillan riding a "bicycle," can be found in *Glasgow Argus*, 9 June 1842, p. 2, col. 4.
5. Quoted in *Northern Wheeler*, 7 Dec. 1892.
6. *English Mechanic*, 10 Aug. 1866.
7. Charles Spencer, *The Bicycle, Its Use and Action*, 1870.
8. G. Lacy Hillier, Badminton *Cycling*, 1889, p. 7.
9. G. Lacy Hillier, Badminton Cycling, 1891, "Racing," p. 171.
10. op. cit., Appendix, p. 409.
11. Andrew Millward, "The Genesis of the British Cycle Industry," *Proceedings of the 1st International Cycle History Conference*, Glasgow, 1990.

Nicholas Oddy

4. The Bicycle— An Exercise in Gendered Design

Almost since their invention, bicycles have been gendered by the existence of specifically ladies' machines, these being designed in such a way to accommodate riders wearing long skirts. The very existence of these machines as early as 1820 points to a realisation that bicycling was not necessarily a gendered activity, but that the bicycle itself was a gendered object; unless stated otherwise bicycles were, effectively, male.

As far as cycle makes were concerned, the gender of the cycle was determined by the skirt, and throughout the 19th century makers attempted to de-gender the activity of bicycling by providing machines for women wearing skirts. The cycle makers' response was, therefore, to provide another gendered object, something which they achieved with great success in the 1890s.

The alternative to this was to de-gender bicycling by de-gendering the object, by attacking the determining factor—the skirt. This strategy was rider-led and was pursued with some success and great publicity in the latter years of the century. However, while it succeeded in establishing divided garments as an alternative to the skirt for cycling, it did not seriously affect the perception of the object: there were and still are male and female bicycles, those which are perceived as not providing or providing provision for skirts.

While many histories of cycles and of cycling pay considerable attention to the latter process, they tend to pay only cursory attention to the former: female bicycles are treated as mutated male machines and, being generally less structurally efficient than their male counterparts, they do not suit the technologically determinist stance which characterises such histories. This paper sets out to begin to redress this balance by focusing on the design of the gendered object. It will explore the process which led to the creation of the type-form male and female machines, and the seemingly unchallenged supremacy of these type forms in the years since the earliest bicycles.

The earliest bicycles proclaimed their gender through frame design. Von Drais, the inventor of the machine, and seemingly all his copyists, employed a frame structure in which the wheels were effectively hung on trunnions below a connecting beam with the saddle mounted on top of the beam. To ride the machine one sat astride the beam, which would interfere too much with a long skirt to make riding practicable for a respectably dressed woman; in addition, mounting the machine by swinging a leg over the connecting beam was considered an unseemly action for a lady. For the machine to be accessible to women who did not wish to completely flaunt social convention, the machine would have to be designed in such a way that one could easily step over its frame and, once astride the saddle, would allow enough "drop" for a skirt to hang uninterrupted. Had Drais designed his machine with a low forked beam which would allow for both these requirements, the concept of male and female machines might not have been established so early but, as it was, both activity and object were clearly defined as male.

Synopsis

The ladies' bicycle seems to possess a somewhat contradictory role in many cycling histories. On the one hand it is perceived as a major component in women's emancipation and dress reform in the late 19th century, on the other it is seen as a design compromised by the very social pressures it is seen to be a tool in dismantling. Since that time, the concept of what is a female or a male bicycle has remained intact; indeed it could be argued that female machines have become more feminine in recent years, in spite of the erosion of those factors which created the ladies' bicycle in the first place. This paper explores the creation and remarkable persistency of gendering in cycle design.

The earliest attempt at providing a female machine was probably made by Denis Johnston of London. His female machine was built as early as 1819, only 2 years after Von Drais first demonstrated his invention; however, in that time the precedent had become established. Johnston's female machines were, effectively, developed out of, and were therefore second to, their male counterparts. As far as cycling histories go, this assumption has never been challenged.

If the frame was to determine the gender of the earliest machines of circa 1820, technology might be considered the chief factor in gendering the driven machine of the mid to late-19th century. Here the wide-scale adoption of front wheel drive was, to all intents and purposes, to preclude female bicycles altogether. With cranks and pedals mounted each side of the hub of the front wheel, it was almost impossible to ride the machine in a long skirt. The few builders who attempted to produce female counterparts to these machines either tried to make sidesaddle versions with a crank arrangement on one side of the front wheel, and a compensatory offset rear wheel, or fundamentally altered the arrangement by adopting a lever drive to the rear wheel with the rider sitting forward. Both designs posed difficulties for mounting and balance when setting off, and this might explain their seeming unpopularity. None established enough following to make a gender classification requirement for either the "boneshaker" of the 1860s, or the high-wheeled "ordinary" bicycle of the 1870s and 1880s; bicycles and bicycling remained unquestionably male.

Could it be argued that the gendered nature of the object was the key determinant in establishing the gendering of the activity during this period, over social pressures which might have been effective no matter what the design of the machine? Here it is worthwhile to consider tricycling, where the designs of the machines contemporary with the clearly male ordinary did not fall into any obvious gender classification. Tricycles were generally "open" forward of their saddles and therefore did not challenge female dress conventions, while their safety and reliability, particularly on poorer roads, appealed equally to male and female riders. Tricycling seems to have been equally popular for both sexes at this time, suggesting that it was the bicycle itself rather than cycling as an activity that was the key male factor in the ordinary period.

The type forms which we recognise today as male and female bicycles, or to use the terminology of the 1890s still common today, "gentlemen's" and "ladies'," were established in the period 1885–95 when the rear-driven "dwarf safety" bicycle became established as the preeminent bicycle design. This type of machine was first successfully marketed by Starley and Sutton as the "Rover" in 1885, but it was by no means the first design of its type. Other makers had produced machines employing the same principles in the 1870s, and notably in 1884 H. J. Lawson had manufactured an open-frame rear chain-driven safety bicycle, the design of which seems to have had no clear gender implications. In 1884, Lawson does not seem to have realised that this design might be construed as female.[1] Lawson was interested in safety and possibly designed the frame with ease of mounting in mind for a male rider; equally the design's conspicuously curvaceous and elegant frame structure could be a response to the ridicule Lawson's earlier ungainly "crocodile-like"[2] bicycle designs had met with in the 70s. Lawson was later to claim that his 1884 design was a ladies' machine, but this might well be the application of hindsight on to a design which was actually aimed at the existing male cycling culture, but which was not marketed in the right way to appeal to it. Lawson's 1884 machine must remain as one of the few truly genderless bicycle designs of the 19th century, if only because of the contradictions between its physical and social construction. In the former case its physical design might gender it as neutral or female, but had Lawson successfully managed to establish the machine in the existing market, it would presumably have become socially constructed as a male object.

Lawson's 1884 design comes at a date where "closure"[3] as far as the design of safety bicycles were concerned had not been achieved, and there was nothing to say whether or not rear-driven safety bicycles for male riders were to have open or closed frames. The determining gendering factor for Lawson's machine was its intended rider.

Starley and Sutton's "Rover" bicycle, on the other hand, was clearly gendered in design and by its marketing. None of Starley's[4] designs at this time had provision for a rider wearing long skirts, although the Mark 2 machine (on which the rear driver's success was founded) could easily have been redesigned for such a requirement. More importantly, Starley seems not to have been aiming to expand the bicycle market beyond its existent athletic male boundaries, but was interested in carving his sales out of existing cyclists. Starley and Sutton mounted an aggressive sales campaign which emphasised those features which would appeal to this market, notably speed and performance. The "safety" feature of the Rover was not emphasised, but Rovers were entered in high profile races against the established type form of the high-wheeled ordinary and rival front-driven safeties in order to demonstrate their superiority.[5] Other manufacturers followed suit, and the rear-driven safety's potential in terms of a broader market was not to be fully realised until the 1890s. In this way Starley's Rover should not be seen as radically changing cycling culture in the 1880s, as seems to be suggested in many histories. Rather, Starley lodged his machine firmly within the existing male cycling culture, and in so doing established the rear wheel chain-drive bicycle as a male machine, no matter what its design. Starley's Rover was, in cultural terms, no different from the ordinary.

An illustration of this type of cultural construction of frame design, not dissimilar to the H. J. Lawson 1884 bicycle mentioned above, is the cross-frame pattern safety, a type of rear wheel chain-drive machine popular in the 1885–90 period. The cross frame was perceived as purely male at this time, but, when what was effectively the same frame was adopted by Alex Moulton in the 1960s, its gender was reinterpreted as unisex while many more conservative established cyclists considered it a women's bicycle.

What factors allow for such a change of interpretation to take place? As has been mentioned, in the late 1880s the type form of safety bicycle had not reached "closure," but it was assumed that all bicycles were male. The few designers who experimented with broadening their product range to include bicycles for female riders in the 1885–90 period had to make it clear that such machines were specifically for ladies. This was soon to change: by the mid-1890s the diamond frame had come to dominate cycle design, its high crossbar proclaiming its maleness. Female bicycles were effectively the same design with the crossbar removed or, more commonly, "dropped" to provide a step-through frame with skirt clearance. Pinch and Bijker claim that by 1898 "closure" had been achieved in bicycle design, and the type-form bicycles with which we are still familiar today had become established.[6] From this time on male machines had crossbars, female machines did not. Thus, when after 70 years of non-use Moulton resurrected the cross frame, its lack of crossbar proclaimed it as not being male, while in the 1880s the crossbar did not carry such cultural meaning. It can be argued that the more or less universal adoption of the diamond frame in the 1890s is the key element in the establishment of the gendered bicycle in the post-ordinary period.

Could it be that, had the safety bicycle continued to be developed along the "cross frame" pattern which offered more clearance for a skirt, women might have taken to using these machines, and the social construction of bicycles as male would have been eroded? This is possible, but I would contend that such a reinterpretation could only have been achieved had makers never offered a "ladies'" bicycle as an alternative design to those of unstated but assumed male configuration. As it was, those makers who realised the potential of the safety bicycle for female riders set about producing machines designed particularly to address clothing conventions and specifying them as being for ladies' use. While this was certainly a sensible marketing move given the highly gendered social conventions

Fig. 4.1. Lady riding sidesaddle about 1872 (from Bicycle Books collection).

of the time, and the likely criticism of female bicyclists being "masculine" had they not been provided with a specifically feminine bicycle, the provision of defined women's machines was to confirm that those designs not labelled as ladies' bicycles were, per se, gentlemen's bicycles, even if this was challenged by actual use. An example of this can be found in Parisian bicycling activity in the 1890s. Here, the adoption of divided garments was seen as fashionable and was quite commonplace amongst female cyclists, many of whom rode diamond-framed machines.[7] However, this did not lead to any real attempt to reclassify the gender of the diamond frame amongst French or indeed any other manufacturers or commentators. Such riders were women riding men's bicycles.[8]

Returning to the cross frame, it is likely then that even had this design continued to be a standard type form during the 1890s and beyond and been adopted by female riders, it would have remained a male design. The reason why its gender could be reinterpreted in the 1960s was that it had died out of common use before closure of the gendered design forms had been achieved.

The closure of design around the diamond frame is therefore not so important in terms of establishing the principle of gendered bicycles, but rather it establishes the key signifier of the object's gender, namely the crossbar. The longevity and success of the diamond frame in fact seems to have had the effect of reversing the assumptions made regarding gender in bicycle design. Prior to the diamond frame, all bicycle designs were presumed male unless stated otherwise; since the establishment of the diamond frame, any bicycle which does not have a clearly defined "crossbar" in the manner of the "classic" diamond frame is likely to be presumed feminine. An example here is the so-called "mixte" frame which, though originally designed as unisex, was quickly feminised because it lacked the crossbar. Since the 1970s at least, few bicycle builders have considered the mixte frame bicycle as anything other than a female machine.

Why has the mixte become female, yet the Moulton, introduced as unisex, has managed to retain its genderless classification? Here we need to consider relationships to type forms. The mixte frame bicycle is basically a diamond-frame bicycle with the crossbar replaced by 2 tubes running from steering head to rear fork ends; as such it fits the assumption that female machines are essentially diamond-frame bicycles with the crossbar removed. The Moulton, on the other hand, is not a diamond-frame machine at all. This, coupled with its small wheels, makes it so radically different to the type-form diamond-frame machine that assumptions regarding its gender are not easily made, and it can remain a unisex machine. However, I would question whether or not the Moulton could ever have been considered as a male machine, as its "step-through" low frame gives a reading of skirt clearance similar to that of the "dropped-frame" ladies' machines which have become the type-form female bicycles.

It has been noted that today the gender classification of bicycle design revolves round "assumptions about women's clothing which were current a century ago and are now severely out of date, if not completely irrelevant."[9] This points to an interesting possibility that a design form's closure takes with it the social construction of the context of its "closure" until an opportunity occurs for the design to be reopened. If this does not happen for a long time, as in the case of cycle design, then what was a social construction becomes so obscure and irrelevant that it can only be accounted for in terms of "tradition."[10] It would seem that as the practical origins of what we recognise as male and female bicycles fade into history, designers have begun to turn to aesthetic considerations in keeping the gender classifications active.

A purchaser of a ladies' bicycle in the 1890s would buy a bicycle similar in finish to that of its gentlemen's counterpart. Differences would be found in componentry and frame design, but in terms of paintwork, plating, transfers, and publicity the machines would be treated as one and the same. This might be because female bicycles were designed in the context of the existing male cycling culture. Bicycle builders assumed that the ladies' machine should aim at providing the same as the gentlemen's equivalent, given the practical constraints of clothing and mounting. There seems to have been no attempt to reconsider whether or not male cyclists might find open frame designs more convenient and easy, possibly because bicycle makers seem to have assumed that male bicyclists in the 1890s were an identical group to those who rode ordinaries, and valued sporting specifications more than any other. The almost universal black finish which characterises machines of this period also had its origins in the ordinary period—it was seen as practical and serviceable; anything more flashy was presumed by many commentators to be at the expense of constructional qualities. It was argued that the best makers did not need to waste effort in making the machine "best please the untrained eye."[11] With this as the guiding rule, it is no surprise that almost all makers aspired to such a finish, regardless of the use that the machine was to be put to. When female bicycles started to be introduced, their finish was viewed similarly.

Much the same could be said for catalogues and publicity. Here there are few efforts made to respond to female stereotyping—machines are illustrated in a flat-on technical manner with a list of specifications given next to them. Where descriptions between ladies' and gentlemen's machines vary most are limited to a word or two added to the female specification such as "elegant" or "artistically finished" (in spite of being no different to the finish of the male models).

In comparison, since WWII, and particularly in the last 25 years, it has been more common for manufacturers to design "femininity" into female machines and their related sales literature, while "masculinity" is also more stated for diamond-framed machines than previously. This is achieved by the use of different colours and transfers for the two genders (white and "brights" being used for female, black and darker tones for male); naming policies; and more emphasis being placed on technological specification in the description of male bicycles; and on appearance and comfort for the female.[12]

Remarkably then, it would seem that as the practical reason for female machines being so classified diminishes (i.e., the provision for very full skirts), the dropped-frame machine is being made more, rather than less, feminine. Why is this? Might not a male rider find an open frame an advantage? Surely one would expect makers to attempt to drop the "ladies" classification and try to sell the drop frame to a broader constituency?

To address these questions one needs to return to the 1890s, as it is here that a hierarchy which has continued in cycle design to this day was firmly set. Ladies' bicycles were not a design form in their own right: in spite of being more difficult to build, generally better equipped, and more expensive than gentlemen's bicycles, they were a male design compromised by social conditions. Invariably they were seen as lesser machines to their male counterparts. Through the 1890s various makers attempted to design a female frame which was as rigid as the diamond frame, as rigidity was a feature of the diamond-framed machine; in the same way there was a pressure to lighten diamond-framed machines, as lightness was a feature of the best track machines. This hierarchy of specification took little account of the actual use of the bicycles, most of which were probably employed for promenading and light touring, for which comfort is much more a requirement than rigidity or lightness (one could argue that for this purpose the drop-framed machine was ideal), but was based on a 1870s and 1880s athletic male market profile: effectively the social construction of cycling, at least in the eyes of cycle builders, had reached "closure" during the era of the high-wheeled "ordinary."

In this hierarchical structure of design forms it was possible to aim up, i.e., to the athletic sporting male machine, but it was certainly not so easy to go down. As social conditions changed it became more acceptable for female cyclists to ride the male diamond frame, but for a male cyclist to ride the female dropped frame was, and still is, a different matter. Here there are obviously close connections with cross-dressing, and it could be argued that the important feature of the dropped frame was not that it was designed for easy mounting and dismounting, or to offer a more comfortable ride, but that it was designed to be ridden in a skirt. No matter how obsolete this feature of the design has become, it seems to be firmly rooted in the minds of both manufacturers and purchasers.[13] As a result the

Fig. 4.2. Early 20th-century ladies' bicycle design—and the correct dress for a young lady of the day (from Bicycle Books collection).

dropped-frame bicycle has become as feminine as the skirt it was intended to accommodate, and manufacturers have begun to divorce the type form from its diamond-frame counterpart. No longer is the female bicycle treated as a compromised male machine; rather it has become an exercise in femininity in its own right. It is no surprise that few manufacturers are willing to try to reassess the gender of the dropped frame, but instead turn to stereotyping the femininity of the design.

Notes

1. Roberts, *Cycling History—Myths and Queries*, p. 43.

2. Pinch and Bijker, "The Social Construction of Facts and Artefacts" in Bijker, Hughes, and Pinch: *The Social Construction of Technological Systems*, pp. 17–50, p. 39. This description probably derives from *The Cyclist*, 21 April 1880, cited in Ritchie, *King of the Road*, p. 124.

3. Closure is the term used to describe the point at which a dominant design becomes the type form against which all others are measured.

4. John Kemp Starley was both principle designer and leading partner of Starley and Sutton.

5. Ritchie, *King of the Road*, pp. 129, 130.

6. Pinch and Bijker, op. cit. p. 39.

7. The fact was commonly observed by British commentators, for example Mary E. Kennard in *A Guide Book for Lady Cyclists*. "If it were the fashion in this country for ladies of good standing and position to wear knickerbockers, and if they could appear as freely in them as in France, without shocking the non-cycling portion of the community, then, no doubt much might be adduced in their favour" (p. 44); and Lillias Campbell Davidson in *Handbook for Lady Cyclists*, "In France it is the skirted woman who is conspicuous, and who becomes the subject of general remarks about her attire." (p. 30).

8. In spite of some makers turning out diamond-framed ladies' machines in the mid-1890s, e.g., Messrs Marriott & Cooper make a light full diamond frame for the use of those affecting the so-called "rational dress" (Erskine, *Bicycling for Ladies*, p. 25), this seems to have had little effect on perceptions of the gender of the diamond frame; indeed some manufacturers were evidently not entirely committed to the concept of a female diamond frame themselves. John Barratt & Co.'s "Wulfruna Lady's Rational Safety" is described in their 1896 catalogue as "La Petite Parisienne Scorcher. It is light, though strong and reliable, being built with large tubes: it is also strong enough for gentlemen's use. 28 in. front and 26 in. back wheels, butt ended tangent spokes, which I consider makes it adaptable for ladies' use, and easy to reach, mount and dismount" (p. 13).

9. Rosen, *Cycling Round the Boundaries: The Mutual Construction of People and Machines*. Conference paper delivered to the British Sociological Association Annual Conference, University of Central Lancashire, March 1994, p. 12.

10. By 1927 "Kuklos" (Fitzwater Wray) was able to comment: "Nine out of ten of the people who want bicycles still trustfully enter a shop and buy one of the brand new machines of 1895 design…complete with 'dress guards'…Observe the lady who has accepted the Standard Roadster of the big maker, 1927 pattern…the chain is covered with more obsolete relics of 1895—either a Ford body in tin or an attache case of synthetic leather. These are 'to keep her skirt out of the chain,' although that disappearing garment never comes within a foot of the chain, and may generally be observed as in a state of retreat, joyously nonchalent, to the vicinity of the waist." *Kuklos Papers*, "Of Wriggling," pp. 167–87, pp. 179–80. By the 1930s *Cycling* handbooks often give no reason at all for the use of the drop frame as a ladies' machine beyond it being usual, for example. In 1936 F. J. Camm noted, "Although it is customary to regard it as essential to drop the top bar for a lady rider, this is a drawback from the point of view of design…where the lady rider wears breeches or a proper riding skirt the standard diamond pattern may be employed." *Every Cyclist's Handbook*, p. 22. In spite of this advice, "The Keen Lady Cyclist" is illustrated on p. 31 wearing breeches alongside a standard "straight" tubed drop frame machine.

11. Davidson, *Handbook for Lady Cyclists*, p. 40. See also: Sturmey, *The Complete Guide to Bicycling*, pp. 35–38; Erskine, *Tricycling for Ladies*, p. 5; Erskine, *Lady Cycling*, pp. 35–36.

12. A good example of this can be found in Raleigh publicity since 1982—notably the 1983 catalogue, *The Raleigh Collection*.

13. It is worth noting the way in which the open frame and diamond frame are advertised to the same female market. In *Elle* magazine (June 1988) Raleigh advertised the semi-curved drop frame "Caprice" with a wickerwork handlebar basket full of flowers alongside its rider befrocked in a full ballgown, under the caption "Endless love." The same magazine carried another Raleigh advertisement (July 1991) for their ATB/Mountain bike range with a diamond-frame machine standing in a docklands warehouse flat, with a wardrobe full of other machines in the range—no rider visible—beneath the caption, "What do you wear under your trousers?"

Bibliography

Alderson. *Bicycling, A History*. Newton Abbot: David Charles, 1972.

Anon. *The Wheelwoman's Handbook*. London: Mowbray House Cycling Association, 1897.

Bartleet, H. W. *Bartleet's Bicycle Book*. London: J. Burrow & Co., 1931.

Beeley, Serina. *A History of Bicycles*. London: Studio Editions Ltd., 1992.

Bijker, W., T. Hughes, and T. Pinch (eds). *The Social Construction of Technological Systems. New Directions in the Sociology and History of Technology*. Cambridge, Mass. and London: MIT Press, 1987.

Bijker, W., and J. Law. *Shaping Technology/Building Society: Studies in Socio-Technical Change*. Cambridge, Mass. and London: MIT Press, 1992.

Bike (The). *A Journal for Scottish Cyclists*. Glasgow, No. 1, 9 Mar. 1889; No. 35, 3 Nov. 1897.

Camm, F. J. *Every Cyclists's Handbook*. London: Newnes, 1936.

Caunter, C. F. *The History and Development of Cycles as Illustrated by the Collection of Cycles in the Science Museum* (2 sections). London: HMSO, 1955–58.

Clayton, Nick. *Early Bicycles*. Princes Risborough: Shire Publications, 1986.

_____. *Cycling Histories—Myths and Queries*. Correction Notes. Cheshire: Nick Clayton, 1991.

Crump, Basil. *The Queen's Cycling Book*. London: Horace Cox, 1900.

Davidson, L. C. *Handbook for Lady Cyclists*. London/Glasgow: Hay Nisbet, 1896.

Erskine, F. J. *Tricycling for Ladies*. London: Iliffe & Son, 1885.

_____. *Bicycling for Ladies*. London: Iliffe & Son, 1896.

_____. *Lady Cycling*. London: Walter Scott Ltd., 1897.

The Gentlewoman. "Cycling for Women" by "Ariel." London. Various issues through the 1890s.

Griffin, H. H. *Bicycles and Tricycles of the Year, 1885*. London: L. Upcott Gill, 1885.

Hindle, Kathy and Lee Irvine. *A Thorough Good Fellow. The Story of Dan Albone, Inventor and Cyclist*. Bedford: Bedfordshire County Council, 1990.

The Hub. An Illustrated Weekly for Wheelmen and Wheelwomen. London: Newnes. no. 1–143 and New Series no. 1–26, 8 Aug. 1896–28 Oct. 1899.

Kennard, Mary E. *A Guidebook for Lady Cyclists*. London: F. V. White & Co., 1896.

Keppel, William Coutts and George Lacy Hillier. *The Badminton Library of Sports and Pastimes—Cycling*. London: Longman Green & Co., 1887, 1890 and 1895.

McGurn, James. *On Your Bicycle (An Illustrated History of Cycling)*. London: John Murray, 1987.

Oddy, Nicholas, "The Machine Aesthetic: Marketing the Bicycle in the Late 19th and Early 20th Centuries," *Proceedings of the 2nd International Cyclist History Conference*, Musée d'Art et d'Industrie, St. Etienne, 1991.

Palmer, Arthur Judson. *Riding High: The Story of the Bicycle*. London: Vision Press, 1958.

Pinch, Trevor, and Wiebe E. J. Bijker. "The Social Construction of Facts and Artefacts or How the Sociology of Science and the Sociology of Technology Might Benefit Each Other," *Social Studies of Science*, no. 14, pp. 399–441. London: SAGE, 1984.

_____. "Science, Relativism and the New Sociology of Technology," *Social Studies of Science*, no. 16, pp. 347–60. London: SAGE, 1986.

Ritchie, Andrew. *King of the Road, An Illustrated History of Cycling*. London: Wildwood House. Berkeley: Ten Speed Press, 1975.

Roberts, Derek. *Cycling History, Myths and Queries*. Birmingham: Pinkerton Press, 1991.

Rosen, Paul. "Cycling Round the Boundaries: The Mutual Construction of People and Machines," paper, The British Sociological Asssociation Annual Conference, University of Central Lancashire, March 1994.

_____. "Diamonds Are Forever: The Socio-Technical Shaping of Bicycle Design," paper, *Proceedings of the 5th International Cycling History Conference*, Cambridge University, 1994.

Russell, Stewart. "The Social Construction of Artefacts: A Response to Pinch and Bijker," *Social Studies of Science*, no. 16, pp. 331–46. London: SAGE, 1986.

Spencer, Charles. *Bicycles & Tricycles, Past and Present*. London: Griffith & Farren, 1883.

Sturmey, Henry (ed). *The Tricyclist's Indispensible Annual and Handbook—A Guide to the Pastime and Complete Cyclopaedia on the Subject*. Coventry: Iliffe & Son, 1883.

Sturmey, Henry. *Indispensible Guide to the Safety Bicycle.* London: Iliffe & Son, 1889.

_____. *The Complete Guide to Bicycling.* London: Iliffe, 1885.

_____. *The Cyclist's Indispensible Handbook and Year Book for 1899–1900.* London, 1899.

The Wheelwoman & Society Cycling News, London, no. 1–64, 23 May 1896–17 Aug. 1897.

Wilkinson Latham, Robert. *Cycles in Colour.* Poole: Blandford Press Ltd., 1977.

Woodforde, John. *The Story of the Bicycle.* London: Routledge and Kegan Paul Ltd., 1970.

Wray, W. Fitzwalter. *The Kuklos Papers.* London, J. M. Dent & Sons Ltd., 1927.

Alastair Dodds and Alex Brown

5. The Edinburgh Tricycle

The first International Conference on Cycle History was held in Glasgow in 1990 amid an atmosphere of controversy about the nature of machine built by Kirkpatrick MacMillan, and indeed whether he built any machine. It was perhaps an appropriate time for Nicholas Oddy to first show Alex Brown's mysterious wooden relic, which had sufficient features to suggest that it may have been a bicycle, tricycle, or quadricycle.

The discovery of the relic makes an interesting story but gives no clues to its origins. Alex Brown's usual instinct—to hunt down every possible lead to a cycle "find" to its finality—was a little shaken when his telephone rang one evening. On the other end, from a licensed premises, was a friend of his, a non cycle-collector and himself none the better for plainly having made a number of retail purchases there, who said that he had fallen into conversation with an individual who claimed he had "a bike a lot older than anything Kirkpatrick MacMillan had ever made."

However, follow the long trail he did, and it was a very long one. The culmination was finally to meet a gentleman, after 3 previous arrangements when he said he would turn up, but never did, and he was 2 hours late when he finally arrived at a very derelict terraced house in Lochwinnoch, in Renfrewshire, not many miles west of Glasgow. Within, there was amassed a collection of material of astonishing diversity and content, sadly suffering very badly from the effects of rain and vandalism—a room full of perhaps 40 or 50 long case clocks, all incomplete—a tramp had broken into the building, sold all the brass dials for scrap, and, to provide heat, had burnt the easily removeable parts of the cases. Evident were 5 dismantled Austin 7's on the premises; there was a room full of early amusement machines; 2 or 3 motorcycles, one of which could be identified as a Rex "Acme"; and other items.

And eventually, fortunately in a dry corner, a curious relic—a main timber beam, bifurcated towards the rear to form a fork, and on the underside near the end of each fork, a bearing that partly faced downwards, of brass with an iron cap. At the forward end of the beam, an elegant post around 18 in. high, with a crosstree of iron, and suspended from one side of this transverse bar was a single timber member, again elegantly and lightly formed, wider at its lower end, in which was an opening accommodating a foot-shaped paddle, rocking on bearings at its "instep." From the end of the vertical member, which was free to swing to and fro from its crosstree, was an iron connecting rod extending approximately as far back as the rear bearings.

Two timber "horns," pointing forward in the horizontal plane, were fixed to the middle part of the main frame. These both had strips of iron fitted to their undersides. The main frame was pierced here and there, horizontally and vertically. These, together with witness markings, meant little at the time. The whole was finely detailed and constructed, suggesting the work of a cabinetmaker.

There was little or nothing to suggest that here were the remains of a cycle (Fig. 5.1). The design and construction of the rear bearings suggested that they supported a vertical loading on their upper surfaces—so perhaps the thing was a manumotive. Or was it a human-powered predecessor of the stationary engine?

Despite Alex's protests to this effect they were but nought to its owner, so convinced was he that here indeed were the remains of a "bike from the 1700s when people's feet were smaller." Yes, the paddles were a little on the small side, he had to

Fig. 5.1. The relic shortly after it was discovered.

agree. Haggling over the price resulted in a £100 increase each time he tried to argue downwards. Alex had never met anyone who did it this way. So £200 worse off, on top of an already hugely inflated sum, saw him become the proprietor of an object the purpose of which was quite unclear!

Although there was nothing to suggest that this relic had any connection with MacMillan, equally there was nothing to say that it was not his work. Indeed there was no evidence to indicate who had built this intriguing machine. Further study strongly suggested that this had almost certainly been a tricycle. Even the approximate size of the rear wheel was now known, from marks on the inner surface of the fork.

The desire to find the holy grail of cycling history, MacMillan's original machine, could not be allowed to cloud the facts and the need to undertake some serious research into the origins of the machine. In the absence of any documentary evidence at that time, it was decided that the only way to discover the original form of the machine was to build a replica of what was extant in order to experiment further.

The relic was left in the hands of a local craftsman for the wooden parts to be replicated, while the ironwork was commissioned from a blacksmith. The intention was to create an exact copy as far as possible perfectly matching the materials and skills evident in the original. This was necessary to ensure that the function of the machine was an accurate representation of the original.

Work on the copy had now gone as far as was possible from the evidence gleaned from the original. The copy included a rear wheel, missing from the original, having used witness marks in the wood of the rear fork to ascertain the diameters of what were clearly the hub and felloes. An educated guess, and looking at contemporary practise, dictated that the wheel should comprise 12 wooden spokes. Working on the basis that the relic was probably the remains of a velocipede, and not a turnip cutter or knife grinder, several people now got together to try to interpret how the various marks and fittings could relate to the functions of a vehicle.

Although a consensus was reached that this was certainly a treadle driven 3-wheel velocipede, there was still insufficient evidence to justify the commissioning of further iron and woodwork. What was now urgently required was some documentary evidence of how the missing seat, steering mechanism, and axle with front wheels would have been constructed.

At this time in late 1992, luck and coincidence intervened. Peter Matthews of Dublin had discovered at an antique fair an old photograph illustrating a tricycle velocipede (Fig. 5.2). The photo was embossed "Taylors Photographic and Art Studios, 62 Jamaica St., Glasgow," and Peter had sent the photo to Nick Clayton, who recognised its significance and immediately passed it on to Alex Brown to see if he knew anything further about the photographers. Taylors were in business at that address[1] around the 1870 period, the height of the velocipede mania.

The similarity between the machine in the photo and the relic were very close, with only minor detail differences. The 2 machines had almost certainly been built by the same person. Although the maker remained unknown, the photo revealed enough detail to enable work on the replica to continue. Front wheels could now be constructed, based on the number of spokes illustrated and an interpolation of the wheel diameter.

Both the style of the seat and the form and length of the rear cranks could now be determined, and the purpose of the two wooden horns referred to above discovered. These have iron rubbing strips fixed to their underside, and bear on the front axle to provide rotational support for the main chassis beam. The exact details of the construction of the axle could still not be seen, and a simple wooden baton was substituted to support the wheels.

The photograph reveals very little of the exact arrangement of the steering mechanism, with only a shaped handle in the rider's left hand being visible; from the position of the right hand it may be presumed that there is a corresponding handle on the other side. Witness marks in the wood again give a clue to the exact arrangement used. The sides of the

Fig. 5.2. The Peter Matthews photograph showing a machine almost identical to the relic.

main beam show circular marks surrounding the hole under the seat area, suggesting large washers possibly of wood were used behind the handles.

Under the beam there is a further circular mark and iron pin, which points to the possibility of another washer or a pulley being fitted here. Wear marks where the horns join the beam are likely to have been made by the rubbing of cord or thin rope.

A mock-up was tried with a pair of handles fitted with pulley wheels sized to the marks, which were at first thought to have been washers. Cord was then fed back to a pair of pulley wheels, one above the other, on the underside of the frame. Initially only one pulley wheel was tried, but the wear marks on each horn suggested a different angle each side and therefore different heights of pulleys.

The final part of the mock-up involved experimenting with various possible lengths of front axle. When the optimum length was arrived at, to prevent the wheels fouling the frame, the cord was then attached to a midpoint of the axle. With the two handles operating independently, possible due to a void inside the main beam, this gave a steering operation where one handle was pulled back as the other was pushed forward to turn in one direction, and the converse for the other direction.

At this stage there was still no evidence for a maker, or even a country of origin. An intriguing paragraph was then found in Griffin's book, *Cycling*,[2] which states, "Bicycles were alone thought of in 1874–76; tricycles were scarcely heard of, the longest to survive being one named the 'Edinbro',' but it had slipper foot-plates on long levers, and belonged to the 1860 or so period."

This briefest of descriptions did show similarities with the surviving relic and provided a tantalising possibility for a maker. The Scottish connection with the photo, the place of discovery of the relic, and the probability of this hitherto unknown maker working in Edinburgh in the 1860 period demanded closer investigation. Another sentence in the same edition of *Cycling*,[3] "This is the modern development of the Edinbro' (1865–75)," narrows the field for possible production dates even further.

At this time a hitherto unknown piece by Griffin was discovered which at last brought to light a captioned photograph of "The Edinburgh Tricycle." This was in an article on the cycle industry published in 1901 as part of a *Morning Post* supplement on commerce.[4] The photo was very similar to the Peter Matthews one, but with an important difference (Fig. 5.3).

The Matthews photo clearly shows the rider grasping a handle at the side of his seat. In this new photo there is no handle by the seat, but there is an upright support for a small handle or "tiller" near the front of the main beam. This was clearly the steering handle which turned a pair of pulley wheels above the beam with cord leading to the axle via outrigger guides.

This alternative steering arrangement and minor detail differences were sufficient to throw doubt on whether the relic, or the machine in the Matthews photo, were Edinburgh built. The paragraph accompanying the Griffin article did however suggest the origin of his photo and information to be *The Field* magazine; "The most practical of all these was called the 'Edinburgh' (illustrated in *The Field*, 28 November 1874), from the place of its origin. It had a single large rear (driving) wheel and two small front ones, a type which was followed by the 'Harrison' (January 1877), 'Dublin' (Blood's, 1878), and later by

Fig. 5.3. The photograph which accompanied Griffin's article, with original caption.

Fig. 5.4. The line drawing which appeared in The Field.

the 'Phantom'; (1886), and 'Olympia' in after years, all on somewhat similar lines."

The article in *The Field*[5] produced the final evidence needed to link the Matthews photo and the relic to the Edinburgh Tricycle. The article was illustrated with an engraving, "obtained from the makers," which shows a machine almost identical to the Matthews machine (Fig. 5.4). Perhaps more significantly, the figure illustrated seated on the machine bears such a close resemblance to the figure in the Matthews photo that it was almost certainly taken from the photo.

The article incorporates a letter from an owner which includes much detail, including weights and a description of its use. The article is of sufficient interest to justify inclusion in its entirety.

THE EDINBURGH TRICYCLE

At the request of several of our subscribers we have obtained from the makers, 57, St. Leonard's Street, Edinburgh, an engraving of the above tricycle, which we now reproduce for their information. Not having seen it in action, we can express no opinion on its powers, and must refer to the letter of our correspondent, which we inserted in *The Field* of 24 Oct., for a description of them, as follows:

SIR,—I have driven an Edinburgh for four years past, and under every conceivable variety of circumstances except an upset. My friends have once or twice contrived to upset my little trap; but to myself it has never happened, nor been near happening, neither with common care need such a catastrophe every occur. My tricycle weighs 83 lb., and, when loaded for a summer journey of several days, it is made to carry myself (14 st.) and an overcoat, spare clothes, a book, sketch book, colours, &c., to the extent of 25 lb. This, as you say, is a good burden; but I do not find it necessary to be at all particular about a few pounds. I have always a comfortable seat to sketch from, or to rest in when I need, with great ease in driving. You may think it hard to move such a weight as I have mentioned. Given a good road, it is not so, even up a moderate slope, but I admit that a deep road will always beat me. In such a case, and in the ascent and descent of dangerously steep hills, I get out, and make use of a light line, the ends of which are fast to the extremities of the fore axle, and by which the vehicle is effectually and easily controlled both up and down hill. For those who have not seen the Edinburgh, I may mention that the two wheels are in front, and these are acted on by the steering gear; the driving wheel behind, the 9 in. cranks being connected by rods with treadles in front. For easier stowage in a railway van, I have my driving wheel of 36 in. only, therefore the speed is but low. Although I can put it along on level ground at the rate of eight or nine miles an hour, I seldom cover more than six in travelling; but the road must be very bad to reduce me to four. This would not content many, but it is quite sufficient for my purpose, and to me far more enjoyable than racing over the country at fabulous speed. We must not expect in the cob the swiftness of the hunter; but, for his own purpose, the cob is the better horse. So it is with me and my tricycle. Yet if my age were not what my signature denotes, and my weight materially less than that stated above, I think I should still prefer the three wheels. For locomotion only, there cannot be a question that the bicycle is best; but enjoying, as I do, a sketch from nature and a good book, and objecting to the scanty apparel I sometimes see on the bicyclists, I am more than satisfied with things as they are. But I hold at the same time, that it is possible, and that we ought to try, to make them better. The plan of the Edinburgh is good, graceful in appearance, and very convenient for use, and the steering apparatus especially ingenious and effective. But the vehicle must be much improved. The body, I think, might be lighter; but, above all, more accurate fitting and better workmanship is desirable. The want of this implies an increase of friction, and consequent waste of power.

SOIXANTE.

Those who are acquainted with mechanics will at once see that it is merely the old "4-wheeler" converted into a "3-wheeler," but in a very convenient form. Until the general introduction of the bicycle these 4-wheelers were much used, and especially by artisans in going to and returning from their work. In common with the Edinburgh, they had the defect known as the "dead point"—that is to say, when the two cranks are drawn into the same straight line there is a tendency for the machine to stop altogether, which it would do but for the momentum previously acquired, which carries the crank over that point. Hence, as described by our correspondent, the Edinburgh cannot be ridden up a steep hill or over a bad road, because in these cases there is not sufficient momentum, and the "dead point" cannot be got over. Like the Velociman this tricycle has the advantage of the two wheels in front, which conduces greatly to safety, but the former beats it in the absence of the dead point. The Velociman is, however, considerably heavier and more costly in its manufacture, so that we should imagine there is not much balance in favour of either. Both are a long way behind the bicycle in speed, the "dead point" in that machine being got over by the back draw of the lower foot, and moreover they could not compete with the remotest prospect of success with its simple mechanism over a distance of ground.

We are still continuing our experiment on this subject, with a reasonable prospect of success; but machinists are always slow in their operations, to say nothing of the expense attending on them.

This article not only gave an almost certain attribution to the relic, but was also the earliest contemporary reference to an Edinburgh Tricycle. Subsequently one of the "request of several… subscribers" mentioned at the start of the article, was discovered by Nick Clayton in an 1872 edition of *The Field* [6]: "THE EDINBURGH TRICYCLE—Can any of your readers afford me any information respecting the Edinburgh three-wheeled velocipede, Gibson's patent, made in Edinburgh by Mr. Brown? It is said to do fourteen miles an hour on good roads, and to weigh from 14–17 lb. less than an ordinary bicycle.—T.E.T."

If one is to believe the statement by "Soixante," in the 1874 article, as to the machine weighing 83 lb., then the contemporary ordinary bicycles weighed about 100 lb. This is clearly not correct and calls into question the estimates of weight.

Perusal of the *Scotsman* newspaper for 1869 reveals an advert[7] for the machines: "VELOCIPEDES—Edinburgh 3-Wheel Velocipede is pronounced by Mechanics to be the Best and Lightest Machines made. Weight 50 lb. Manufactured by M. Brown, 57 St. Leonard's Street." Here we have the maker, Matthew Brown, stating that his machines weigh 50 lb., surely a much more realistic weight both for the tricycle and for the contemporary bicycles at 14–17 lb. heavier.

The *Scotsman* from the previous week[8] carries the earliest advert, and earliest contemporary reference, for the "Edinburgh": "VELOCIPEDES—Something New! The Edinburgh Velocipede, Lightest and Most Comfortable Made. Matthew Brown, 57 St. Leonard's Street." The strong suggestion here is that this is an entirely new machine, not just a revamp of an earlier model, and just recently put into production.

It is interesting to note that Griffin describes the machine in 1892, in *Cycling*,[9] as "belonging to the 1860 or so period" and also "the Edinbro' (1865–75)." By 1901[10] Griffin was being quite specific with the photograph caption "THE EDINBURGH TRICYCLE (1869)." Together with the evidence of the Matthews photograph being circa 1870, this places the Edinburgh firmly in the 1869–70 period. There is no firm evidence of a date when production stopped.

One further intriguing but inconclusive aspect of the dating comes from the short letter in the 1872 *Field*,[11] where the correspondent describes the machine as being "Gibson's patent, made in Edinburgh by Mr. Brown." A search of the patent office records showed no sign of a Gibson's Patent, but a patent by one Edward Gilman[12] dated August 1866, for an Improved Velocipede, sounds remarkably like the Edinburgh. Could the name Gibson be a misprint for Gilman?

There is no obvious link between Matthew Brown in Edinburgh and Edward Gilman in Surrey. Brown was listed[13] as being a cabinetmaker, upholsterer, house agent, auctioneer, appraiser, and wood merchant, all useful trades for someone branching out into the velocipede business. Could it be that Brown met Gilman through one of his areas of business, assuming that Gibson is indeed Gilman?

Sadly, there are no tangible links between Matthew Brown and the present day other than the surviving relic; even the premises at 57 St. Leonard Street in South Edinburgh are now demolished. It is fascinating to ponder on the fact that Brown may have been at the centre of a large industry in Scotland producing tricycle velocipedes, of which his were "pronounced by Mechanics to be the Best and Lightest Machines made."[14]

Brown was certainly not alone manufacturing velocipedes in Edinburgh. Alexander Munro, a coachbuilder and harness maker, also advertised himself as a Velocipede Maker. Unfortunately there is no evidence as to how many wheels his machines used. Typically most advertisements in 1869 were for

Fig. 5.5. The replica Edinburgh Tricycle at the stage that it had reached in early 1994.

French and American machines, e.g., "VELOCIPEDES! of the most Approved French and American Designs etc." and "VELOCIPEDES! (Two-Wheel)—Jas Soutter & Sons 102 Princes Street Edinburgh are expecting daily from Paris a Large Stock of the best make."[15]

There is evidence that 3-wheeled velocipedes were in use in Edinburgh at this time. A contemporary advertisement[16] offers a "VELOCIPEDE (Strong Three-Wheeled) to contain two for sale, James White, 8 St. Anthony Place." As White is not known to be a builder, it is presumed that this was a secondhand machine.

One thing that is clear is the fact that there were at least 3 Edinburgh Tricycles built, because the 1901 Griffin photo,[17] the Peter Matthews photo, and the relic are all slightly different. This could indicate that we have evidence for several production versions, or possibly each is a development machine from different stages of the gestation period.

There is strong evidence on the relic of changes having been made, e.g., the marks and position of the pin under the beam (probably the steering pulley) show it to have been moved forward. It is possible that at the same time the grooves for the cord were deliberately cut deeper.

In the absence of any further information coming to light, the remaining unknown details of the machine will need to be replicated on a best guess basis (Fig. 5.5). Contemporary carriage practice, along with what can be seen in the photographs, should enable the main axle to be constructed. Other details gleaned from the photographs include the small block on the back of the seat backrest which would seem to have been a brake, probably operated by flexing the seat. Doubt still remains as to how the seat was formed, and from what material.

One thing is certain—the finished replica will provide a unique opportunity to discover how effective a 3-wheeled velocipede was at the height of the velocipede mania.

Notes

1. Glasgow Post Office Street Directories.
2. Griffin, H. H., *Cycling* (1892): 32.
3. Ibid., 50.
4. Griffin, H. Hewitt, "The Cycle Industry," *Great Britain, Her Finance and Commerce*, a souvenir edition of *The Morning Post*, London (1901): 351.
5. *The Field, The Country Gentleman's Newspaper* (28 November 1874): 575.
6. *The Field* (23 November 1872).
7. *Scotsman* (10 April 1869): 4, c2.
8. *Scotsman* (3 April 1869): 4, c4.
9. Griffin, H. H., *Cycling* (1892): 32, 50.
10. Griffin, op. cit. (note 4).
11. *The Field*, op. cit. (note 6).
12. *An Improved Velocipede*, 1 August 1866, Patent No. 1981, by Edward Gilman, Prospect Place, Wandsworth Road, Surrey.
13. *Edinburgh and Leith Post Office Street Directory*, 1871–72.
14. *Scotsman*, op. cit. (note 7).
15. *Scotsman* (1 March 1869): 1, c4.
16. *Scotsman* (3 March 1869): 4, c4.
17. Griffin, op. cit. (note 4).

6. Diamonds Are Forever: The Socio-Technical Shaping of Bicycle Design

Paul Rosen

My aim in this paper is to raise some questions about what exactly constitutes "a bicycle." Debates within cycle history circles show that this is a burning issue when it comes to the progression of early bicycle designs. What I want to do is to look at things from a different perspective. Rather than try to trace the development of bicycle design from *Draisienne* to boneshaker to ordinary to safety, I want to look at some of the factors that have prevented the bicycle from developing otherwise.

What I suggest is that despite several attempts over the last hundred years to destabilise the diamond-framed safety bicycle, it has still maintained its place as the dominant design and will probably continue to do so. The reasons for this have little to do with the technical details or engineering principles that underlie the design. Rather it has resulted from a combination of some of the social factors of cycling culture, in particular racing regulations, manufacturers' assumptions about their customers, and the tacit knowledge and techniques of bicycle framebuilders.

I'll be relating these issues also to debates within the academic field of technology studies, in particular the question of our relationship to the machines we live with. My argument will be that bicycles offer a prime example of how technology is so interwoven with our lives that it's sometimes difficult to distinguish the boundary between people and machines.

A point to note here is that I'm not looking at all at 19th-century bicycles, because until the safety design had become fairly stable, the possibilities were more or less boundless. Rather, my story starts in 1900 with the founding of the UCI—the *Union Cycliste Internationale*—the international cycle racing regulatory body.

Regulations and Constraints

The UCI appears to have been formed specifically to restrict technical development in the design of racing bikes (Sanders 1991: 49), with the rationale that this would prevent cycle racing from becoming an elite activity closed to those unable to afford expensive machines. In retrospect, this can be seen as a major factor in shaping the boundaries of the bicycle.

In the 1930s, a number of people began to experiment with aerodynamic fairings and with recumbent bicycles, beating conventional designs in several key races such as the Hour record. The UCI's response to the racing successes of recumbents was to specify new rules for the definition of bicycles in UCI-administered competitions. These rules stated that a bicycle should have tubes of specified diameters, built into a diamond frame, with wheels of a minimum size. In other words, the definition of "a bicycle" was no longer to include recumbents.

This redefinition of the regulations led to recumbent designs being more or less abandoned after the 1930s, until the International Human-Powered Vehicle Association (IHPVA) was set up in the mid-1970s, matched by national bodies such as the British Human Power Club (BHPC). The aim of these groups has been to encourage a return

---

Synopsis

In this paper, I examine the problem of what exactly counts as "a bicycle." I use recent innovations in cycle design to show that the defining features of bicycles are unclear. Moreover, these examples, and others concerning bicycles designed for women, show that distinctions between bikes and their riders can be blurred. Cyclists and their bikes might be more usefully regarded as cyborgs, that is, as hybrid entities comprising people, machines and events.

to the creativity of cycle design that was common in the 1870s and 1880s. The IHPVA has only one rule—that machines be powered only by human energy.

There is a wide variety of HPV designs, with little standardisation, and machines are as likely to be homemade as to have been bought off-the-peg (see Fig. 6.1 for some of the machines used at the BHPC's national championships in Lancaster, England, July 1994). Recumbents continue to be much faster than diamond-framed bikes, and have been known to exceed 65 mph (Ballantine & Grant 1992: 135).

It isn't just recumbents that have been excluded from races administered by the UCI, though. The restrictive definition of "a bicycle" that was intended to exclude recumbents also faced Mike Burrows in the early 1980s, when he built the prototype of the Lotus Sport bike on which Chris Boardman won the 1992 Olympic Pursuits. This bike had a carbon-fibre monocoque frame, i.e., it consisted of a single piece of material. Because it wasn't made of tubes, the bike was deemed illegal by the UCI. It was only in 1990, when the regulations were relaxed to make allowances for new technology, that the monocoque was legalised.

UCI's regulations now state that a bicycle must be "viable, marketable and able to be used by all types of sporting cyclists" (British Cycling Federation 1994: 229[1]). At the same time, though, the dimensions are specified closely enough to prohibit the use of recumbents.

Another design banned by the UCI, in April 1994, is that of Graeme Obree. Obree hand built his bike himself, using a bizarre combination of materials. The frame combines old BMX tubing with conventional tubes hammered into a more aerodynamic shape. Bearings and other parts were taken from a washing machine, whilst the handlebar stem was made out of a BMX seatpin. The left-hand crank was made from a piece of steel Obree found in the gutter (*Cycling Weekly* 5291, 24/7/93: 5; *Cycling Today*, April 1994: 34–5). Obree rides hunched over the handlebars in a "knock-kneed" position caused by his having sawn the bottom bracket shell and axle in half so as to reduce aerodynamic drag on his legs. This is the machine, known in the cycle press as "Old Faithful," that Obree rode when he set the Hour record in July 1993, beating Francesco Moser's 1984 record.

The UCI objections to the Obree bike in part go back to their original founding rationale—"to limit the design of bikes on the road to more or less what exists at the moment," as a means of keeping the cost of cycling within "the range of the man in the street" (UCI President Hein Verbruggen, quoted in *Cycling Weekly* 5318, 5/2/94: 5).

Overriding this is the issue of the "Obree position." The position Obree rides in is seen as contravening UCI's Rule 49, the rule that excludes recumbent bikes. What it is that UCI has banned, then, isn't clear—is it the bike or the riding position? The distinction between the rider and the

Fig. 6.1. Recumbent bicycle racing at the BHPC National Championships, Lancaster, England, July 1994 (photo Paul Rosen).

machine is blurred, and this blurring is exacerbated by the ongoing development of the dispute, with the latest developments occurring at the World Pursuit Championships in August 1994. Firstly, Obree was prevented from using the unconventional saddle he'd brought with him. The dispute then moved to the issue of whether or not daylight was visible between his chest and his arms (*Cycling Weekly* 5344, 20/8/94: 5). The issue has yet to be resolved. It isn't clear, for example, whether it would be legal if Obree used the "Obree position" on a conventional bike equipped with tri-bars. And what if he rode "Old Faithful" in a conventional position? What these examples highlight is that the question of what counts as a bicycle is open for negotiation.

Innovation and the Cycle Industry

Cycle design is commonly seen as having more or less stagnated from the turn of the century until the invention of the Moulton small-wheeled suspension bike in the late 1950s. This stagnation is sometimes set up as the logical consequence of the development of the diamond frame—F. R. Whitt, for example, saw this as the perfect design, needing no improvement (cited in Sanders 1991: 49). So for some observers it is the diamond frame that constitutes the essential meaning of "bicycle."

Many cycling commentators, however, see the stagnation of cycle design not as intrinsic to the machine itself, but as something that derives directly from the UCI regulations. Rather than protecting the interests of "the man in the street," they believe UCI has served to protect the investments of the cycle industry in tooling up for mass production. This is seen to have stifled technological development, since mass production can't cope with unusual designs that are often expensive to produce in small quantities (Alderson 1972: 186; Caunter 1955: 51; Ballantine 1992: 39).

This argument has its merits, but also one or two flaws. As the Moulton example shows, innovations in designs for the public are often very successful without bearing much relation to the world of racing. While the costs of retooling can be high, it's only occasionally that racing regulations are a significant factor in the decision about whether to innovate. An alternative view, suggested to me by Mike Burrows (personal communication—also see his contribution in this volume), is that it is the conservative traditions of cycle framebuilders that have primarily held back both the design of racing bikes and innovation in the cycle industry more broadly. Bicycle builders are generally trained by other bicycle builders, thus ensuring the ongoing diffusion of a particular body of knowledge around cycle engineering—that bicycles should be built out of steel tubes put together into a diamond frame.

Key innovators in cycle design tend, on the other hand, to have obtained their ideas from outside these traditions of framebuilding. Alex Moulton had worked in the car industry; Obree was an unemployed amateur cyclist trying to build a high quality machine with little money and support except for the use of a friend's workshop; Burrows himself had experience as an engineer in the packaging industry, and worked with boat and car design before coming to bicycles (QED 1993).

A key source of major innovation in cycle design recently has been in the world of mountain bikes. Mountain bikes have been central to many of the technological developments in cycling over the last decade, and these innovations, especially in materials and in production techniques, have often been borrowed from the Californian aerospace industry. At one level, innovations here relate again to the financial interests of manufacturers. Mountain bikes have developed alongside more flexible manufacturing methods in the cycle industry that don't rely on tooling up for mass production. Rather, the same equipment can be used to build a wider range of designs, allowing opportunities for companies to gain a competitive edge over their rivals through innovation.

Interestingly, though, in contrast to the UCI experience, mountain bikers attribute much of the innovation not to the industry but to racing regulations. Riders in mountain bike races are subject to a "no outside assistance" rule that requires them to start and finish on the same machine and to carry out their own repairs using only spares they've brought with them. This need for self-sufficiency is believed in mountain biking circles to have spurred innovations such as suspension systems and developments that have made mountain bikes faster, stronger, and safer. If they were allowed to change machines during a race, or get outside help for repairs, riders believe that designers "would no longer be forced into finding technological advances to better their rivals" (Murrell 1992: 39).

So racing regulations can both constrain and allow the expansion of the boundaries of bicycle design. Recumbents and other unconventional designs are for the most part excluded from this boundary, whilst improvements to the existing form—brakes, gears, the types of material used in the frame—are allowed or even encouraged to develop. There's nothing inherent, then, in the technical design of the diamond-framed safety that can account for its continued dominance in the face of challenges from recumbents, monocoques, or the Obree bike. What counts as "a bicycle" depends instead on who is trying to define it.

Constructing Riders

If the definition of bicycles is contingent, shaped by a variety of interlinked factors, so too are definitions of their riders. My original question of "what constitutes a bicycle?" extends also to "what constitutes a cyclist?", since it is often impossible analytically to distinguish one from the other, as the Obree case shows. I'm going to explore this argument in relation to bikes for women, since women's bikes raise some important questions about cycle design. This also relates back to the point about framebuilding traditions.

Looking through cycle catalogues, it is possible to find implicit specifications for riders alongside the more explicit specifications of the machines. Bikes may be described as "aggressive" or "recreational"; descriptions of components may focus on high-tech gears, brakes, forks, tyres, and so on, or they might concentrate on the comfort of the saddle and the addition of mudguards, reflectors, and rear racks.

Designers and marketers of bikes thus construct their intended customers according to their assumed interests and riding activities at the same time as they construct their products technically.

This building of specifications for riders into the design of bikes is perhaps most evident in women's and girls' machines. Women's bikes are likely to be described in terms linked to leisure use rather than to racing. The appearance of women's bikes also tends to differ quite considerably from that of men's bikes, with pastel colours and more "feminine" names.

The gendering of bicycles goes deeper than the paintwork, though. Bicycles designed for women have existed throughout the history of cycling. Nevertheless, the way designers have tended to meet women's requirements has been informed primarily by the need to build machines around the constraints of women's clothing from the 19th century. This still remains the case despite its irrelevance nowadays.

Nevertheless, there are a number of problems with so-called "ladies'" bikes. Firstly, a bike without a top tube is less strong, making it unsuitable for more serious use. More importantly for most women riders, just removing the top tube doesn't address women's physiological requirements of a bicycle. It has lately become accepted knowledge in the cycling world that a woman and a man of the same height will on average have different physical proportions, and thus need different frame geometries on their bikes (see Fig. 6.2). More and

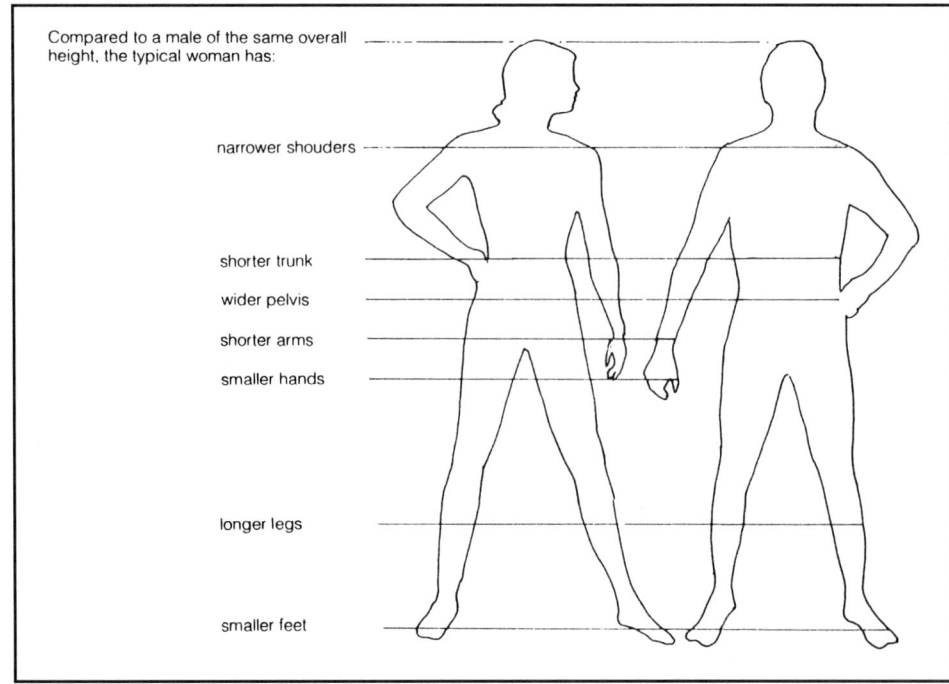

Fig. 6.2. Typical differences between the physiques of an "average" man and woman with the same overall body height (reproduced with permission from Rob van der Plas, Bicycle Technology).

more companies are now beginning to address these issues, yet the differences between men's and women's requirements of a bike remain unacknowledged by most manufacturers, and this highlights the degree to which gender assumptions are built into bicycle design at every level.

This point echoes Mike Burrows's argument that it is the traditions of framebuilding that have held back innovation in cycle design, since gender assumptions are often implicit in framebuilders' design tools. For example, Richard Talbot's influential guide to framebuilding, *Designing and Building Your Own Frameset* (1984), translates anatomical measurements into frame dimensions (Fig. 6.3). This framebuilding method is actually not gender-specific in practice, but the tables Talbot provides in his book begin with a figure for the combined length of torso and arm (B + C) which is too large for many women. This (probably) unconscious exclusion of women is matched by the fact that the figure in Talbot's illustration is clearly a man, complete with neat side parting. Other framebuilding guides make similar implicit gender assumptions (for example the Bioracer system, described in Stone 1992).

The response of some women framebuilders to this gender bias has been to design bicycles that are explicitly aimed at women. Consequently there are now a few ranges of bikes, *with* top tubes, that do meet the needs of women cyclists, although how to address women's needs isn't universally agreed. Isla Rowntree, a framebuilder and racer from Birmingham, builds bikes with an unusually steep seat tube to bring the rider's arms closer to the handlebars and allow her to sit in a more upright position (*Mountain Biker*, June 1993: 43).

Other designers and engineers regard Rowntree's solution as the wrong approach. Chris Juden of the Cyclists' Touring Club sees these kind of adjustments to frame geometry as an attempt "to build a frame that will somehow arrange standard-sized components around a small-sized rider" (1994: 21). He advocates an alternative approach that maintains a standard frame geometry for smaller riders by using a smaller front wheel. This is the approach of the American manufacturer of bicycles and components for women, Georgena Terry. Without engaging in the technical debate between these two perspectives, they highlight the degree to which social considerations are built into the most minor points of cycle design, even though this is rarely as conscious a factor for manufacturers that don't specifically target women.

So gender is an implicit element of the definition of a bicycle, and the technical disagreement between Rowntree and Terry[2] suggests that even the issue of how to define a female cyclist is open to question. Do women sit on their bikes and ride them the same way as men, and therefore need a conventional geometry with smaller wheels, or should the geometry of women's bikes reflect the differences between women's and men's bodies?

Beyond these physiological distinctions, too, women's bikes embody assumptions regarding taste, interests, clothing, and cycling activities that may not be appropriate. Manufacturers usually treat women cyclists as recreational rather than sporting riders, and hence see them as concerned with comfort rather than with technology. Yet despite this, there are many examples of strong women racers, particularly in the world of mountain biking. A recent Cyclists' Touring Club survey indicates also that women are taking a greater interest in cycling issues, including the technical side (*Cycle Touring & Campaigning*, June/July 1993: 21–2). The assumptions built into their bikes, then, may be somewhat inaccurate.

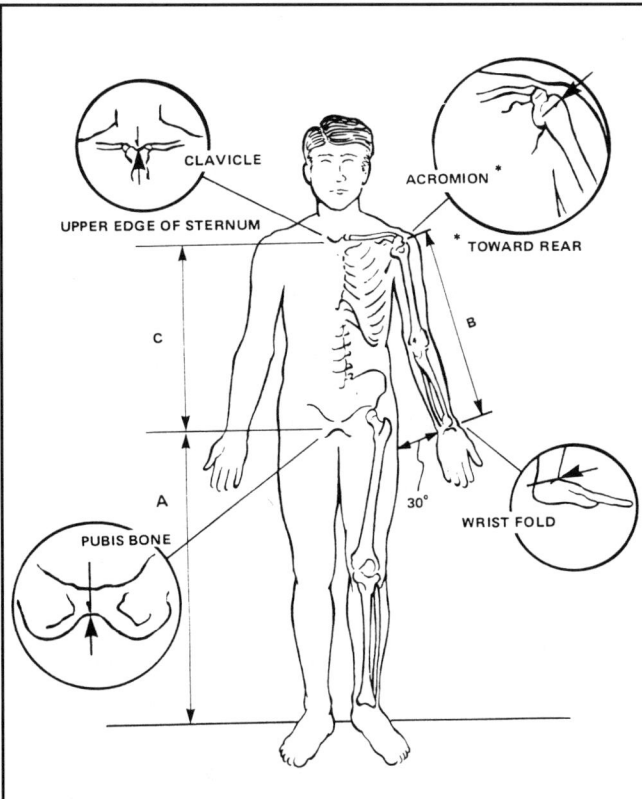

Fig. 6.3. Diagram of anatomical dimensions (reproduced with permission from Richard P. Talbot, Designing and Building Your Own Frameset).

Cycling Cyborgs

I want to try to relate what I've been discussing to some current issues in academic technology studies, particularly with regard to the relation between people and machines. Donna Haraway, in particular, argues that in our "postmodern" world, the boundaries between people and the machines we live with have become far less clearly defined than we might like to think.

Haraway's main example comes from what she calls "the informatics of domination," in other words the networks of new information technologies that in their manufacture and use bring together what appear to be incongruous elements. Information technologies, machines used to transmit messages through the cyberspace of computer networks "are made of sunshine; they are all light and clean because they are nothing but signals, electromagnetic waves, a section of a spectrum." At the same time, though, their manufacture is the cause of material suffering, of "immense human pain in Detroit and Singapore," exploiting inner city and "Third World" workers for the benefit of Western shareholders (Haraway 1989: 178). Haraway characterises the workers in these factories—generally poorly-paid women—as cyborgs, people whose lives cannot be defined without reference to technology. The same applies to all of us—we all live in a world where society and technology are irreversably intertwined.

For technology to underlie our very identity seems a worrying prospect given common fears about the power of technology to take on its own trajectory and become "out-of-control" (Winner 1978). For Haraway, though, while cyborgs are an outcome of the meeting between modern technology and globalisation, taking on cyborg identities offers opportunities for resisting and subverting not just technological determinism but also the domination that results from the social relations of global production. At one level, the work of Rowntree and Terry is an example of this, making explicit the gender biases of bicycle design that are usually left unnoticed. They thus subvert the albeit often unconscious male bias of cycle designers. This deconstruction of technology, exposing myths and creating new counter-myths, is crucial to the cyborg politics that Haraway calls for.

Bicycles are in many ways an appropriate technology to relate to Haraway's ideas. The bicycle served as a key transitional point in the development of both mass production and mass transportation (Hounshell 1980). Moreover, the cycle industry has over the last two decades become an exemplary case of a global industry where over 90% of components and probably 50% of frame tubing on new British bikes is produced in the Far East (Sanders 1991, and my own research).

Aside from the structure of the cycle industry, the notion of cyborgs also provides a means of interpreting new developments in cycle technology, and the ways these relate to cyclists. An example is the case of Chris Boardman's 1992 Olympic gold medal, which he won on the Lotus Sport bike originally designed by Mike Burrows. Just as the prototype of this machine pushed the boundaries of the bicycle, so did Boardman's use of it raise questions about the boundary between "man and machine"—this was a phrase frequently used with regard to whether Boardman could have won without that particular bike. The British non-cycling media in particular latched onto the notion that it was the bicycle itself that won the race, although Boardman's fellow cyclists were unanimous in the feeling that he would have won whatever he was riding, even a butcher's bike (Tony Doyle in *Bicycle*, September 1992: 98).

More interestingly, perhaps, was the way Boardman's achievement was constructed by Lotus Sport, who built the bicycle, in terms not of his strength as a rider but of aerodynamics in their wind tunnel. The engineers were convinced Boardman would win just on the results of their aerodynamic tests, made whilst the bike was stationary indoors, without the stresses of an international competition (QED 1993). Boardman's Olympic success can be regarded, then, as comprising several disparate elements: his strength as a rider; the relaxation of the UCI regulations to permit the monocoque frame in the Olympics; the work of Burrows and then Lotus Engineering in developing the prototype; aerodynamic theory; and of course the "superbike" itself. None of these elements alone is sufficient to explain how Boardman won the gold medal, but together they comprise, in the words of Bruno Latour (1993), a hybrid entity made up of people, objects, and events—in other words, a cyborg.

This example shows again that the boundary between a bicycle and its rider is often difficult to pin down. The construction of the Lotus Sport bike crucially involved Boardman's physical capabilities as well as the technical specifications of the machine. Lotus Sport couldn't take for granted that the riding position of the machine was necessarily achievable. Boardman had to train his body to fit the machine (QED 1993). Had he been unable to spend four-and-a-half minutes on this bike riding extremely fast in a very uncomfortable position, then the bike would have been a failure.

Conclusion

This last point relates to work in the sociology of technology that argues that rather than regard the "success" of a technical artifact as the explanation of its subsequent development (i.e., "the superbike was aerodynamic, therefore it won the race"), it is precisely that success that needs to be explained (Pinch & Bijker 1987). The same goes for the success of the diamond-framed safety bicycle: diamonds may be forever empirically, but this shouldn't be accepted without question. Cycle historians have traced the developments that led to the emergence of the diamond-framed safety out of the plethora of cycle designs that existed in the late 19th century (e.g., McGurn 1987, Ritchie 1975). Sociologists have shown that this development was shaped not just by the technical differences between diamonds and other designs, but more importantly by the needs and interests of various social groups (Pinch & Bijker 1987).

What I hope I've done in this paper is to take the story forward into the 20th century, to identify some of the means by which the dominance of the diamond frame has been maintained. Most prominent among these are the regulations of racing bodies and the assumptions and techniques that are implicit in the methods and knowledge of cycle framebuilders. The definition of "a bicycle" goes beyond simply its physical shape, though. Any technological artifact assumes certain characteristics for its users as well, and these too can be found implicitly present in framebuilding methods.

Returning to the subject of cyborgs, given that conceptions of people are built into bicycles, I've tried to follow through the implications of Haraway's point that what we are as people includes also conceptions of technology. For Chris Boardman, as perhaps for all of us at this conference, this includes bicycles.

Notes

1. This is part of Rule 7 of the British Cycling Federation's Racing Rules, but Rule 49 of the UCI.
2. Note the chocolate connection with both names!

References

Alderson, Frederick. *Bicycling: A History*. Newton Abbot: David & Charles, 1972.

Ballantine, Richard. "The Lotus position," *New Cyclist* 26 (October 1992): 38–40.

Ballantine, Richard and Richard Grant. *Richard's Ultimate Bicycle Book*. London: Dorling Kindersley, 1992.

British Cycling Federation Handbook, 1994.

Caunter, C. F. *The History and Development of Cycles, as Illustrated by the Collection of Cycles in the Science Museum*, Part 1—Historical Survey. London: HMSO, 1955.

Haraway, Donna. "A manifesto for Cyborgs: Science, Technology, and Socialist Feminism in the 1980s" in Elizabeth Weed (ed), *Coming to Terms: Feminism, Theory, Politics*. New York: Routledge, 1989.

Hounshell, David. "The Bicycle and Technology in Late Nineteenth-Century America" in Per Sörbom (ed), *Transport Technology and Social Change*. Stockholm: Teknisa Museet, 1980.

Juden, Chris, "Petite Test," *Cycletouring & Campaigning* (February/March 1994): 19–26.

Latour, Bruno. *We Have Never Been Modern*. Hemel Hempstead: Harvester Wheatsheaf, 1993.

McGurn, James. *On Your Bicycle: An Illustrated History of Cycling*. London: John Murray, 1987.

Murrell, Deb. "Pit Stop?" *Mountain Biker* (February 1992): 38–40.

Pinch, Trevor J. and Wiebe E. Bijker. "The Social Construction of Facts and Artefacts: Or How the Sociology of Science and the Sociology of Technology might Benefit Each Other" in W. E. Bijker, T. P. Hughes and T. Pinch (eds) *The Social Construction of Technological Systems*. Cambridge, Mass.: MIT Press, 1987.

QED. "The Bike," TV programme and transcript, first broadcast BBC1, 10 March 1993.

Ritchie, Andrew. *King of the Road: An Illustrated History of Cycling*. London: Wildwood House, 1975.

Sanders, Nick (ed). *Bicycle: The Image and the Dream*. Place not named: Red Bus, 1991.

Stone, Hilary. "Fixing your Fit," *Cycling Plus*: 1 (February 1992): 50–56.

Talbot, Richard P. *Designing and Building Your Own Frameset*. Place not named: The Manet Guild, 1984, 2nd ed.

Van der Plas, Rob. *Bicycle Technology*. San Francisco: Bicycle Books, 1991.

Winner, Langdon. *Autonomous Technology: Technics-Out-of-Control as a Theme in Political Thought*. Cambridge, Mass.: MIT Press, 1978.

Mike Burrows

7. New Tubes for Old

I should like to begin by not apologising for the lack of any real "science" in this paper. This is because a) I am not a scientist, and b) experience suggests that using the words "science" and "bicycle" in the same sentence is seldom productive.

This therefore is an attempt to reconstruct the process that led to my Windcheetah monocoque cycle, with the occasional observation on how I think the design process should work. The bicycle as we know it today dates from 1885 and has remained, apart from detail improvements, virtually unchanged in all that time. This is not, as is often suggested, because real engineers turned their attention to cars and aeroplanes, and so on. It is because the bicycle is almost perfect; that is to say, it does what a bicycle should do with almost 100% efficiency in most areas, i.e., the drive chain, rolling resistance, overall weight, and even ergonomics are quite good, considering! This is why the only alternative to the diamond-frame safety bicycle to succeed is the Moulton or small-wheel cycle. These are not "better" but offer certain advantages—folding, and so on. All other attempts failed because attempts were made to improve something that could not be improved.

The bicycle does have an Achilles' heel though—its aerodynamics. Both the cycle and the rider are as bad as everything else is good, despite the fact that the first thing a cyclist says when looking over a new bike is "what does it weigh?" It is the air resistance which does most to slow him down even at quite low speeds. At 10 mph it is approximately half the total effort required to propel a cycle, and at 30 mph something like 85%. This has been understood for a long time. Indeed in the early 1900s, cycles were fitted with complete enclosures to set new records, but all of this was seen as cheating and such "add ons" were banned, and the idea of streamlining was given a bad name.

The next thing was the Americans rediscovering the fairing in the mid 70s and forming their own club, the IHPVA (International Human Powered Vehicle Association) for the purpose of racing these "illegal" cycles. This in turn made the regular cyclists take note, and a new generation of "funny bikes" appeared. Few had any real merit, but at least people were starting to think along the right lines.

This is where I came in. I started cycling in 1976 and had made my own touring bike. By 1979 I was riding in time trials and building my first racing bike—all very conventional with Reynolds tubing and filed lugs! Then in 1980 the first HPV (Human Powered Vehicle) races were held in this country, with the top American machines invited over to show us how to do it. These James Bond bicycles were very impressive, and I was soon building my own attempt at the world's fastest bike. This became a parallel hobby with my regular cycling, and what had been pure speed machines soon became road useable runabouts. This is where I really learned about the effects of aerodynamics; for it is one thing to read about them in books, and quite another to be able to ride past the fastest cyclist in England in a 3-wheel "pedal car."

This "understanding" then started to influence the design of my regular cycles, and it was not long before I produced a genuine aero bike, with the non-streamlined frame reduced to a minimum and with an extra long 250 mm seat pin made, like the handlebars, from solid aluminium and machined to an aerofoil section. The next bit of inspiration came from seeing carbon fibre at first hand in 1982. This was still very much an aerospace material, but a friend had acquired enough to produce a fairing for his HPV. The resulting shell was the stiffest and lightest I had ever seen, and so I went away determined to find a way of using this magic material. This I should point out is not a good approach to design. Using things for their own sake seldom does any real good. What a designer should do is analyse the problems and then look for a way of solving them. But rules are made to be bent at least, and in this case it worked. The bike I was currently riding had a very small (40 cm) frame and was an ideal candidate for "filling in." Had I still been riding a traditional 60 cm frame, it would have seemed a lot less logical thing to do.

This first monocoque was a copy of its predecessor, having the same small front wheel on conventional forks and with a "slot" for the rear wheel. I was riding "fixed wheel" so there were no gear mounting problems. My father had made the wooden "plug" or male master, and a friend, Mike Nelthorpe, an experienced moulder, made the mould and the frame itself. The idea was to pre-mould a polyurethane foam core which could be wrapped in carbon fibre cloth with metal inserts for spindles, and so forth, and the whole replaced in the mould for curing.

It was great theory but lots of problems putting it into practice. Also the HPV movement was growing and these "speedies" were a lot more fun than regular cycle racing, and so it was late 1984 before I was able to ride a monocoque. Mayday 1985 saw me riding it in competition for the first time and to a second best ever personal ride despite an almost 2-year layoff from bike racing proper, even beating our club record holder.

Great smugness! I had finally made a faster bicycle. There followed a lot of running around showing the "new wheel" to those who should have been interested, only to be met with a mixture of apathy and ignorance, with the notable exception of Jim Hendry, the British Cycling Federation boss, who took the bike to Italy for the World Championships where it was banned!

Sod you then, back to the HPVs, which are not only more fun but offer more scope for design and no problems with the establishment, because I am it. 1985, and I get an unusual offer from the Veteran Cycle Club to take part in a ride to commemorate 100 years of the safety bicycle, the VCC being a club for peole interested in cycles rather than cycling. They were among the few people who understood what I had done, and John Pinkerton thought the monocoque would represent the next 100 years. On the subsequent ride we visited the Coventry Museum of Transport where I saw the "Invincible" cycle of 1898 which had one "fork" blade and a similar cantilever arrangement for the rear wheel. This is a very alien concept for a cyclist, but I had been using the very same concepts on my recumbents for several years, and could see the benefits, and soon realised they included improved air resistance if this monoblade was a large airfoil section. A second frame was then made from the original mould and a monoblade was machined from a solid block of aluminium, and once more I tried to interest the establishment to no avail, returning yet again to the creative haven of the HPV world.

Shortly after this, though, the rules were changed in this country to allow disc wheels on the rear of bikes for time trialing. This was the final piece of the jig now needed to create the all cantilever monocoque. It also illustrates well how I try to design, that is by storing a series of ideas well to the back of my mind and not allowing any real direction to be taken until I have solved all the main problems. Being self employed, this is a luxury that I can afford. How to translate this into a major design house would be quite a challenge.

I had already considered the idea of a cantilever rear end as a way of solving one of the production problems, i.e., the "slot" for the rear wheel. This meant that the mould had to be a complicated 3- rather than a simple 2-wheel affair. But it was only when the possibility of using the disc wheel, which would effectively form one side of the frame aerodynamically, that there was enough incentive to go through it all over again. I had also realised by then that the small front wheel that had allowed the original frame to be small was not necessary now that the frame itself was streamlined. Also by now, 3-spoke wheels were available. Again production problems slowed things up as we were trying to find a better way of moulding than the foam core technique, but unsuccessfully, and so the final frame was produced in 1990 with p.u. foam core and a combined monoblade/handlebar assembly compression moulded from some 40 layers of carbon fibre filed to an airfoil section, and a drum brake built into the front wheel. That bike was ridden for the first part of the 1991 season, and despite the engine by now being very old and worn, managed some very good times.

It was eventually seen by a cycling friend, Rudy Thomann, who took it to Lotus to see what they thought of it, but as they say, that is another story.

Walter Ulreich

8. The Bamboo Bicycles of Grundner & Lemisch, Austria

The top sensation of the 1894 London Stanley Show (23 November–1 December)—besides a lot of wood rims, modern features like a bigger diameter of front chain wheels, frame tubes of a larger diameter than the previous year, improved tandem systems, and the new design of Palmer tyres—was bamboo cycles from the Bamboo Cycle Company of London. Among 1,300 exhibited bicycles, the extraordinary design of bamboo cycles made them the eyecatchers of the show. Yellow bamboo tubing connected by shiny aluminium lugs gave them an unusual appearance. Even Austrian bicycle magazines reported on this novelty. The machines weighed 10.2 kg and were able to carry a 101.6 kg man.[1] All the manufacturing companies mentioned light weight as one of the top promotional points in advertising bamboo cycles; nevertheless, surviving bamboo cycles are not much lighter than comparable contemporary bikes—one compared was less than 1 kg lighter.

England

The Bamboo Cycle Co. Ltd. had its manufacturing plant in Wolverhampton and offices at 59 Holborn Viaduct in London, according to Dick Swann, "the H.Q. of British Cycledom."[2] Three patents of 1894 and 1895 are known to have been issued in England to build the first bamboo cycles; all the other patents I found are later. The English patents are:

☐ No. 8274, dated 26 April 1894, R. Harrington and A. Anthony

☐ No. 8832, dated 3 May 1895, G. McAnney

☐ No. 8906, dated 4 May 1895, H. W. Dover

All these patents are improvements for connecting the bamboo canes and lugs, or methods preventing splitting of the bamboo. No British patent is known on a bamboo frame. *Wheelmen* librarian Ross Hill checked British Cycle Patent books of the period and found the preceding patents listed. In Wallis-Tayler, 1897, these 3 patents are the only ones described.[3]

The Bamboo Cycle Co. Ltd. built a big range of different models—Road Racer, Special Road Racer, Light Roadster, Special Light Roadster, Lady's Safety, Lady's Popular Bamboo Safety, Special Lady's Safety, High Frame Roadster, Special High Frame Light Roadster, Youth's Machine, Young Lady's Machine, and Light Roadster Tricycle, as offered in the company's catalogue for 1897. A second company in England, Smith Brothers of Peckham, made bamboo bikes, "until the original patentees caught up with them."[4] Different reports are known about the financial success of the company: Bartleet reports that the bamboo bicycle "was not taken up by the public, only very few being sold."[5] Swann says: "the machines sold well."[6] However, only a few machines are found in collections (1 frame in Coventry,[7] 6

Synopsis

Bamboo bicycles made their first appearance at the London Stanley Show of 1894. The manufacturer was the Bamboo Cycle Company (Wolverhampton and London), who offered them in a wide range of sizes. These bikes first appeared on the Continent in 1895, the first European distributor being A. Tönnies (J. T. Otté) of Groningen. In the same year Franz Grundner and Otto Lemisch made their first tests with bamboo as a material for bicycle frames. In 1896 Franz Grundner and Carl Bäuer received a patent ("Privilegium") for "Bicycle frames and rims made with bamboo." The newly founded company, "K. k. Priv. Bambus-Fahrräder-Fabrik Grundner & Lemisch" was a successful business until 1901. That year, Otto Lemisch took sole control of the company. A number of Grundner & Lemisch bamboo bicycles or frames are known to exist in European and American collections. A comparison of these machines reveals four distinct periods of manufacture.

bamboo cycles in private collections in England,[8] and 1 machine in the Henry Ford Museum in the U.S.A.[9]) The Bamboo Cycle Co. existed until 1899, when they "crashed"; the investors were described as "being bamboozled."[10]

America and Germany

Little is known about bamboo cycles in the U.S.A.: only one patent within the period 1892 to 1896 was found by *Wheelman* Cliff Miller checking United States Patent books up to 1896:

No. 565,783 dated 11 August 1896, A. J. Oberg and A. W. Gustafson

Bamboo cycles were produced by a company in Milwaukee, Wisconsin, which "used bamboo stalks as jackets over small diameter steel rods."[12]

Nothing is known about bamboo bicycle makers in the origin countries for the raw material. Reports on cycling in Japan and China in an Austrian bicycle magazine in the years 1900–1902 does not mention any manufacturing. If there had been, I think bamboo cycles would have been curious enough to report it.[13]

I have only heard rumours about bamboo manufacturing in France, at a company in Castres. A bamboo bicycle in the Swiss Edy Bühler collection is said to have been made by the German Bismarck Works in 1910. I have not checked the machine or documentation.[14] At the 3rd bicycle exhibition in Dresden, which opened on 9 March 1895, the company August Bayer from Gruna-Dresden showed bamboo bicycles; it is not known who the maker was.[15] A utility model with a combined frame (the upper part made of maple wood, the lower part of bamboo tubing) was reported in 1896 in Germany:

Class 63.53139, 3 February 1896, No. B–5749, Armin Büttner from Cölln at Meissen[16]

Austria

An Austrian bamboo-making company seems—according to the number of surviving machines—to have been the most successful producer. The company started with the rather unconventional interests of Franz Grundner. He was born on 7 September 1861 in St. Johann in Saggautal, today still a small village in the Leibnitz district of Styria. He was trained in mechanics and lathe turning. Interested in bicycles from an early age, he owned a high bicycle before 1891, which in his home village must have been a sensation. In the same year he moved to Klagenfurt, the capital of Carinthia, and established a shop and workshop for bicycles and sewing machines at Wienergasse 10. In night school at the "Staatsgewerbeschule" (Federal Trade School) in Klagenfurt, he developed his knowledge. His workshop eventually became a well-known meeting point for people who liked to discuss all sorts of mechanical problems, improvements, and inventions. He was also one of the founders and the first captain of a local bicycle club, the "Vorwärts" (Go ahead!), founded in 1895.

Among his friends and colleagues were some of the early Austrian pilots, like Hauger and Sablattnig, and technicians, one of them Ing. Otto Lemisch. Lemisch was born in 1866 in St. Veit an der Glan in Carinthia, and had studied mechanical engineering at the technical universities of Berlin, Karlsruhe, and Vienna. As a member of a wealthy Carinthian family, he seems to have financed the realisation of fantastic ideas which were discussed in the little Grundner workshop.[17]

In 1895, the Stanley Show again showed bamboo cycles from the Bamboo Cycle Co. Twenty-five machines were on display, with a special trial machine of 22 lbs., tested over 1,000 miles. The frame, forks, handlebars, and saddle pin of that machine were reportedly made from bamboo; the lugs were still of exotic aluminium. The first continental representative was the Dutch company A Tönnies (J. T. Otté) from Groningen, which offered bamboo cycles for 400 marks.[18]

At Christmas 1895, the first Grundner & Lemisch trial bamboo bicycles appeared and were a sensation in Klagenfurt.[19] The priority of the Austrian "Privilegium" (forerunner of the patent in Austria) also dates from 30 December 1895 (Fig. 8.1). The patent was issued in 8 countries (Austria, Germany, Italy, Switzerland, Russia, France, England, and Belgium).[20] I did not find out which came first.

The Austrian "Privilegium" was issued on 16 April 1896; the descriptive text is dated 27 March; it was presented to the Trade Ministry one day later. The envelope notes that the first descriptive text is dated 3 March and was corrected on 27 March.

The patentees were Franz Grundner, his profession given as mechanic, and Carl Bräuer, a hatter, both from Klagenfurt. The title of the "Privilegium" was "Bicycle frame and bicycle rims made from bamboo canes." Carl Bräuer's part of the patent rights were bought by Otto Lemisch within the year of issue.

The patent drawing shows a bamboo frame, with bamboo handlebars and bamboo rims. The tubes are connected with lugs, which are pressed collars of steel with bolting flanges. They are slotted and bolted collaterally, once or twice at each open end of a lug. This method of connecting the bamboo tubes is effective and conventional: the exciting point in the "Privilegium" is the use of bamboo tubes for making rims.

Manufacturing these rims is described as follows: the bamboo tube is bent to a circle, the ends are cut at an angle, then the outer half of the tube is cut away and the connecting point strenghtened by a piece of riveted sheet steel. The whole inside of the rim is laminated with canvas. It is not known whether that method was successful: no photo shows such a rim, and no remaining parts are known, nor are they ever described in bicycle magazines. The few contemporary photos of Grundner & Lemisch bicycles show bamboo-like painted (steel) rims.

Karl Bräuer some months later got a "Privilegium" (number 46/3738, issued 24 September 1896) again, described the same way, but with a varied material, "Pfefferrohr," a darker relation of bamboo (literally "pepper cane"). The lugs in that patent are bolted through the canes, not with

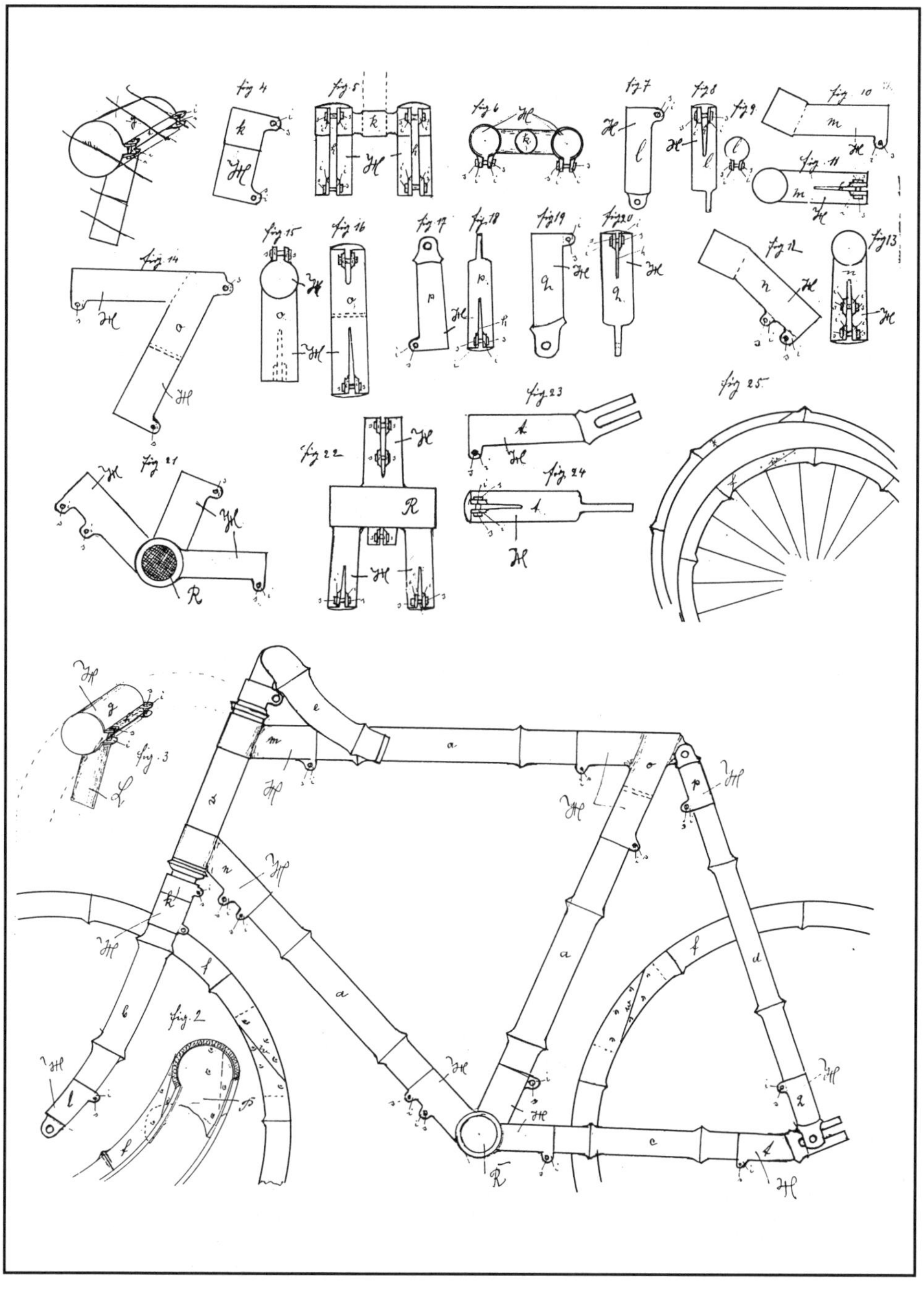

Left: Fig. 8.1. Patent drawing from Austrian "Privilegium" 46/1512 (reproduced with permission of the Austrian Patent Office Library).

Below: Fig. 8.2. Headbadge No. 1 on the Grundner & Lemisch bamboo bicycle frame in Ferlach (photo by the author).

collateral flanges as in the Bräuer and Grundner patent. Apart from the different material and lugs, it is mainly the same patent, described as "Bicycle, whose frame and rims are made from pepper cane." Bräuer seems never to have made use of that patent. In 1905 he is known to have had a store offering all sorts of sporting items, arms, fishing accessories, and bicycles—but bamboo or pepper-cane bicycles are not mentioned.

Grundner & Lemisch had tested their new bamboo cycle for 4 months on the worst tracks and in the worst weather with loads up to 180 kg. An article on the "Privilegium" in a bicycle magazine in May 1896 praised the ability to interchange all parts, and the possibility of replacing the bamboo parts by simple sticks of wood in case of an accident. The price was quoted as much lower than normal bikes.[21]

A report in a newspaper of 1896 explains that the bamboo bike was cheaper because the bamboo stalks do not need enameling.[22] That sounds logical as enameling before 1920 was a time-consuming and expensive procedure using natural resin. An article from about 1910 describes 27 different steps for a finished coat of lacquer in the automobile industry,[23] the same process used in the bicycle business.

The bicycle factory of Franz Grundner and Otto Lemisch was registered on 3 November 1896.[24] The name was "K. k. priv. Bambus-Fahrräder-Fabrik Grundner & Lemisch." The factory was in Unterferlach on the premises of the famous (then and now) gun manufacturers of Ferlach. The office, store, and repair shop of the company were at the Grundner shop at Wienergasse 10 in Klagenfurt.[25]

In December a utility model of the Grundner & Lemisch bamboo bike was registered:

Klagenfurt No. G.3648, 19 December 1896[26]

The company grew fast, from 6 workers in the beginning to 63 in 1898. Their own turbine was used for energy supply. Modern American tooling machines of high quality enabled Grundner & Lemisch to produce the entire bicycle except the leather and rubber parts (Fig. 8.2).

The raw material, the bamboo canes, came from Shanghai and were protected against the influence of heat and humidity by a secret method. What is known is that first the bamboo tubes were cut to the exact length for certain frame parts, both ends being turned for a defined external and internal diameter. The ends were strengthened by short, glued-in wooden cylinders. These perfectly prepared tubes were pressed with great force into the lugs. All connections were secured by a special cement. The last step fixed the connections by bolts and nuts. Both front fork bamboo canes were bent hot, but not by steam.

The lugs had to be strong, light, and cheap. Grundner & Lemisch used the best Mannesmann or weldless tubing, a high quality material that was pressed in dies to give them the right shape with bolting flanges, which were then drilled and had slits cut longitudinally. The parts were finished by polishing and nickeling.[27]

In 1897, the company took part in the world exhibition in Brussels[28] and was awarded a medal.[29]

In 1898, Grundner & Lemisch expanded and opened a branch in Vienna, at Dominikanerbastei 21.[30] As capital of the monarchy, Vienna was a prime marketplace, and it was important for an expanding company to be there. Advertising was much easier, and one day a Grundner & Lemisch bamboo tandem turned up at the Viennese Waffenrad racing track, the first ever at a race, and won one race. An additional sprint lap was suddenly stopped, as the frame began to crack, and the riders dismounted rapidly.[31]

In winter 1898–99, the company established a winter riding school in Vienna at Taborstraße 11a, which was lit by fashionable electric light, and had a comfortable reading room and every convenience. There were free lectures for customers, and bamboo cycles to hire.[32]

In December 1898 a new bicycle club was founded: "Die Bambusradler" ("the bamboo cyclists").[33] The bicycle reached its peak of popularity in Austria from 1896 to 1898, with the best year, 1897, when each social group and bicycle company had its own club (Fig. 8.3).

Grundner & Lemisch took part in 3 exhibitions that year: the "Jubiläumsausstellung" in Vienna, and international sport exhibitions in Innsbruck and Vienna. At each event, bamboo bicycles were awarded prizes.[34]

In the following year, when Grundner & Lemisch wanted to test the quality of their product, they went to the "Technologisches Gewerbemuseum" (a technical school in Vienna which had the knowledge and ability to make scientific technical examinations). The tests lasted from 1–27 March 1899. Technicians tested the frame, increasing the load weight in steps of 50 kg. It was noted that at a weight of 550 kg, the bottom bracket lowered by 7.7 mm, but there was no permanent lowering. At 900 kg the bottom bracket was 20 mm lower, and after removing this weight a permanent lowering of 7.4 mm was noted. The reason was that the front fork became bent. Even increasing the weight to 2,800 kg only caused the breaking of the front fork bamboo tubes. The certificate showed that the frame had high elasticity, and attested no danger even in the case of fractures, because of the respectable holding capacity. To illustrate this result, Grundner & Lemisch used a photo of a well-known athlete of the time, Georg Jagendorfer, a man of 126 kg, on a bamboo bike.[35]

Franz Grundner was not a man to be satisfied with one success: he always had new ideas and the personal power to undertake them. In 1900, a patent was issued on a water bicycle for Franz Grunder and Franz Fichtner of Seeboden (9 February 1900).[36] One year later, Grundner tested his water bicycle on the Wörthersee in Carinthia. Both tin floating bodies of the machine were divided in 4 isolated chambers. The propelling screw was moved by the drive unit from a bicycle; even the back wheel seems to have a function, possibly braking the boat. Steering was by means of normal handlebars. The man in the picture postcard is Mr. Grundner himself.[37] Later on Grundner advanced his "water bicycle" to a "water car," which he presented to an amazed public in 1904. This boat engine reached a velocity of 20 km/h.[38]

A new raw material, paper mâché, reported in 1900, was used to improve the building of light bicycle frames. Extremely light frames of that unique material were produced by a company in Springfield, Massachusetts. Very thin coloured paper was used, soaked with an ammonia-like salt, which was dipped in warm glue and rolled in up to 40 layers over moulding tubes. The soft paper canes were pressed by 2 roll barrels. After pulling out the moulding tube, the paper tubing became a very hard and light material for frames, handlebars, and even wheels and pedals. The weight of a robust touring bike was about 10 kg, while a normal machine weighed between 6 and 8 kg.[39]

In 1901 the branch in Vienna was closed, and Grundner and Lemisch separated. Grundner, still at Wienergasse 10, had a bicycle dealership and repair shop with special conditions for the Austrian Touring Club, and was a supplier of the "Union of the Austrian k.k. federal officials."[40]

Otto Lemisch, after a short and not very successful try to establish a bicycle factory in America in 1899,[41] took over the bamboo bicycle factory in 1901 and called it "K. k. priv. Bambus-Fahrräder-Fabrik Otto Lemisch." The old company in Unterferlach stopped production in the same year.[42] The new premises were in Ebenthal near Klagenfurt. The factory had a riding school in Klagenfurt, a repair shop, its own plating and enameling facilities, and gave a 1-year guarantee on bamboo cycles.[43]

A 1902 advertisement with big letters, "Otto Lemisch/Ebenthal," for the new bamboo company shows the newest fashion in bicycle styling, the full chain wheel, which was introduced by Johann Puch one year earlier (Fig. 8.4).[44] Most Austrian and Bohemian bicycle companies used the pretty chain wheels, and some examples are even known in Germany.[45] One Lemisch bamboo cycle is preserved in a private collection in Switzerland.

Franz Grundner died in 1945 in Weitensfeld in Carinthia, and Otto Lemisch died in 1940 in

Fig. 8.3. Presumably a company photograph of Grundner & Lemisch of about 1899 (reproduced with permission of Helge Schulz, Ludwigsburg).

Pörtschach.[46] The Grundner shop in Klagenfurt at Wienergasse 10 continued as a bicycle shop until a couple of years ago.

Surviving Bamboo Bicycles from Grundner & Lemisch and Otto Lemisch

- ☐ Büchsenmachermuseum, Ferlach: Grundner & Lemisch, Gents, frame
- ☐ Deutsches Museum, Munich: Grundner & Lemisch, Gents—Inv. No. 1933/65543
- ☐ Private collection, Franz Heini, Wolhusen: Otto Lemisch, Gents
- ☐ Private collection, Gottfried Keller, Bauma: Grundner & Lemisch, Gents
- ☐ Museum für Verkehr und Technik, Berlin: Grundner & Lemisch, Ladies
- ☐ Narodní Technice Museum, Prague: Grundner & Lemisch, Gents, I.C. 18598; Grundner & Lemisch, Gents, without I.C.; Grundner & Lemisch, Gents, I.C. 18533
- ☐ Nationaal Fietsmuseum Velorama, Nijmegen: Grundner & Lemisch, Gents
- ☐ Verkehrshaus der Schweiz, Luzern: Grundner & Lemisch, Gents
- ☐ Private collection, Michael Zappe, Vienna: Grundner & Lemisch, Gents, frame

An Attempt at a Dating System

Comparing pictures of most of the machines mentioned before and knowing about the history of the two companies enabled me to develop an approximative system for dating Austrian bamboo bicycles. For this purpose I compared the plates, if they were still attached, and the lugs and fork crowns.

Two different types of plates are known:

No. 1 has the text

"K. K. PRIV./BAMBUS FAHRRÄDER FABRIK / GRUNDNER & LEMISCH/KLAGENFURT"

and 2 exhibition medals on it.

No. 2 has the text

"BAMBUS FAHRRÄDER FABRIK/K. K. "PRIV./ GRUNDNER & LEMISCH/KLAGENFURT"

and 3 exhibition medals. On the top of the plate is a stamped number, maybe a production number: no recorded system is known.

No. 1 predates No. 2. The 2 medals, I think are from Brussels 1897, and one of the 3 exhibitions of 1898. The third medal is from the year 1898 too, so I think the change of plate was made in that year.

No plate is known of Otto Lemisch bamboo bikes: the only surviving machine has a plate No. 2, which I believe is wrong for that bicycle.

Bottom bracket assembly: The main variants of the bottom bracket assembly are type A with straight chain stay tubes and type B with cranked chain stay tubes.

Rear ends are 2 types: Type A straight or type B bent upwards.

All lugs additionally can differ in 3 variants: Type A for plain tubing (as in the drawing of the "Privilegium") and bolts; type B for a strain relieving cutout and bolts; type C for plain tubing, no bolts.

Fork crown: Type A has flat tops and plain tubing; type B has flat tops and 1 cutout on each side; type C has flat tops and 2 cutouts on each side; type D has bevelled tops and plain tubing; type E has bevelled tops and 1 cutout on each side; type F has bevelled tops, no cutouts, no bolts; type G has horseshoe form, no cutouts, no bolts.

Fig. 8.4. Advertisement for Otto Lemisch's bamboo bicycle published in Das Stahlrad in October 1902, page 153. It includes references to a "full chainwheel" and "lugs without cutouts or bolts."

Conclusion

I believe there to be 4 production periods:

- ☐ The earliest Grundner & Lemisch has plate No.1, bottom bracket type A, rear ends type A, all lugs type A, and fork crown type A. Built from 1896–1898. The only machine with that specification is Prague (I.C. 18533). I believe this to be the oldest surviving machine, with the design nearest to the drawing of the "Privilegium."

- ☐ Grundner & Lemisch with plate No. 1 or No. 2, bottom bracket type A, rear ends type A, all lugs type B, and fork crown type A, B, or C. Built after 1898, I do not know when the change to the next period is to date. Machines of that period are: Luzern, Prague (without I.C.), Berlin, Zappe, and Ferlach.

- ☐ Grundner & Lemisch with plate No. 2, bottom bracket type B, rear ends type B, all lugs type B, and fork crown type D or E. Built until 1901. Machines of that period are: Keller, Prague (I.C. 18598) and Nijmegen.

- ☐ Otto Lemisch, plate unknown, bottom bracket type B, rear ends type B, all lugs type C, and fork crown type F or G, full chain wheel with the text "Otto Lemisch/Ebenthal." Built from 1901 to at least 1902. The only known machine of that period is the Heini.

Acknowledgments

For help in preparing this paper I want to thank: Gert Jan Moed (Nijmegen), Cliff Miller (Clinton Township, Michigan) and Carl Wiedman (Bloomfield Hills, Michigan) for checking British and American patent books, Tobias Greuter (Schöftland) for sending me photocopies from *Der Schweizerische Radmarkt*, again Gert Jan Moed for photocopies from Bamboo Cycle Co. catalogue, John Pinkerton and Andrew Millward (Birmingham) for information about bamboo cycles in British collections, Pryor Dodge (New York) for information about his bamboo cycle, Valerie P. Dalzell Pears and Michael P. Dalzell (Groby, Leicester) and Terry Wright for brushing up my English text, Roswitha Schmidt (Klagenfurt) and Dr. Werner Watzenig (Villach) for helping me with information about the family and company of Franz Grundner, the library of the Austrian Patent Office for permission to use texts and illustrations of the 2 Austrian Privilegia, all the owners of Austrian bamboo cycles for the opportunity to examine and photograph their machines, and all the owners of the illustrations for their kind permission to use them in this paper.

Notes and Sources

1. *Die Ostmark* no. 33 (1894): 736–37.
2. Swann, 1968, p. 32.
3. Wallis-Taylor, 1897, pp. 88–89.
4. Swann, 1968, p. 33.
5. Bartleet, 1931, p. 66.
6. Swann, 1968, p. 33.
7. Bartleet, 1931, pp. 66–67 and Plate 28.
8. Information courtesy of John Pinkerton and Andrew Millward, Birmingham.
9. Adams, 1981, p. 224. A second machine in the U.S.A. is in the Pryor Dodge collection (Information courtesy of Pryor Dodge, New York).
10. Swann, 1968, p. 33.
11. Ibid.
12. Adams, 1981, p. 222; compare Swann, 1968, p. 32.
13. Berthel, Carl, "Das Rad in China," *Radfahr-Sport* no. 4 (1902): 38–39 ; and "Japan" (extract of an article by Arthur Divsy in *Wheeling*), *Radfahr-Sport* no. 38 (1900): 418.
14. *Tour* no. 2 (1984): 40.
15. *Deutsch-österreichischer Radfahrer* no. 7 (1895): 174.
16. *Deutsch-österreichischer Radfahrer* no. 7 (1896): 157.
17. The 3 paragraphs above are compiled from information in Genser, 1972 and Watzenig (in progress).
18. *Radfahr-Sport* no. 1 (1895): 11; compare advertisement in *Deutscher Radfahrer-Bund* no. 2 (1895): 20.
19. *Die Gross-Industrie* (1898): 163.
20. Ibid.
21. *Die Ostmark* no. 15 (1896): 282.

22. *Klagenfurter Zeitung* no. 129 (1896): 1099.
23. *Kunstharz Nachrichten*, February 1986.
24. Watzenig (in progress).
25. Handbuch, Graz, 1898, no page.
26. *Deutsch-österreichischer Radfahrer* no. 10 (1897): 236.
27. About the fabrication according to *Die Gross-Industrie* (1898): 163.
28. Officieller Special-Katalog, 1897, pp. 55 and 68.
29. *Die Gross-Industrie* (1898): 163.
30. *Österreichisch-Ungarische Radfahrer-Zeitung* no. 29 (1898): 11.
31. *Centralblatt für Radsport und Athletik* No. 10 (1898): 6.
32. *Centralblatt für Radsport und Athletik* No. 23 (1898): 5.
33. *Radfahr-Sport* no. 52 (1898): 1118.
34. *Die Gross-Industrie* (1898) S. 163.
35. *Der Schweizerische Radmarkt* no. 6 (1904).
36. *Deutsch-österreichischer Radfahrer* no. 5 (1900): 69; compare *Radfahr-Sport* no. 11 (1900): 127.
37. *Radfahr-Sport* no. 39 (1901): 438.
38. Genser, 1972 and Watzenig (in progress).
39. *Deutsch-österreichischer Radfahrer* no. 14 (1900): 214; compare ibid., no. 19 (1900): 292; compare Wallis-Taylor, 1897, p. 80.
40. Tourenbuch, Klagenfurt, 1901, p. 159.
41. Watzenig (in progress).
42. Ibid.
43. Tourenbuch, Klagenfurt, 1901, p. 160.
44. *Das Stahlrad* no. 10 (1902): 153.
45. Ulreich, 1995 (in print).
46. Franke, 1987, pp. 128–29.

Bibliography

Magazines

Centralblatt für Radsport und Athletik. Wochenschrift für alle Sportzweige mit Ausnahme des Pferdesports. Vienna, 1899.

Deutsch-österreichischer Radfahrer. Illustrierte Fachzeitschrift zur Förderung der gesammten Radfahrsache und des Betriebes der Fahrraderzeugung. Vienna, 1895–1897.

Deutscher Radfahrer-Bund. Amtliche Zeitung des Deutschen Radfahrer-Bundes. Magdeburg, no. 2 (1895).

Hygiea. Wien no. 13 (1899).

Kunstharz Nachrichten. Frankfurt on Main, February 1986.

Österreichisch-Ungarische Radfahrer-Zeitung. Fachblatt für die Gesammt-Interessen des Radfahrsportes. Vienna, 1898.

Die Ostmark. Organ der selbständigen deutschen Landes-Verbände Oesterreichs. Illustrierte Fachzeitschrift für Radfahr- und Ski-Sport. Vienna, 1894–1896.

Radfahr-Sport. Organ für das gesammte Radfahrwesen. Vienna, 1901–1902.

Der Schweizerische Radmarkt. Bern, no. 6 (1904).

Das Stahlrad. Fachzeitschrift für die Gesamtinteressen des Radfahrers. Offizielles Organ des Verbandes Deutscher Fahrradhändler. Leipzig, no. 10 (1902).

Tour. Rund ums Rad. Munich, no. 2 (1984).

Books, Catalogues, and Articles

Adams, G. Donald. *Collecting and Restoring Antique Bicycles*. Blue Ridge Summit: 1981.

Adler, Joh. W. Tourenbuch von Kärnten und Oberitalien sowie der österreichischen Alpenländer für Radfahrer und Automobilisten. Klagenfurt: 1901.

Bartleet, H.W. *Bartleet's Bicycle Book*. London: 1931.

Catalogue of the Bamboo Cycle Co. Ltd. London: 1897.

Franke, Jutta. *Illustrierte Fahrradgeschichte*. Berlin: 1987.

Genser, Margarethe. *Klagenfurter Bicyclisten*. "Kärntner Tageszeitung," Klagenfurt 6, May 1972.

Die Gross-Industrie Oesterreichs. Festgabe zum glorreichen fünfzigjährigen Regierungs-Jubiläum seiner Majestät des Kaisers Franz Josef I. dargebracht von den Industriellen Oesterreichs. Band III. Vienna: 1898.

Handbuch des Cartells der vier selbstständigen Herrenfahrer-Verbände Deutsch-Oesterreichs. Graz: 1898.

Officieller Special-Katalog der Österreichischen Abtheilung auf der Weltausstellung Brüssel 1897. Vienna: 1897.

Swann, Dick. *Days of Davies*. U.S.A.: 1968.

Ulreich, Walter. *Das Steyr Waffenrad*. Gnas: 1995 (in print).

Wallis-Taylor, J. A. *Modern Cycles: A Practical Handbook on their Construction & Repair*. London: 1897.

Watzenig, Werner. *Die K. k. privilegierte Bambus-Fahrräder-Fabrik Grundner & Lemisch* (in progress). *Jahrbuch der Kärntner*

Elektrizitäts-Aktiengesellschaft für 1995. Klagenfurt: (to be published in 1995).

Documents

Austrian Privilegium no. 46/1512, issued 16 April 1896.

Austrian Privilegium no. 46/3738, issued 24 September 1896.

Appendix:
Text of the Austrian Privilegium 46/1512:

(Envelope:)

Privilegiumswerber Carl Bräuer, Hutappreteur/und Franz Grundner, Mechaniker/beide in Klagenfurt Zur Erfindung betitelt "Fahrradrahmen u. Fahrradfelgen aus Bambusrohr"

Pr(iorität): 30. December 1895

Klagenfurt am 3. März 1896

Corr(igiert) am 27. März 1896

[stamp] HANDELSMINISTERIUM pr(äsentiert): 28.3.96 No. 17465 um 10.30

[Privilegium number] 46/1512 geheim [issued] 16/4/96

(Page 1:)

[stamp] K. K. Priv: Archiv: [in long hand] 46/1512

Carl Bräuer, Hutappreteur, u./Franz Grundner, Mechaniker/beide in Klagenfurt. Fahrradrahmen u. Fahrradfelgen aus Bambusrohr.

Die in der Fig. 1 gelb hervorgehobenen Fahrradbestandtheile u. zwar die—Rahmentheile (a a) die vorderen Gabeltheile (b b) die hinteren Gabeltheile (c c) die hinteren Verbindungsstangen (d d) die Lenkstange (e) und Fahrradfelgen (f) werden aus Bambusrohr hergestellt und wird die Verbindung der Rahmen u. Gabeltheile sowie der Lenk u. Verbindungsstangen untereinander rsp. mit den brigen Fahrradbestandtheilen mittelst Stahlhülsen (H), welche mit Schlitzen (h) Lappen (i i) u. Schrauben (s) versehen sind bewerkstelligt, wodurch die Möglichkeit geboten ist, die einzelnen Bambusrohrbestandtheile beliebig auszuwechseln und für Nothfälle auch durch andere Holztheile zu ersetzen.

Diese Stahlhülsen-Verbindungstheile sind in der Fig. 1 weg gelassen u. in Fig. 3—24 zur besseren Ersichtlichmachung der Schlitze (h) Lappen (i i) und Schrauben (s) in verschiedenen Ansichten gezeichnet.

(Page 2:)

Fig. 3. Das Lenkstangen Verbindungsstück; Fig. 4. Der Gabelkopf (Seitenansicht); Fig. 5. Dt (Hinteransicht); Fig. 6. Dto (obere Ansicht); Fig. 7. Die geraden Gabelscheidenenden (Seitenansicht); Fig. 8. Dto (hintere Ansicht); Fig. 9. Dto (obere Ansicht); Fig. 10. Die obere Steuerungsverbindungsmuffe (Seitenansicht); Fig. 11. Dto (untere Ansicht); Fig. 12. Die untere Steuerungsverbindungsmuffe (Seitenansicht); Fig. 13. Dto (untere Ansicht); Fig. 14. Die Sattelstützmuffe (Seitenansicht); Fig. 15. Dto (obere Ansicht); Fig. 16. Dto (hintere Ansicht); Fig. 17. Die oberen Enden der hinteren Verbindungsstange (Seiten Ansicht); Fig. 18. Die oberen Enden der hinteren Verbindungsstange (vordere Ansicht); Fig. 19. Die unteren Enden der hinteren Verbindungsstange (Seitenansicht); Fig. 20. Dto (vordere Ansicht); Fig. 21. Das Tretlagergehäuse (Seitenansicht); Fig. 22. Dto (untere Ansicht); Fig. 23. Die hinteren Gabelenden (Seitenansicht); Fig. 24. Dto (untere Ansicht).

Die Radfelge f wird entweder aus einer einzigen oder aus zwei zusammen geschifteten Bambusrohren folgender Weise hergestellt: Das Bambusrohr wird

(Page 3:)

gebogen sodan werden die zusammengefügten Enden von oben nach unten schräg durchschnitten (wie Linie (w) der Figs. 1,2 u. 25 zeigt) übereinandergepaßt und verleimt hierauf wird die convexe Seite des Ringes z Fig. 25 abgenohmen. Die hiedurch enstehende offene Rinne an der Stelle der Schifftung mitelst eines Stahlbleches (P) verstärkt und vernietet und durchaus mit Segeltuch ausgefütert.

Patent Ansprüche:

1. Ein Fahrrad, bei welchem die Bestandtheile (a-a) des Rahmens, die Hülse (b-b) der Vorderradgabel und (c c) der Hinterradgabel. Die Verbindungsstangen (d d) und die Lenkstange e ferner die Felgen (f) der Räder aus Bambusrohr bestehen.

2. Zur Befestigung des Tretkurbellagers (R.) der Achsenhalter l, p, t des Gabelkopfes k. der Verbindungsmuffen m, n, des Steuerrohres v, des Rohres a, zur Aufnahme der Sattelstütze u. der Verbindungsoesen p an den Bambusrohren u. zur Befestigung der Bambus-Lenkstange e mit der Steuerstange L bei einem Fahrrade nach Anspruch 1. Die Anordnung von Klemmhülsen H an diesen Bestandtheilen, welche Hülsen gekennzeichnet sind, durch einen Schlitz h ein oder zwei Lappen i i und durch die letzeren gehenden Schrauben s.

(Page 4:)

3 Bei den Rädern eines Fahrrades nach Anspruch 1) eine Felge f, welche aus einem oder mehreren durch Spaltung eines Bambusrohres in der Faserrichtung enstandenen Rohrstücken besteht, wobei die zusammenzufügenden Enden schräg (nach Linie w der Figs. 1, 2 u. 25) abgeschnitten, übereinandergepat u. verleimt sind u. hernach zur Verstärkung dieser Verbindung ein Stahlblech P. eingelegt und mit beiden Rohrenden vernietet wird.

Wien, am 27. März 1896 Karl Bräuer Franz Grundner.

Ron Shepherd

9. The Dancing Chain: One Hundred Years of Derailleur Gears

Derailleur gears are standard components of modern bicycles, yet until a few years ago little had been published about their history. After a lifetime of using derailleurs for bicycle touring, I was keen to discover their origins. From suburban Melbourne it was surprisingly straightforward to obtain the necessary information by correspondence with patent offices, museums and libraries, and with bicycle enthusiasts around the world. I wish to express my thanks to the many people whose kindness and cooperation enabled me to piece together the story of the dancing chain.

The Origins of Derailleur Gears

In 1990 an outline of the origins of derailleur gearing was compiled and published,[1] tracing back to Jean Loubeyre's Polyceler of 1895 (Fig. 9.1).

This initial article stimulated reports of two other 19th-century chain gears—a French derailleur in the U.S.A.[2,3] (Fig. 9.2) and an English derailleur in France[4] (Fig. 9.3).

Two inferences may be drawn from this brief excursion into cycle history: 1. the need for further study; and 2. the importance of studying cycling in the 20th century.

The Need for Further Study of Cycle History

Unlike politics, warfare, or the arts, everyday technology attracts little attention from historians. Yet technology, including bicycle technology, has also had its discoveries, innovations, triumphs, and disasters. Through lack of study, key artefacts and information are in danger of being lost forever. There are 3 chain derailling mechanisms from the 19th century which still exist—the Berry bicycle and the Whippet already mentioned, and the Gradient in the Science Museum in London (Inv. 1924–69). Perhaps there are more to be discovered, although most cycling components from the 19th century would have been discarded long ago. Virtually nothing is known of the inventors of these early derailleurs. For example, who manufactured Ed Berry's bicycle? Who

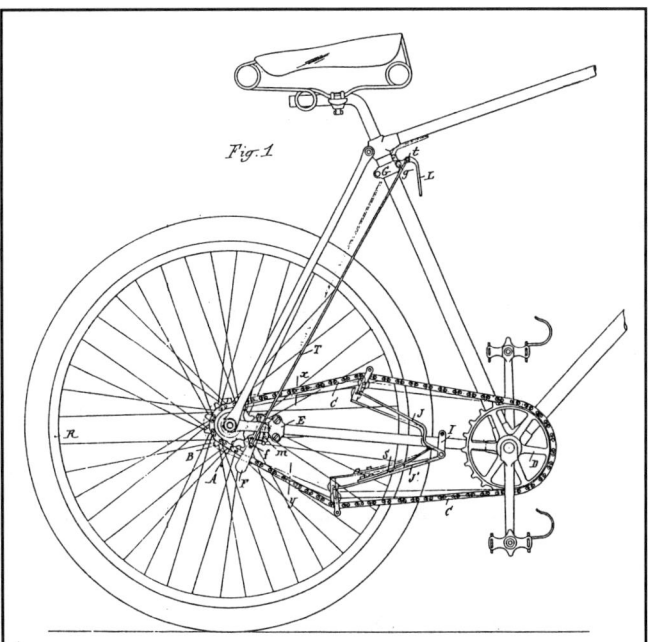

Fig. 9.1. Jean Loubeyre's Polyceler (Brevet no. 1299 of 1895, Institut Nationale de Propriété Industrielle, Paris).

Synopsis

This paper traces the development of derailleur gearing. While front derailleurs have hardly altered this century, double-pulley, chain-bending rear derailleurs have been steadily improved to become the only type now produced. Earlier alternative types of rear derailleurs had either no pulleys or only one pulley to minimise chain resistance. Other types maintained the chain in line by sliding the sprockets sideways.

Fig. 9.2. The author (left) and Ed Berry in New York with Berry's mysterious derailleur-equipped bicycle.

Fig. 9.3. The English Whippet bicycle discovered by Raymond Henry in the Musée d'Art et d'Industrie de Saint-Etienne.

was Loubeyre? What is known of Edmund Hodgkinson and Charles Linley? If they had been Wolfgang Mozart or Toulouse Lautrec or the Duke of Wellington, every detail of their lives would have been chronicled.

The Importance of Studying Cycling in the 20th Century

Cycle history is often regarded as belonging in the 19th century—hobbyhorses, boneshakers, high bicycles, then safety bicycles. In a recent issue of *News and Views*,[5] Vic Polanski referred to the emphasis on these old bicycles. To illustrate the concentration on the 19th century, the dates in a recent, authoritative source—Derek Robert's *Cycling History: Myths and Queries*[6]—are shown in Fig. 9.4.

Although most cycle components, including pneumatic tyres, steel tubes, ball bearings, disc wheels, and suspension, were invented in the 19th century, it has taken a hundred years of development and refinement to convert many of them into practical realities. In particular gears, brakes and tyres are incomparably better than what was available a century ago. Nick Clayton commented in a recent issue of *The Boneshaker*[7] that innovation has continued throughout the present century. The 20th century is much more accessible than the 19th

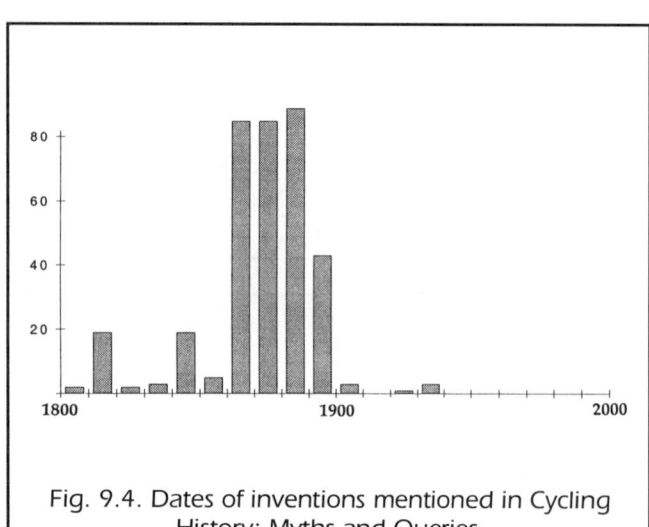

Fig. 9.4. Dates of inventions mentioned in Cycling History: Myths and Queries.

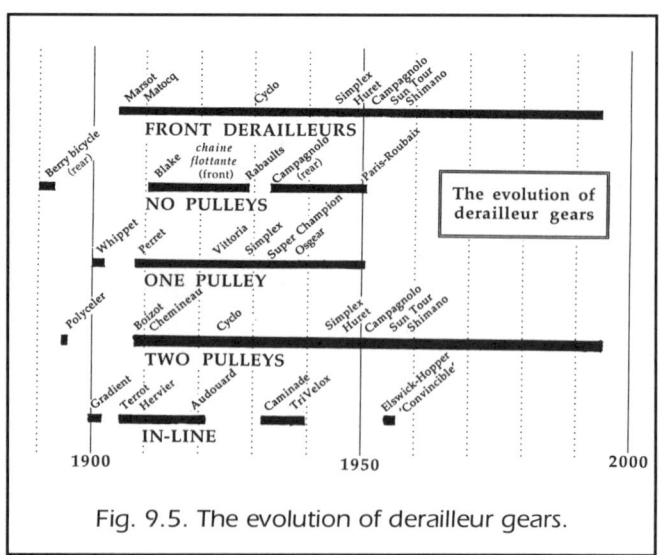

Fig. 9.5. The evolution of derailleur gears.

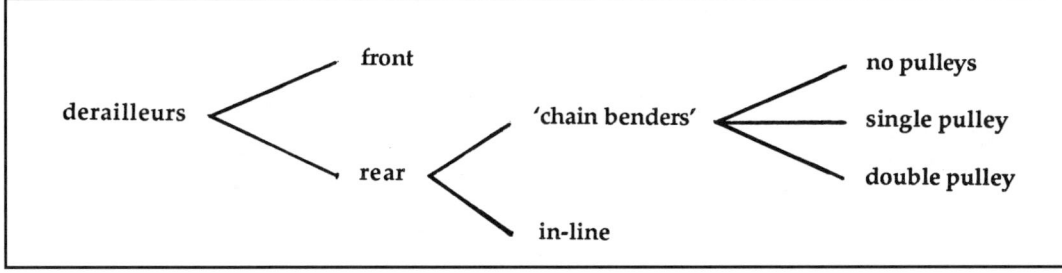

Table 9.1. Overview of derailleur types.

century. There are many surviving artefacts and publications from the present century, and people who can remember much of it. Some cyclists can still recall the 1930s, and we should collect their reminiscences while we can.

By studying aspects of cycling longitudinally, from their origins through to the present, patterns of development can be discerned.

The many different derailleurs produced over the past hundred years can be categorised as shown in Table 9.1. Various derailleurs in these categories are shown in Fig. 9.5.

	MAJOR	MINOR	
1890s		Berry bicycle, France ??? Jean Loubeyre, Paris - Polyceler Edmund Hodgkinson, London - Gradient George Linley, Whippet - New Protean	
1900s		Terrot, Dijon Boizot, Paris - Bidirect P.d'A. Perret	Marsot Matocq Hervier Paul de Vivie?
1910s		Audouard Blanchard-Grange	Panel - Le Chemineau Raimond - Le Routier
1920s	Albert Raimond - Cyclo Lucien Juy - Simplex	As Crack	Izoard Montagnard
1930s	Cyclo (France, UK)) Simplex Super Champion	Caminade - Rectiligne Campagnolo, Italy Constrictor- Osgear Enfield, England Fichtel-Sachs Inax Lautaret Morgan, Wales Nivex	Pelissier Perry Stronglight Super Prior TriVelox, England Vainqueur Victo Vittoria, Italy Zeus, Spain
1940s	Cyclo (France, UK) Huret Simplex	Campagnolo Gi-emme JIC	New-Lewis Osgear Super Champion
1950s	Campagnolo Cyclo (France, UK) Huret Simplex	GB Altenburger Hercules - Herailleur Osgear Resilion	Shimano Spirax Sun Tour
1960s	Campagnolo Huret Simplex	Cyclo (France, UK) Shimano Sun Tour	
1970s	Campagnolo Shimano Simplex Sun Tour	Cyclo (France) Galli Huret Long Yi - Epoch	Roto Sun Race Zeus
1980s	Campagnolo Shimano Sun Tour	Galli Gian Robert Huret Long Yi - Epoch	Mavic Simplex Sun Race Zeus
1990s	Shimano	Blanchard Campagnolo Falcon - Dynamax Joytech - Posidex	Long Yi - Epoch Mavic Sun Race SunTour

Table 9.2. Derailleur manufacturers.

Table 9.2 is a tentative list of the firms who have made derailleur gears. It reveals the flourishing interest in derailleur gears in the 1930s.

Double-Pulley Derailleurs

Modern rear derailleurs are of the chain-bending type, and have double pulleys for shifting the chain sideways and taking up chain slack. The main line of evolution which has led to modern derailleurs could be said to have begun with Charles Boizot's Bidirect of 1908 (see Fig. 9.6). The Bidirect had 2 pulleys, the characteristic feature of modern derailleurs.

By selecting a derailleur every 20 years since the Bidirect, modifications of the basic 2-pulley type can be noted.

In the 1930s, the Cyclo double-cable model was popular for both racing and touring (see Fig. 9.7). The Australian Hubert Opperman (now Sir Hubert) used a Cyclo on his record rides in the United Kingdom, and later in Australia. The Cyclo was also solidly built. Harry Suddaby recently reported in *Fellowship News*[8] that he and his wife had used one on their tandem for 50 years.

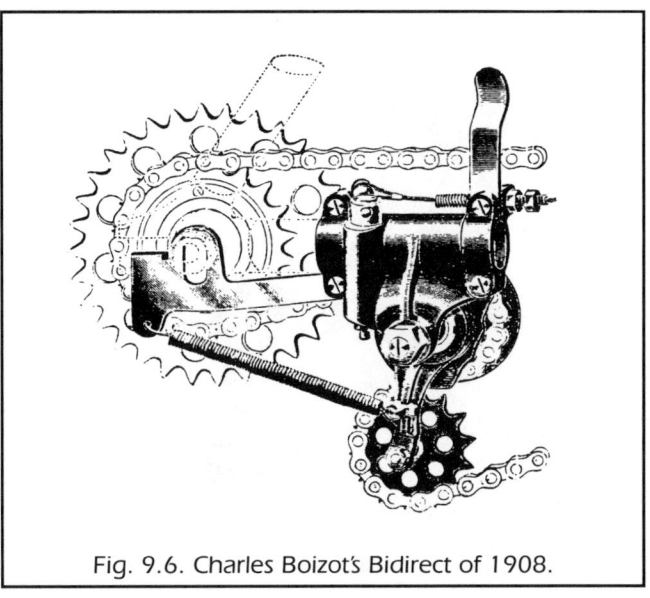

Fig. 9.6. Charles Boizot's Bidirect of 1908.

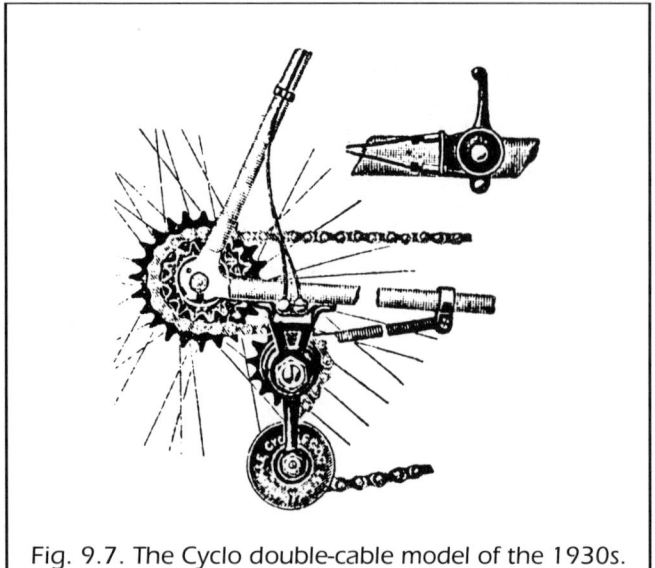

Fig. 9.7. The Cyclo double-cable model of the 1930s.

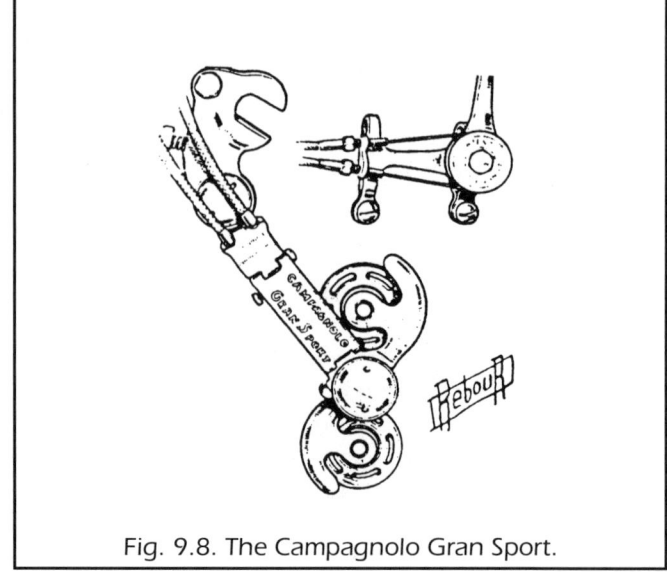

Fig. 9.8. The Campagnolo Gran Sport.

In the 1950s, the Campagnolo Gran Sport became the standard rear derailleur for cycle racers around the world (see Fig. 9.8). Beautifully made, the Gran Sport had a parallelogram action, and was light but strong.

In the 1970s, SunTour derailleurs featured the slant pantograph invented by Nobuo Ozaki and his team at Maeda Industries. The slant pantograph greatly improved shifting across sprockets with large differences in size (see Fig. 9.9). On mountain tours in winter I recall my rear wheel caked in mud, and under the mud a faithful SunTour VGT-Luxe shifted the chain from sprocket to sprocket.

In the 1990s, the pre-eminent rear derailleur is the Shimano XT (see Fig. 9.10). First produced in 1986, this model is now a classic. *Cycling Plus*[9] magazine referred to it as follows:

> For the majority of riders Shimano XT is Nirvana, Heaven, the highest ideal to which their chains can aspire.

The Shimano XT has 2 pulleys, a slant pantograph, a sprung pivot, and indexed shifting. It has a huge capacity, is strong and rigid, and shifts smoothly even when the rider is pedalling uphill. Each year Shimano produces a slightly improved version of the XT. A marque enthusiast is needed to record its history.

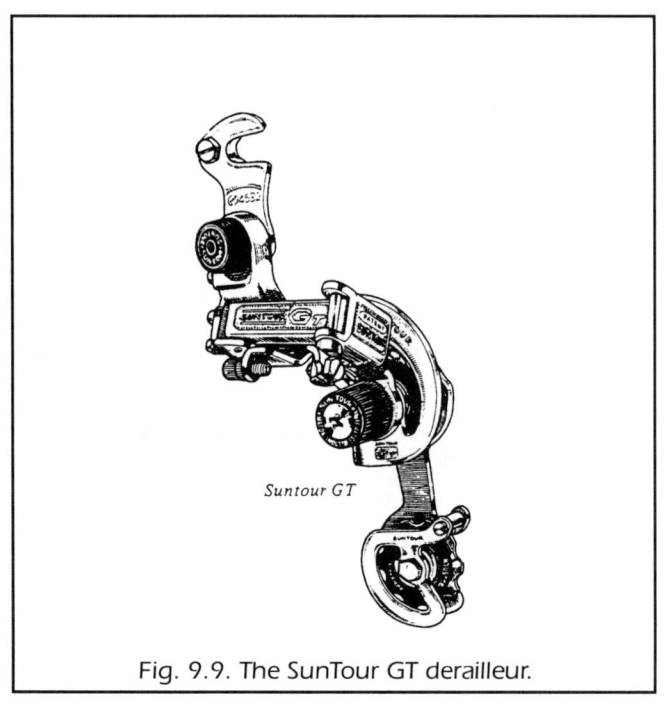

Fig. 9.9. The SunTour GT derailleur.

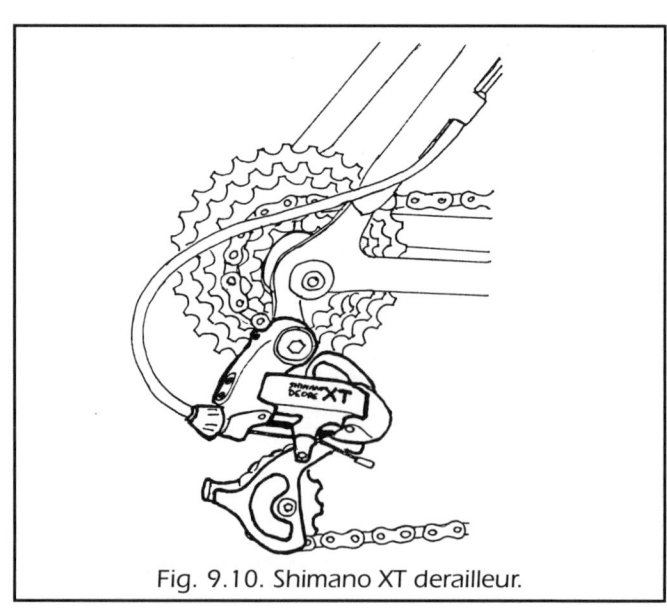

Fig. 9.10. Shimano XT derailleur.

Fig. 9.11. Swinging bottom bracket on the Berry bicycle.

Fig. 9.12. Vernon Blake and the chaine flottante.

Other Types of Rear Derailleur

In parallel with the main line of derailleur evolution, there have been several intriguing alternative designs. In 1908, Paul de Vivie ("Vélocio") objected to *la résistance passive* of the 2 pulleys around which the chain was constrained to move at all times, whether a gear shift was occurring or not.[10] Instead of referring to them as *galets*, Vélocio called the pulleys *galopins* (urchins). Vélocio and others sought a more elegant system that avoided the drag of the 2 pulleys. At various times there have been derailleurs which had only one pulley, or no pulley at all.

No-Pulley Derailleurs

Ed Berry's bicycle has 2 fixed sprockets, and when the chain is shifted to the smaller sprocket the chain slack is taken up by swinging the bottom bracket forward (see Fig. 9.11).

To avoid the use of pulleys, Vélocio and Vernon Blake experimented with the "floating chain," *la chaine flottante*.[11] The dangling chain could be lifted by hand from one chainwheel to another with a small steel roller, *un acier doigt*, to guide the chain onto

Fig. 9.13. Simone and André Rabault.

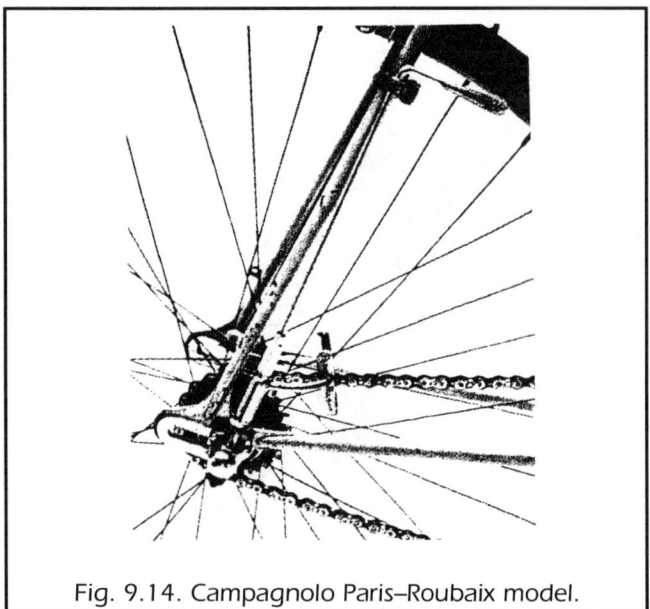

Fig. 9.14. Campagnolo Paris–Roubaix model.

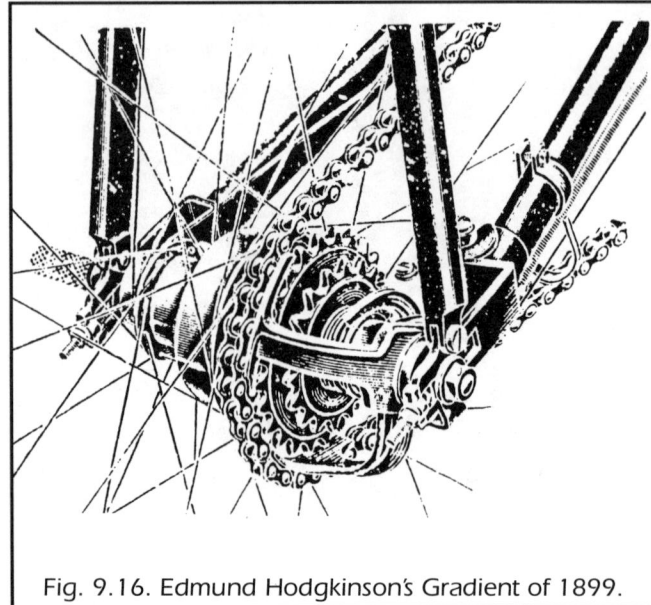

Fig. 9.16. Edmund Hodgkinson's Gradient of 1899.

the rear sprocket (see Fig. 9.12). (A similar roller is used today on single-geared cargo tricycles in China and India.)

In a later development, the floating chain was shifted by a front derailleur. This arrangement was used by Simon and André Rabault on their Bachelier tandem in 1929[12] (see Fig. 9.13).

In the 1930s, Tullio Campagnolo built derailleurs which tensioned the chain by rolling the rear wheel forward and back along a toothed rack on the upper face of the forkend (see Fig. 9.14). This design was used with great success from 1946 to 1950 by Gino Bartali and Fausto Coppi, although the *campionissimo* referred to it as "this complicated device" (and probably less printable descriptions).

Single-Pulley Derailleurs

The single-pulley derailleurs included the early English mechanisms of Hodgkinson and Linley, and the 1908 model made by Perret in Böen. By the 1930s, there were several excellent single-pulley derailleurs, such as the Super Champion. At the British Empire Games in Sydney in 1938, virtually all the competitors in the road race used single-pulley derailleurs (see Fig. 9.15).

Do Double Pulleys Cause too much Drag?

No one knows whether the drag caused by the double pulleys on a derailleur is a real hindrance. In 1919, Vélocio commented that there was a profound

Fig. 9.15. Cycling road race, British Empire Games, Sydney, 1938.

Fig. 9.17. Tri-Velox derailleur

lack of knowledge on whether the pulleys caused significant drag. He added:

> Indeed, during the war which has just ended, M. Planiol, one of our faithful subscribers and a valued mechanic, has put to good use the leisure forced on him by a severe wound to make a first series of experiments…to establish how much a whippet (derailleur) increases the drag at the rim.[10]

In fact the drag caused by the pulleys has never been determined, apparently because the resistance of a bicycle cannot be measured more accurately than +/- 5%, according to Professor Kyle.[13] However, a 5% increase in resistance would be more than enough to lose a race. After eighty years of controversy, it still remains for someone to devise a way of resolving this issue.

In-Line Derailleurs

The other side branch in the evolution of derailleur gearing was the in-line derailleur, in which the sprocket cluster was moved sideways to enable the chain to run straight without being bent sideways. The first such in-line derailleur was Hodgkinson's Gradient (see Fig. 9.16).

In-line derailleurs persisted into the 1930s with the Caminade Rectiligne in France, and the TriVelox in England (see Fig. 9.17).

However the in-line derailleurs were doomed by the heavy hubs and wide forkends they required. Just bending the chain, though crude, worked better.

Finally, it is interesting to note that as derailling mechanisms have improved, the number of sprockets has increased on average every 15 years (see Fig. 9.18).

Conclusion

This paper offers only a broad overview of derailleur gears during the past 100 years. I hope there will be more detailed investigation of these intriguing mechanisms. Every decade contains fascinating stories of the dancing chain which remain to be told.

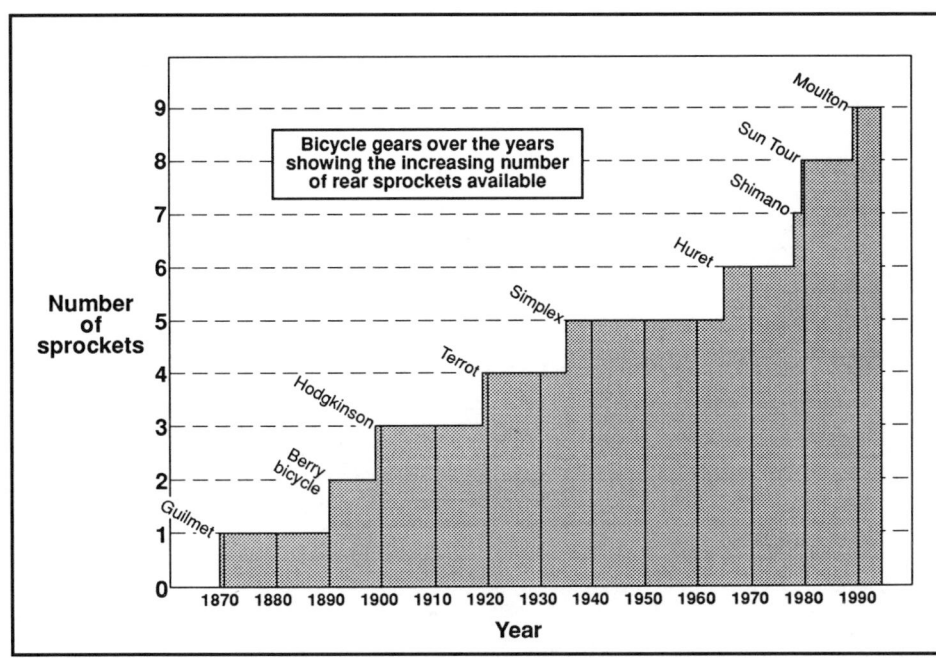

Fig. 9.18. Bicycle sprockets over the years.

Notes

1. Ron Shepherd, "The Origins of Derailleur Gears," *The Boneshaker*, vol. 13, no. 124 (Winter 1990): 4–22.

2. Ed Berry, "Letter to the Editor," *The Boneshaker*, vol. 13, no. 126 (Summer 1991): 23–25.

3. Ron Shepherd, "Le premier dérailleur," *The International Veteran Cyclist*, no. 4/92 (December 1992): 10–15.

4. Raymond Henry, "La bicyclette Crypto et le dérailleur Whippet," *The International Veteran Cyclist*, no. 4/92 (December 1992): 4–9.

5. Vic Polanski, Letter in *News and Views of the Veteran-Cycle Club*, issue 241 (June/July 1994): 46–47.

6. Derek Roberts, *Cycling History—Myths and Queries*, John Pinkerton, 1991.

7. Nick Clayton, Editorial in *The Boneshaker*, vol. 14, no. 133 (Winter 1993): 3.

8. Harry Suddaby, *Fellowship News*, no. 113 (March 1993): 40.

9. *Cycling Plus*, no. 19 (August 1993): 36.

10. "Vélocio" (Paul de Vivie), "Revue des différent systèmes de polyxcation," *Le Cycliste* (Oct./Nov./Dec. 1919): 139.

11. Vernon Blake, "The floating chain," *Cycling* (4 December 1919): 446–49.

12. Jacques Borge and Nicolas Viasnoff. *Le velo: la liberté*. Balland, 1978.

13. Chester R. Kyle, "The power output of bicycle trainers," *Cycling Science*, vol. 3, no. 2 (June 1991): 9–10.

Raymond Henry

10. Touring Bicycle Technical Trials in France, 1901–1950

Touring bicycle technical trials were held all through the first half of the present century. They should be remembered for the major role they played in the advancement of the bicycle in France. At first, the two aspects of cycling, touring and racing, were governed by the same federal body, the Union Vélocipédique de France, a body more concerned, however, with racing. Because of this, the Touring Club de France was formed in 1890, catering to cycle tourists and their needs.

Cycle touring required specially adapted bicycles for fatigue-free travelling on all kinds of roads and over diverse country. In spite of the efforts of a few small makers such as Vélocio, most bicycles of the day, either racing or utilitarian, did not meet these requirements. Major manufacturers remained deaf to this demand, doubtless diffuse and ill-expressed, and were interested mainly in the commercial output of easily made mediatised models of bicycles. Racing cyclists themselves might have liked to use better machines, had they not been trapped in habits, contracts, and sports regulations of all sorts.

The T.C.F. played an eminent part in promoting research for better touring bicycles by organising mediatised technical trials with an emphasis on innovation. Other associations followed, much later. There were three waves of such trials: 1901–05, 1920–24 and 1934–49.

At the beginning of the century, free wheels were ousting fixed gears. Back-pedal braking was on its way out. A bicycle had to be fitted with at least one brake. All types of brakes appeared, fondly and vocally vying for preeminence. Members of the T.C.F. complained of this state of affairs to the club. With the security of cyclists at stake, the Touring Club de France decided to organise brake tests ("concours de freins") on mountain roads.

These took place in August 1901 in the Alps.[1] Three days of gruelling tests drew a crowd of interested onlookers.[2] Mounts and riders entered were strictly controlled. Plunger brakes were not allowed as they were ineffective on deflated tyres.[3] The report on the tests was published in "L'Industrie Vélocipédique" on 25 September 1901. On 18 December, the president of the test committee, the eminent Carlo Bourlet, author of books on technical aspects of the bicycle that are still read today, gave a lecture with the tested bicycles at hand, and explained the pros and cons of every braking device. Rim brakes took first place because of their reliability going down long steep hills. Points were awarded for other qualities such as accessibility of controls, and comfort. Several brakes had blocking devices for long downgrades. Pincer brakes were preferred to the pull-up type. A number of back-pedalling or cable-operated hub brakes passed muster, but others were criticised for their "frying-pan" noise.[4]

The following year, Carlo Bourlet noted that "the success of the brake tests was considerable and their results were so useful that a great number of fellow members and cycle makers have asked us to further such tests…"[5]

The 1901 tests did much to prove the usefulness of the brake, until then much reviled by "scorchers" and their ilk, and strongly favoured the general adoption of pincer brakes in France, though how

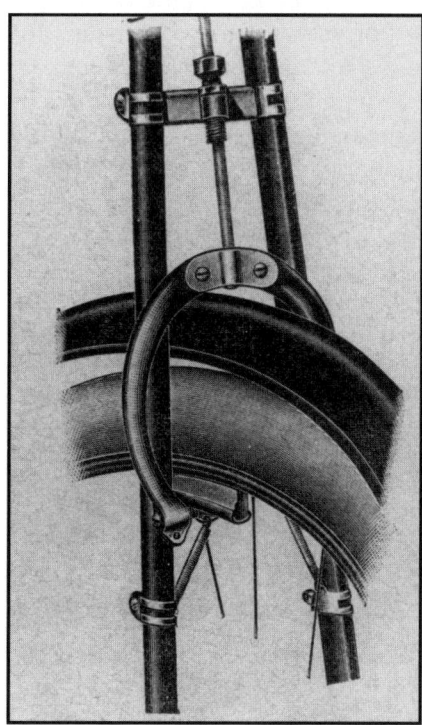

Fig. 10.1. Bowden brake—the first cable-controlled brake (from Le Cycliste, April 1902).

Translated by Roland Sauvaget

much we cannot say exactly. And they also favoured, over the fixed gear, the adoption of the free wheel which could no longer be considered dangerous going downhill with a pair of good brakes.

Thus encouraged, in 1902, the T.C.F. went one better and for the first time ever organised trials concerning the touring bicycle in its every aspect ("concours de bicyclettes de tourisme"). The jury was composed of respected specialists, with Carlo Bourlet of course.[6] Having noticed that cycle makers were producing machines less and less adapted to touring purposes, the jury drew up rules to encourage them to build bicycles adapted in every detail to "long journeys on any roads in all sorts of country." The trials included a preliminary technical examination, road tests, and an after-test comparative technical inspection. They took place in the Pyrenees, from 15–20 August 1902, on a there-and-back two-stage run between Tarbes and Bagnères de Bigorre, with two passings of the Tourmalet Pass: a hard test for multiple gearing.[7]

The organisation was helped by the good reputation built up by the T.C.F. in various administrative and political circles, and was sponsored to the tune of 5,500 frs (of the time) distributed among the riders. Some manufacturers had enrolled well-known racing professionals. Others were content with trained touring cyclists. Prize money according to results encouraged the professionals not to spare the machines. The others preferred to stop for a leisurely lunch between the two stages.[8] There were 52 marshals on the road.

Twenty makes of bicycles competed. Seven machines were not accepted as not comforming to the touring machine requirements set in the rules: a notable proportion of manufacturers did not know what a touring machine was. However, 48 machines were accepted, giving an idea of the event's impact.[9]

The preliminary examination of the machines lasted two days. An exhaustive four-page description of each machine was drawn up, complete with measurements (chain and tube lengths, width of the bottom bracket, overall weight, and so on). Each frame was then twice tagged under T.C.F. seal; the wheels were tagged and sealed; tyres and inner tubes were stamped.

The variety of machines submitted was most interesting. Weight varied from 14 to 21 kg (30.9 to 46.41 lbs.). Bearing witness to the research being carried on, there was a strong emphasis on multiple gearing: double-chains (Terrot No. 11, Hirondelle No. 15 and 17, Hurtu No. 26 and 27, Automoto No. 40 and 41, and De Vivie No. 20), triple chains (De Vivie No. 19), chainless (Peugeot's Percutante No. 34, Durieu's Touricyclette No. 42, both two-speed), two-speed hubs (Clément No. 1, 2 and 3; Gladiator No. 6, 7 and 8; Simpson No. 31; La Française No. 35, 36 and 37; Terrot No. 12; Peugeot No. 32 and 33; Searle et De Cleves No. 38 and 39; Goyon No. 45), two-speed geared bottom-brackets (Le Métais (17) No. 14 and 46 with Variand gear; Coste No. 9 and 10 with Lancelot gear; Guinard No. 24 and 25 with Lacarme/Michel gear); retro-direct gears (Hirondelle double-chain Palmeranze/Svea lévocyclette presented by Floquart but which did not compete). Note that gears went from 2.75 to 7.35 m (22 to 58.8 in.) on the Terrot, De Vivie and Automoto bicycles.

Twenty-nine machines passed the road tests.[10] Many riders walked up the hills.[11] On 20 August the machines were submitted to a technical examination for loose bearings, gear-change misadjustment, rims, wear on brake blocks, and tyres. Seventeen machines went through the second series of tests: front-fork elasticity, lateral rigidity of the frame, tests on the toughness of the balls in the bearings.[12] Up to 40 points were awarded in each test.[13]

Fig. 10.2. Double-chain Terrot No. 11. First prize at the 1902 trial (from Le Cycliste, November 1902).

Fig. 10.3. Retro-direct Magnat et Debon, in Concours de Bicyclettes de Voyage, Rapport Générale, August 1905.

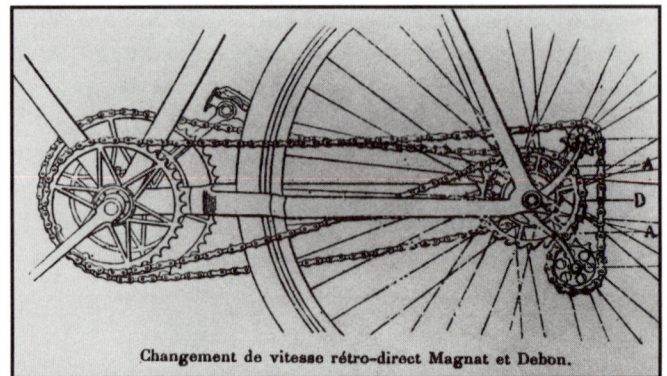

Finally, first prize went to Terrot for their No. 11, double-chain, three-speed bicycle. Second came No. 15: a double-chain, two-speed Hirondelle, and No. 35: a single-chain, two-speed Peugeot. There were special awards for retro-direct Hirondelle and Magnat-Debon bicycles, for Terrot and Magnat-Debon rim brakes, and for the Lacarme/Michel bracket gear.

However, the jury was scathing on front forks with mere holes instead of drop-outs, a practise which thereafter disappeared. It regretted that few makers had really made an effort to meet the specific needs of the touring cyclist. In many cases bottom gears had no relation with the difficulties met, and were too high, thus proving the makers had no idea of this major requisite in cycle-touring. One had the impression that they had "considered these trials as a non-event with no foreseeable sequel and had hardly bothered to build special machines, just entering their usual models built more for sport than touring." Others, "pressed for time, badly served by spare-parts makers interested only in current goods, had made praiseworthy efforts," but had presented ill-researched machines. And indeed, machines sold after these trials still did not meet the needs of their buyers, and the number of practising cycle tourists did not increase as much as had been hoped.[14]

With this in mind, the T.C.F. organised a third series of trials in August 1905. In July 1904, a committee as ably composed as that of 1902 adopted a set of rules suggested by Captain Perrache. The intent was still to encourage the production of bicycles giving every satisfaction in terms of strength, security, ease of adjustment and repair, and allowing the user, without any special training, to cycle on all roads whatever their state or incline.[15] The rules required two brakes.

After a preliminary examination of the machines entered, there were two-day road tests between Grenoble and Chambery, there and back, by the Col de Porte, the Col du Cucheron, and the Col du Frène; again a gruelling test both for riders and machines on the roads of the time, with an aggregate 120 km of steep upgrades. The trials were ruled so as not to degenerate into a mere race. There was no individual list of winners, and walking up hills was forbidden. Twenty-six machines from 10 makes were entered. They were closely checked after the test, with stripping of main parts. No outstanding failure was noticed, contrary to what had happened in 1902 when cogs, brakes, and rims had shown notable marks of wear.[16]

Awards went to makes, not to machines.[17] Gold medals were awarded to Terrot, Hirondelle, Magnat-Debon, and La Touricyclette; silver medals went to Raleigh and to La Touriste (a second make by Georges Durieu); bronze medals were awarded to Jacquier (Paris), Bonnet, Guyonnet and Canonne (Paris), Brossard (Autun), and La Française. Practically every make had its medal. A special award was given to Bowden Ltd. for a rear retarder brake.[18]

The organisation of the 1905 trials marked considerable progress over that of 1902. Attention was focussed on the failings of the machines themselves, not on the achievements of the riders. The machines were expected to be quite different from the usual run of bicycles built for flat racing on perfect surfaces. There was no room for firms who thought they could curry favour from the well-heeled touring customers of the time just by paying reputed cyclists to race on the usual sports bicycles. The material entered in the trials was definitely better and more solidly built (see later for innovations in multiple gearing). The makers took their cue from the 1902 trials observations. The machines—ranging from 16.5 to 23.5 kg (36.4 to 51.91 lbs.)—were as heavy as before, owing to the insistence on strength, quality braking, and effective multiple gearing.

The 1901, 1902, and 1905 T.C.F. trials gave a great fillip to technical research in French bicycle manufacture. Multiple gearing was brought to the fore and shortly after, in 1908, the first really dependable chain-shift mechanism was invented. In 1922, Vélocio wrote that "the 1902 and 1905 trials gave a considerable push to multi-geared bicycles."[19] The 1905 trials really roused public interest; many attentive and interested onlookers lined the mountainous roads of the Chartreuse. At the Salon du Cycle (cycle show) that winter, machines from the trials gathered crowds.[20]

Amusing to say, the bicycle racing world remained aloof, and Henri Desgranges, "father" of the Tour de France, viewed the T.C.F. trials with marked disfavour.

After 1905, the T.C.F. veered mainly towards motor touring, coming back to touring cycle testing only in 1920, when it organised a week-long series of trials in the Vosges mountains: the "Semaine des Vosges." For different reasons, the impact was less than that of the previous trials.[21] In 1922, the "Semaine d'Auvergne" was held, a week-long series of trials on some of the roughest and toughest roads of central France, which proved the fiability and advantages of derailleur gears.[22] That same year, the T.C.F. participated in the organisation of the

"Critérium de la Polymultipliée" at Chanteloup, near Paris. The "Critérium" was a trial meant to put multiple gearing while racing before the public eye.[23]

The "Semaine du Dauphiné" in 1924 was again a wholly T.C.F. affair, and marked a return to mainly technical considerations. The organiser was Gaston Clément, T.C.F. councillor and also president of the Fédération Française des Sociétés de Cyclotourisme (F.F.S.C.), founded just the year before in 1923.

Extra marks were awarded for what was then considered as lightness, for the number of gears available, for ease in stripping the machine using only what tools were in the toolbag, for a brake test, and there were separate classes for mixed tandems, ladies' bicycles, and even for auxiliary engines.[24]

Among the entrants were the ever-present Hirondelle retro-direct (but with a double chain wheel and even a three-speed hub, giving twelve remote-control gears), also an R.P.F. with the new Cyclo gear, a double-chain R.P.F., a double-chain Gauloise with a kick-clutch on the chain wheel, and an Intégral with a floating chain and a triple chain wheel within the stays.

In 1926, the T.C.F decided to entrust all cycle-touring organisations to the Union Vélocipédique de France—the body ruling cycle racing. For most cycle tourists this was high treason, and it estranged them definitely from the T.C.F. and U.V.F. It also meant that there were no touring bicycle trials for some years.

Matters having calmed down, in July 1934 the T.C.F. put its name to one more series of touring-bicycle technical tests, in the Pyrenees. It can be remembered for the appearance of the Schultz one-spar frame bicycle and for the Mochet recumbent two-wheel Velo-Vélocar, but otherwise made no stir at all.[25]

The main reason was that these trials had been completely overshadowed by the "Concours de la Meilleure Machine" organised two months earlier by the Groupe Montagnard Parisien. This was a tiny club, with hardly any financial backing and a membership of about 15, but with useful acquaintances in the cycle industry, and a sure intuition of future trends in bicycle construction. Their book of rules was revolutionary, the emphasis being no longer on strength but on lightness, and on high performance touring bicycles. People shuddered and feared the worst. But the machines entered came in unscathed. The route was from Clermont-Ferrand to Saint-Etienne over 460 km of sometimes very rough mountain roads. Frame measurements had to fall within prescribed limits; a minimum luggage of 3 kg (6.6 lbs.) had to be carried;

tyre minimum width was 35 mm; lightweight construction was at a premium. The rules favoured soldered bosses everywhere. Free wheels had to be easily strippable on the roadside.[26]

This "Concours d'Auvergne," as it was also called, spurred enormous progress in the quality of touring bicycles. It opened up the way to shorter and lighter frames, to the general use of alloy accessories, to the adoption of soldered bosses everywhere—in other words, to the French conception of the modern custom-made touring bicycle made by painstaking, innovative, highly capable and reputable artisans such as, in their time, Barra, Reiss (Reyhand bicycles at Lyon), and others.[27] There was a Reyhand bicycle with one-piece brazed frame in Reynolds HM tubing, complete with mudguards, carrier, front and rear lights, weighing only 9.8 kg (21.6 lbs.). The winning Barra bicycle weighed 10.35 kg (22.8 lbs.).[28]

In following years further trials following the same technical trend were organised by Claude Tillet—a well-known figure on the staff of the Auto cycling newspaper in those days—sponsored by the Société du Duralumin, a trade syndicate furthering the use of aluminium alloy. They took place around Grenoble in 1935,[29,30] Saint-Etienne in 1936,[31] Aix-les-Bains in 1937,[32] Annecy in 1938,[33] and Colmar in 1939.

The riders in these trials were usually prominent sporting cyclists, not professionals. The machines had to be complete with mudguards, lighting set, carrier, and bell. Yet their average weight fell from 10.5 kg (23.2 lbs.) in 1936 to 8.892 kg (19.6 lbs.) in 1938, which gives an idea of the progress made.

Reiss won in 1935 with a "Reyhand" 10.65 kg (23.5 lbs.) bicycle equipped with a Cyclo 5-gear changer and double chain wheel, Stronglight square-socket alloy cranks, and alloy accessories all through. Note that at a date when bicycle tourers

Fig. 10.4. Reyhand bicycle, 1938, with Reynolds tubing, Stronglight cotterless cranks, Idéale saddle, Rosa dural chain wheels, Jeay dural brakes, Cyclo rear derailleur.

already enjoyed double and even triple chain wheels and up to twelve gears if they wished, the derailleur was still forbidden to professionals on the Tour de France. In 1936, Barra entered a completely equipped entirely alloy bicycle with a 60 cm (23.6 in.) frame, and his epoch-making cantilever brake, weighing 9.66 kg (21.3 lbs.). In 1937, Reiss (Reyhand) won for the third consecutive time. All the bicycles entered had Stonglight alloy cranks which the racing fraternity was still averse too. Among touring cyclists, the controversy between alloy and steel was already ancient history. Note that in 1937 the Nivex rear derailleur appeared working on the parallelogram principle which later inspired Campagnolo.

In the 1938 trials, bicycles could be entered either as "prototype" or as "production" (i.e., for sale). The Narcisse bicycle built according to the ideas of rider René Herse weighed only 7.94 kg (17.52 lbs.) with a 55 cm (19.7 in.) frame, and had pedals, cranks, and a handlebar stem of his own conception. With the reputation thus gained, Herse was able to set up as a builder in his own right. Narcisse also entered a 13.975 kg (30.8 lbs.) tandem. Out of 36 entered machines, 11 had alloy frames (Barra, Caminargent, Hurtu, Emeriau). Narcisse won in the prototype category and Lionel Brans, a newly established maker, was first in "production" with a bicycle with a Caminargent frame ridden by Jo Routens.[33] In 1939, Narcisse again won in prototypes.

In 1946, the trials, now called "Le Duralumin," were held again at Colmar. New records of lightness were established: 6.875 kg (15.17 lbs.) with a Singer, and 12.3 kg (12.15 lbs.) for a Herse tandem.[34]

In 1947, trials were held at Grenoble. The Herse prototype machines weighed 7 kg (15.45 lbs.) for the gentlemen's model, and 6.97 kg (15.38 lbs.) for the ladies', and the Hugonnier-Routens winning bicycle in the production series weighed 9.44 kg (20.83 lbs.). Each constructor had devised his own very light front shift.[35] The miniature front carrier had been adopted by everyone.

That same year, the Ligue Vélocipédique Belge held touring bike trials in Belgium after the manner of the French, except that weight was not considered.[36] Nor was the quality of the machines the same. Trials were held anew in 1948, and this time weight counted. Mignon bicycles won the first three awards with machines made by Singer, of France.[37] The bicycle classed first weighed 9 kg (19.86 lbs.).

The "Duralumin" was not organised in 1948. The "Cégédur" firm (former Société or Compagnie du Duralumin) was losing interest in bicycles, and in 1949 gave up holding further trials. The Fédération Française de Cyclo-Tourisme then hastily organised trials of its own in the suburbs of Clermont-Ferrand in August. A Hugonnier-Routons machine weighing 7.4 kg without the tyres (16.33 lbs.) took first place.[38] In the following years, cycle touring declined and there was no longer any question of holding touring bicycle trials.

However, all taken together, these touring bicycle trials from 1900 to 1950 promoted considerable progress in the conception and making of touring bicycles. For many years, these were years ahead of the others, and this progress spilled over into the making of racing and utilitarian bicycles. One must underline that this was mainly due to the aggregate experience of artisans who specialised in high quality custom-made touring bicycles who were, more often than not, themselves practising cycle tourists. They were mostly known through various semi-confidential magazines: nevertheless, in the end they influenced the major firms to "pull up their socks," as the saying goes. Speed gears were a case in point. The 1902 and 1905 T.C.F. trials drew attention to this technical problem which had been neglected by major manufacturers. Professional Tour de France riders had to wait until 1937—and even then they had to use a compulsory, low quality mechanism. Cycle tourists had been using Chemineau gears since 1911. Even in 1946, no racing derailleur could compare with the Cyclo, invented in 1923, and Campagnolo was still fussing about with fork-operated chain shifts. The 1934 "Concours de la Meilleure Machine" was a great stride forward in the improvement of frame geometry and overall lightness.

Charles Antonin, president of the F.F.C.T. and no mean technician, wrote in 1949: "We must not forget that comparison of prototypes—and of prototypes only—has been the mainspring in the evolution of bicycle manufacturing…The pattern of present-day utilitarian bicycles, only ten years ago, was reserved to cycle tourists considered as perfectionists by some and as maniacs by others."[39] Discontinuing touring bicycle trials caused cycle-touring machines to lose their technical advance. Progress comes, nowadays, from all-terrain activities, and racing.

Remarks

Until 1901, it was common to have no brakes at all. They came into fashion that year, and all sorts of models appeared, each one presented as the best.

There were front and rear brakes. The first were of the plunger type, with a cup acting directly on the tyre. When effective, they were dangerous on bends, but in the general run they were ineffective. Vélocio was against front brakes, no matter the type, considering them as dangerous.

Rear brakes fell into three types: brakes acting on the tyre; hub brakes; and rim brakes. There again, there were many models.

Tyre brakes, favoured by the suppleness of the tyre, were rather used as retarder brakes. Vélocio had imagined a makeshift brake of this sort fitted beneath the bottom stays. It consisted of a 10–15 cm leather-lined softwood brake block controlled with a well-oiled cord—the Carloni brake was also of this type. The drawback of these brakes was that they became ineffective when a puncture deflated the tyre.

Hub brakes usually had leather loops acting either on a drum (Lehut, Merveilleux), or on a grooved drum (Lemoins), and heated rapidly. There were also cone-friction brakes (Morrow), and rear-pedalling brakes (Juhel, Otto, Trébert). Vélocio thought highly of the Morrow brake.

There were many rim brakes. Whippet and Villardère had been available for several years. Singer, Components, and B.S.A. were foot operated. Bowden was a hand-operated brake controlled by a cable running through a supple coil sheath: Vélocio considered this system far superior to all others and, in fact, it is common nowadays. Brakes, like the Bowden, with blocks adjusting to rims when they were out of true, were considered the best.

The Lamplugh brake, with a rumoured reputation in England, required a special rim. On one side there was an S-profiled groove, one side of which was lodged between the side of the tyre and the inner side of the rim. The reverse outward-looking groove held a noosed steel cable which could be tightened by mean of a lever.

The object of the August 1901 T.C.F. brake trials was to weed out the tares and find which was which in this host of different systems. Terrot were at the fore in 1905 as a touring-cycle maker with their H-model; their lever bicycle directly issued from the Swedish Svea; and a four-speed retro-direct model. Hirondelle had simplified their retro-direct model (1903 patent). The Magnat-Debon three-speed geared bottom bracket seemed effective. The Raleighs were equipped with three-speed Sturmey-Archer hubs. Durieu's Le Touriste model had a double chain wheel, and a double free wheel with only one long chain giving four speeds. The Bonnet, Guyonnet/Canonne, Brossard, and Jacquier machines had relatively simple two speed chain wheels. The Brossard had a satellite system lodged in the bottom bracket. The French Fagan two-speed on the La Française did not equal the Sturmey-Archer.

Notes

1. From 17–19 August, between Grenoble and Chambéry, through the Chartreuse Range, down Laffrey Hill and the Col du Lautaret. *Le Cycliste* (1901): pp. 109, 162, 163.

2. Ibid: pp. 137 and 154.

3. Ibid: p. 109.

4. *Le Cycliste* (1902): p. 7.

5. "Concours de Bicyclettes de tourisme, rapport general" (Touring-bicycle Trials, General Report) by Carlo Bourlet; T.C.F., Paris, Introduction, p.1.

6. Ibid, p. 1. The members of the jury were: Appell, Sorbonne professor for rational mechanics, member of L'Institut; Koenigs, Sorbonne professor of experimental mechanics and physics; Forestier, Roads and Bridges general inspector; Ferrus, artillery commander, director of the "Revue d'Artillerie"; Perrache, retired artillery captain; Carlo Bourlet, Ph.D.Sc, Beaux-Arts professor of mechanics and mathematics professor at the Lycée Saint-Louis.

7. The route followed was: Tarbes, Lourdes, Pierrefitte, Luz, Col du Tourmalet, Gripp, Bagnères de Bigorre, Lourdes…and return. Neutralised from Col du Tourmalet down to Gripp owing to danger: twenty locals had been hired to keep cattle off the road and to hoist "Slow!" placards on dangerous bends, thus accidents were limited to only 4 non-serious falls.

8. Every entrant received 200 frs expenses if he covered the route within the imparted delays, i.e., fourteen-and-a-half hours. The rider could be changed at Lourdes on the return stage, but in that case time limits were one hour less (General Report, p. 8). There was last-minute news that summer migration of 2,000 sheep were expected on the Tourmalet road: the shepherd was given 100 frs to delay his journey a full day.

9. Firms admitted to enter: Clément et Cie (Levallois), Georges Richard (Paris), Gladiator (Paris), Coste et Lancelot (Lyon), Terrot et Cie (Dijon), Le Métais (Paris), Manufacture Française d'Armes et Cycles de Saint-Etienne, De Vivie (Saint-Etienne), Magnat et

9. (cont.) Debon (Grenoble), Guinard (Campiègne), Hurtu (Paris), Floquart (Paris), Darrigade (Pau), Bureu (Bordeaux), Simpson (Paris), Peugeot (Valentigney), La Française (Paris), Scarles et De Clèves (Neuilly), Automott (Saint-Etienne), Duroeu (Neuilly), Brown Brothers (Paris), Floquet (Paris), Goyon (Paris), and Elvish (Bordeaux).

10. Paul de Vivie's (Vélocio) three machines were ridden to the start from Saint-Etienne by a few of Vélocio's friends. They did only the first stage. In *Le Cycliste*, 30 September 1902, p. 166, Vélocio wrote: "My intent was just to cover the set route with my friends so as to prove that such stages had nothing extraordinary. I entered officially only to please the president of the T.C.F." The De Vivie machines were the personal bicycles of his friends, had seen wear and probably bore the scars of the journey from Saint-Etienne to Tarbes. De Vivie was not much of a hand at repairing, and his bicycles would probably not have passed unscathed at the preliminary inspection. He probably only wanted to show his goods at the gathering. His friends and he went on with their journey the next day. Among them was Mlle. Hesse, the only lady.

11. Viviant, a young friend of Vélocio's, walked only 2,200 m. But Muller, a professional who came in first, walked 11,700 m, and Fisher, 5,650 m. Mlle. Hesse walked only 100 m but did only the first stage.

12. To catch up on time, when a firm had entered three identical machines, only one was inspected.

13. Fastest times in the road test earned up to 20 points. State of the machine on arrival and walking were marked out of 20. Up to 40 points were awarded in the technical reliability inspection of gear changes, brakes, free wheels, and tyres. Finish and quality of touring accessories were marked from 0 to 20. (General report, p. 14.)

14. "Concours de bicyclettes de voyage, 1905, rapport general" (Travel bicycles trials, General Report, 1905) by Captain Perrache, T.C.F., Paris, p. 1.

15. Ibid, p. 1.

16. Ibid, p. 3.

17. "Mr. Métais, machine and spare parts agent for the German manufacturer N.S.U. of Neckarsulm, presented two complete [Original N.S.U.] machines with Variand bottom bracket, N.S.U. hub brake and optional free wheel." General report 1902, p. 38.

18. Peugeot did not figure among the ten firms on the list of awards. Vélocio wrote that the firm withdrew their machines just before the start, which, "though good, solid and reliable, could not meet the requirements of the trials." He also said that "the Raleigh and the La Française got over the cols only through sheer muscle power." *Le Cycliste* (XII–1905): p. 222.

19. *Le Cycliste* (III/IV–1922: p. 21.

20. Vélocio in *Le Cycliste* (XII–1905): p. 221.

21. *Le Cycliste*, (VII/VIII-1920): p. 49 and T.C.F. Revue No. 317, (VII/IX–1920): p. 150.

    The Concours des Vosges was organised after the manner of the 1905 trials and under the sponsorship of the well-known newspaper *Le Petit Journal*. It was a 1011 km, 8-stage trial followed by a technical inspection. Five, out of 13 bicycles entered, finished the trial unpenalised: an Audouard (Saint Etienne), a Desvages (Paris), 2 bicycles and a Chemineau tandem (Saint Etienne). The gold metal went to Audouard, and the Petit Journal cup to Panel for his Chemineau derailleur. Desvages was angry not to figure among the awards.

22. The Semaine d'Auvergne included 4 stages totalling 750 km and 10,000 m accumulated climb on rough roads, very trying for both machines and riders. At least 3-speed gear was required. Forty-six machines were entered. The Grand Prix was awarded to Audouard for an 8-speed derailleur of his own make. There were gold medals to a R.P.F. with a 4-speed as derailleur, to a Terrot with a 4-speed Terrot H.T. derailleur, to a Chemineau with a 6-speed derailleur, to a Kéops with 6 speeds by front and rear derailleurs not precisely named, and to a 6-speed Hirondelle by combined retro-direct and hub gear. Silver medals went to: a Thomann with a 3-speed Sturmey-Archer, and a Magnat-Debon with a 3-speed bottom- bracket gear. Bronze awards went to a Royal-Fabric (Saint-Etienne) with a Chemineau derailleur, to a 6-speed Erpelding with combined Erpelding and As gear shifts, to an Automoto with an expanding chain wheel, to a Toutain with a B.S.A. 3-speed hub, and to a Desvages with a Chemineau. *Le Cycliste* (I/II–1923): p. 15.

23. In April 1922, the T.C.F. participated in the organisation of the "Critérium de la Polymultipliée" sponsored by the sports paper *L'Echo des Sports*. This event was meant to promote multiple gearing and to compare the different solutions proposed. It was in fact a race between professionals hired by different cycle firms and competing alongside sporting cyclists using touring bicycles. The T.C.F. did the technical checking and the appraisal of innovations. The T.C.F. took responsibility for the whole organization in

1925. The Critérium had a chequered career. In the end, there was a professional race and a sporting cyclist category in which small firms of custom-made touring cycles competed. Technical inspection of touring bicycles was practised till the end of the organisation in the sixties. *Le Cycliste* (various numbers) and T.C.F., No. 325, p. 235.

In 1926, "Le Cyclotouriste," a cycle-touring club of Lyon, organised trials much less ambitious than those of the T.C.F. and which afterwards became known as the "Poly Lyonnaise." They had little impact.

24. The "Concours International de Bicyclettes de Tourisme" took place at Grenoble in June 1924. Any bicycle with more than 3 remote-controlled gears had a bonus of 10 points per extra gear (with a maximum of 50). Failure of parts was penalised. The road tests included the first 3 days of mountain roads at a minimum speed of 13 kmh (8 mph), then a 172 km race with 3,700 m of aggregate climb in the Chartreuse range, with a braking test on the way down the Col de Porte. Stripping and reassembling were timed and carried a verdict in points. *Le Cycliste* (III/IV–1924): p. 33, and (V/VI): p. 1.

25. The "Concours des Pyrénées," between Biarritz and Carcassonne (750 km and 17,500 m aggregate climb) drew only about 15 participants, probably because speed counted for too much and too much depended on the whims of the jury. An Uldry bicycle won the Grand Prix, and R.P.F. won the cup. There were special prizes for the Schultz one-spar frame bicycle, the Funiculo derailleur, and the Mochet Vélo-Vélocar.

26. Rules and entrance form of the above trials.

27. *Le Cycliste* (XII–1934): p. 556, wrote under the pen of its new director Philippe Marre: "The 1934 trials were turned towards lightweights. They scored a success. Present-day cycle tourists have lightweight machines markedly better than those of a few years ago."

28. Trials control sheet. Raymond Henry collection (André Rabault, "Concours d'Auvergne" file).

29. Claude Tillet, who edited the cycling page of the *Auto* sports paper, waxed enthusiastic over the form of the "Concours d'Auvergne" and asked the G.M.P. for permission to take it over. With the help of the Société du Duralumin and of the "L'Industrie du Cycle" revue, he then organised the "Critérium des Alpes." *Le Cycliste* (VII/VIII–1969): p. 137.

30. The venue was at Grenoble in August 1935. Saving on weight was paramount. This time speed came into line but no professional racing cyclists were admitted. Seventeen makers entered. Thirty-two machines passed the tests including two Ravat-Wonder recumbents (14.725 kg (32.5 lbs.) and 15.4 kg (34 lbs.). The trials made quite a splash in the press. Table of machines, *Le Cycliste* (1935): p. 577.

31. In 1936, the "Critérium Cyclotouristique de l'Auto" took place around Saint-Etienne. There was a night stage so as to promote research into lighting sets, and there were bonus points for front carriers and for front shifts. The best bicycle was the Barra piloted by Oudart with a weight of 9.58 kg (21.14 lbs.) with 6 speeds and 3 brakes, and the 10.04 kg (22.16 lbs.), 8-speed Reyhand piloted by Bernadet. *Le Cycliste* (1936): pp. 252, 287, 346, 425, 503.

32. Forty-one machines were entered at Aix-les-Bains in 1937. Hurtu presented the lightest bicycle and tandem: 9.045 kg (19.96 lbs.) and 15.260 kg (33.68 lbs.) respectively, the tandem piloted by Mr. and Mrs. Herse. Hurtu entered 2 bicycles with brazed alloy frames, and Caminargent 2 with bolted octagonal tubing. Average weight was 10.431 kg (23 lbs). *Le Cycliste* (1937): pp. 274, 312, 357, 397, 445.

33. *Le Cycliste* (1938): pp. 263, 302, 349, 388.

34. The "Duralumin" was still organised by Claude Tillet, but sponsored by *Le Cycle* and by *L'Equipe*. *Le Cycle* (1946): No. 20, p. 3; No. 21, p. 5; No. 22, pp. 3–9; No. 23, pp. 4–7; No. 24, p. 4.

35. In 1947, the actual route was kept secret until the start. There was again a brake test and a night stage, and minor changes. *Le Cycliste* (1947): pp. 132, 156, 184.

36. Eleven firms participated. The trials were won by the Van Hauwaert firm. *Le Cycliste* (1947): p. 31; *Le Vélo* (I–1947): No. 20, pp. 23–25.

37. Note that Alex Singer had piloted a Mignon machine in the previous trials. *Le Cycliste* (1948): p. 59.

38. Gain on weight counted less. Tests showed there was still room for a lot of progress in lighting sets. The heat was intense and everybody agreed to stop the road test after 24 hours. Only 4 machines took part. First was a Hugonnier-Routens of 7.4 kg (16.33 lbs.) in 4/10 mm Vitus tubing piloted by Jo Routens and Rota, then a 9.5 kg (20.97 lbs.) Pitard in alumag alloy tubing, a 10.1 kg (22.29 lbs.) Pitard in 4/10 mm Vitus tubing, and a 9.6 kg (21.19 lbs.) C.D.F. in 6/10 mm Vitus. *Le Cycliste/Cyclotourisme* (1949): pp. 131, 139 (book of rules), 177, 193.

39. *Le Cycliste/Cyclotourisme* (VI/1949): p. 131.

11. Tribology and the Cyclist

Ken James

The efficiency of cycle components, such as the parts making up the drive train and the hubs, receives relatively little attention. Possibly this is because the majority of cyclists are primarily concerned with cost, and the parts that make up a normal drive train are very cheap, and get very dirty.

Performance is measured by how long a bit lasts, and by lasting I mean lasting to failure—seldom is replacement based on the perceived quality of ride.

I can confidently state after two year's intense work on hubs, etc., that there are more polysided lumps of rusty steel being made to rotate in so-called bearings, than there are well lubricated ball races. The average neglected hub has a life of not more than a few months, if the weather is good.

The combination of man or woman and bicycle is extraordinarily self adjusting, and will keep going long after one or both parties to the partnership are so decrepit as to deserve scrapping. Thankfully the scenario is not entirely black: there exists in all categories of cycling activities a percentage of people very aware of that superb bit of practical engineering we call a bicycle. What other means can carry one so many miles on a few sandwiches?

It is from these discerning groups of cyclists that we hope to get recognition of the value of our inventions or developments, and if these good people adopt the invention as being desirable to the point of becoming a necessity, then it will gradually be integrated into the commonplace.

The possible benefits to cycle drives from the use of hard smooth coatings was investigated simply because I am a keen touring cyclist, with an addiction to the French cols, and have at my disposal the resources of a company specialising in various surface treatments. Surface treatments of metals to enhance performance in hostile or arduous situations are some times classified by the thickness of the coating deposited on or generated in the component being treated.

Two classes of treatment were investigated—the deposition of thin hard layers, approximately 4 microns thick, and the creation of nitride layers from 50 microns to 375 microns thick.

The thin coatings, that is approximately 4 micron thick layers, investigated were 2 methods of depositing titanium nitride, and 1 method of depositing a ternary alloy coating, tungsten-titanium-carbide.

The relatively thick nitride layers were generated using the plasma nitriding process. This choice was dictated by the ability of this process to form a mono-phase white layer on steels, and thus do away with the need for white layer removal, and at the same time substantially increase the fatigue resistance.

The use of the plasma nitriding process is actively under investigation as a means of treating the titanium alloy parts, and results are most encouraging.

All the processes demand very expensive apparatus and highly trained staff for consistent and successful operation. I very much doubt if the purchase and relatively complex setting up of a processing department would be justified for use on cycle parts alone. At my company, we regard the provision of a service to treat cycle parts as being of great interest, but it is only of commercial value to us as we already own the coating equipment.

As already stated, there are a number of processes for the deposition of the binary alloy, titanium nitride. Most depend on melting and vaporising metallic titanium using an electric arc or an electron beam gun. The resulting vapour cloud contains microscopically coarse particles, which are consequently deposited onto the object surface.

Synopsis

This paper outlines the possible benefits to the bicycle by making use of modern metallurgical processes, and in particular the reduction of friction losses by interposing hard surface coatings between sliding surfaces, such as the tooth flanks on sprockets and chainrings against the sideplates of the chain. An elementary outline of the processes involved follows, and some discussion on lubrication.

Under the microscope the surface is a bit like the pictures of the moon.

The hardness of the titanium nitride deposit is approximately 2,500 on the Vickers diamond scale, and therefore the presence of these particles on the surface can cause very rapid wear. The occurrence of these hard particles ruled out usage of vaporising processes. It cannot be stressed too strongly that the use of the wrong process can lead to very poor results, while the use of the right technique is proving to be very advantageous.

Another process, of deposition, developed by the Atomic Energy Research Establishment, uses the principle of sputtering. This latter process is very slow compared with the arc or gun processes, but it has the enormous advantages of being peculiarly suitable for the deposition of titanium nitride onto a titanium alloy base, and, of equal importance, it deposits an extraordinarily smooth layer, because the deposit is laid down as atomic size particles, resulting in a featureless surface.

The sputtering process is done in a soft vacuum of about 2/100 millibar in a titanium-lined vessel, the titanium lining acting as the source of titanium for formation of the titanium nitride. Both source and object to be coated are negatively charged: the difference of about 500 volts supplies the energy to ionise the argon gas, accelerates the ions toward the part to be coated or the cathode and effect sputtering. Sputtering is another way of saying displacing or causing removal of particles by bombardment. The conditions in the treatment chamber are controlled in the initial stages so that the argon and titanium ions bombard the object surface and clean it prior to deposition. High voltages are then applied to both cathode and object with the voltage on the object being about 75 volts lower. This difference allows a dense coating to grow as the rate of deposition is slightly higher than the material being resputtered. By supplying a small amount of nitrogen to the chamber, a reaction occurs at the surface to give titanium nitride. At this stage of the process we think that when the object is made from titanium alloy, an extremely thin layer of titanium nitride is formed within the surface of the object that is being coated. This layer acts as an effective inter layer to the deposit of titanium nitride, greatly improving adhesion.

This process of sputtering has the potential for depositing complex alloys of more than two constituents. In theory, the rate at which atoms are sputtered off a source surface is a function of the area of the source. Using this knowledge we experimented with an alloy deposit of tungsten-titanium-carbide. This deposit is not yet so predictable in its properties as the titanium nitride, but it is considerably harder, and again has a featureless surface. The colour of this ternary alloy is that of polished steel, and does not compare in eye appeal with the superb gold of titanium nitride. While we have not yet made practical use of the ternary alloys, we have not abandoned development.

The plasma nitriding process, both as applied to steel and titanium alloys, relies on the generation of an energised cloud of nitrogen gas impinging on the surface to be nitrided, releasing its energy in the form of heat and being absorbed into the surface. The rate of this diffusion is governed by the temperature of the object, but in steel the allowable temperature is seldom higher than about 530° C because higher temperatures affect the core strength of the steel alloy, and also the nitride compounds formed are coarser and less hard. Steels have a fairly high rate of diffusion initially, but this rapidly decreases with increase in depth of the nitride layer, almost ceasing when the depth, even in steels specially formulated for nitriding, reach about 20 thou.

To get nitrogen to diffuse into a titanium alloy demands a much higher temperature, commonly about 850° C, and even at this temperature the available depth of penetration is small, about 5 microns. Notwithstanding this shallow depth the surface produced has remarkable properties, and we are paying great attention to the potential benefits arising from plasma nitrided titanium alloy parts.

The processes discussed are in everyday commercial use: we coat or treat an enormous variety of engineering parts. CNC machines used for mass production use cutting tools coated with titanium nitride; other uses are for perforating knives, moulds, coinage dies, and so on. We have one or two clients who have parts coated purely for the colour. Similarly plasma nitriding is used on articles such as extruder screws down to the hydraulic shuttles in aircraft control systems.

The successful engineering use of these deposits on cutting tools and so on is dependent on the hardness of the core steels, which are usually about 800 on the Vickers scale. Exploitation of the coatings on comparatively soft cycle parts is successful because the forces, etc., on a cycle are so small.

To give one example of the dramatic effect of the everyday use of these coatings, I have brought along some drills, as used in CNC machines. To test the effectiveness of the coating, there is a standard programme whereby a hole is drilled 25 mm deep in a carbon steel plate which has been hardened and tempered to a specified hardness. For this size drill the time allowed to complete the hole is 2.4 seconds. Uncoated the drill will last maybe 3 holes; coated it lasts a minimum of 500 holes, otherwise the batch is deemed to have failed. These drills often go on for 1,500 holes, a truly staggering increase in performance. Your car gears will almost certainly have been generated using coated hobs, and on a more prosaic level, the separation perforations on those home freezer bags will have been made with a coated knife.

At a coating cost of possibly a tenth of the cost of a hob, the user has effectively at least 5 hobs. The process is cost effective in the extreme. When applied to chain rings and sprockets, the quality of the ride lasts a long time, much longer than with an uncoated ring, but long life is not the primary benefit—smoothness and more return for effort applied are more important. We are considering the possibilities of a recoating service if sprockets or rings are returned before serious deterioration of the core material has occurred.

Making maximum use of the properties of these various surface treatments inevitably led to a radical redesign of the drive train, resulting in a most practical and extremely light hub incorporating a choice of sprockets as small as 9 teeth, and a total saving of about 500 grams on the drive train. The bearing arrangements in this hub make for very simple maintenance—the unskilled can replace all parts by making use of the wheel skewers as presses, and a few simple distance pieces.

As the body, etc., of the hub cannot corrode, the hub has virtually an indefinite life, depending entirely on proper lubrication. For lubrication we developed our own oil mix containing water sequestering agents. Grease we found to be utterly unsatisfactory in cycle hubs. In cold climates, the grease never gets to a sufficiently high temperature to cause flow onto the bearings; consequently the races get dry of protective grease and rapidly corrode and rust.

All rotating parts on a bicycle rotate so slowly that they do not get nicely warm like a machine bearing. These conditions impose their own problems, and so far we found that the oil we developed is the best both for our design of hub and for the preservation and free running of any cycle hub.

Our research into lubrication encompassed bearing seals, and here we drew a blank in that we failed to find a low friction seal that could be guaranteed to keep out water. In general, the better the seal the greater the friction. The strategy finally accepted was not to compromise on free running but to accept a degree of oil seepage; this latter ensures that the products of oil/water are constantly being removed. The approach has been very successful, and we have hubs which have required no replacements in over 8,000 miles of all-too-often awful weather conditions.

Coming now to the all important question "Can the use of thin hard films noticeably increase the efficiency of the drive?", the answer is yes—and by a greater margin than we expected. We are all aware of the loss of power which results from an out-of-line chain, the inevitable situation when using low gears in hill climbing. The wear on the large sprockets is predominantly on the inside face, and shows the effect of friction between the chain link and the tooth flank.

Nothing can be done to minimise the loss of effort due solely to the geometry, but the loss due to friction can be reduced by ensuring as low a coefficient of friction as possible between the inner surface of the chain side plates and the tooth flank.

Frictional losses through the interaction of these two surfaces is not constant—it rapidly increases with the roughening of the tooth and side plate surfaces. Both on the chain ring and sprocket tooth sides, surface conditions deteriorate to the extent that often a series of steps are formed, very effectively hindering the smooth passage of the chain over the sprockets.

Measuring improvements resulting from interposing a low friction layer between the chain and tooth were first concerned with observing and measuring the rate of surface deterioration, which we found to be very low compared with untreated surfaces.

The next step was to test on the road, and several long trips were made, including the Pyrenees cols and a long stretch from Calais to Menton over the Jura, Savoie, Alps, and Alps Maritime; the weather on this latter was awful, down to minus 7° C; the last testing trip was along the west coast of France, starting at Plymouth and eventually reaching Montpellier. The weather was even worse—it did not stop raining for 9 days. After all this no sprocket was worn enough to replace or recoat—as a matter of fact they are still on my and my wife's cycles. My own cycle, here on the stand, still has these sprockets fitted. The impression we got, and the impression of a number of much more able cyclists enlisted for trials, was that there was a definite advantage, particularly on hills when using our hubs.

Impressions are not measurements. We set up means of measuring the drive force required under various loads, utilising the same rig as we tested the wear rates of the deposits. Results were good, and then by some extraordinary piece of good fortune we learned that a local institute had been funded to measure the efficiency of all aspects of riding a cycle. They initially contacted us asking for various components to evaluate the effects of crank length on performance.

Cooperating with them has resulted in a series of reports—they measure oxygen requirements for given power outputs and have been able to demonstrate the advantage of low-friction deposits when the chain has to be out of line. They report considerable savings, and are conducting in-depth statistical verification.

12. Founding of the Dunlop Tyre Company

H. D. Higman

During his working life as a veterinary surgeon in Ireland, Mr. Dunlop applied rubber to veterinary problems. This led to experiments with pneumatic tyres, his first patent in 1888 and, after further tests, the formation of the first trading company. Expansion and company name changes then followed. Details for this paper are taken from Mr. J. B. Dunlop's own private notes and papers held by the family.[1]

In my archive, at Oswestry, Shropshire, England, I have approximately 2,000 papers (and a voice recording, made in 1910, of JBD himself) that relate to the story of Dunlop and the reinvention of the air tyre. I say reinvention because, as many will know, Mr. R. W. Thomson invented the air tyre and had it patented in 1845, Patent No. 10990. Unfortunately, the patent was allowed to lapse, and for the next 40 years it was not worked. However, this paper confines itself to Dunlop's contribution, and we should begin with his birth.[1]

John Boyd Dunlop was born on 5 February 1840 in the village of Dreghorn, Ayrshire, Scotland.[1] His family were farmers, and it was on his father's farm that he first noticed that a large roller, rolling the fields, was easier to pull over rough ground than a smaller one. This gave Dunlop an early experience with friction.[7]

Dunlop's health was not robust enough at that time for farming, so his parents decided that after elementary schooling he should enter the academic world.[7] This suited Dunlop well and, at the age of 19, he gained his degree as a veterinary surgeon at the Royal Dick Veterinary College, Edinburgh.[7] By the age of 21, Dunlop had moved from Scotland to Belfast, Ireland, setting up what was to become one of Ireland's largest veterinary practices.[7] Dunlop's working life as a veterinary surgeon involved the use of rubber on a number of occasions to protect and support animals, and in application to veterinary problems.[1] At the age of 47, Dunlop still had vibration problems at the back of his mind when, towards the end of October 1887, he constructed his first pneumatic tyre experiment by making a wooden disc about 16 in. in diameter and 1½ in. thick. He made an air tyre of sheet rubber 1/32 in. thick secured to the disc in a temporary fashion by means of a very thin strip of linen cloth—Dunlop once said that the cloth was part of Mrs. Dunlop's dress. This disc was rolled across Dunlop's stable yard, hitting the far wall. Dunlop then rolled a solid tyred wheel across the yard. The word "pneumatic" was applied by Dunlop to the air tyre, the air being pumped into the tyre with a football pump. When the distance travelled by the air tyre was compared with that which the solid tyred wheel had travelled, Dunlop was convinced on the merit of the future pneumatic tyre. During the late autumn of 1887, he called on Edlin & Co., Garfield Street, Belfast to discuss the fitting of pneumatic tyres to a tricycle for his son. It was often said that Dunlop based his idea of an air tyre on a water hose pipe—a theory he vigourously denied during his lifetime.[1]

Dunlop took delivery of sheets of rubber from Thorntons for his second tyre experiment. He made 2 hooped wheels from 2 strips of American elm, approximately 9 ft. x 3 in. x 2 in., formed by strapping wood around metal hoops. These wheels were then strapped to the 2 rear wheels of the trike. The wheels were 36 in. in diameter. The air tubes and outer rubber were made of 1/32 in. stock sheets, but the front forks of the trike were too narrow to take an air tyre so the solid tyre was retained on the trike. The tyres were made towards the end of December,

---

Synopsis

Based on an archive of approximately 2,000 papers which relate to the story of the reinvention of the tyre by J. B. Dunlop, this paper explores some of the main events that led to the formation of the pneumatic tyre industry by Mr. Dunlop and others.

or early January 1888, and were made large so that they could run softly.¹ The year 1888 saw the first run on Johnnie Dunlop's first trike, now fitted with the new pneumatic tyres. This took place during the night of 28 to 29 January, which was also the night of the eclipse of the moon. Next morning the wheels and tyres were inspected and no cuts could be found.¹ (The Royal Greenwich Observatory, England has confirmed that an eclipse of the moon did take place on 28 January 1888.)

Dunlop then ordered from Edlin & Co., Belfast, who were agents for Quadrant and Centaur bicicles, a Quadrant Trike No. 8 without the rear wheels, and this machine was delivered to him on 20 March 1888. The price of the machine less 2 rear wheels was £18 19s. 8d. Dunlop built the 2 rear wheels himself, the size being approximately 52–60 in. in diameter. The machine weighed 80 lbs. and was completed towards the end of June.² This was his third experiment with pneumatic tyres.

Dunlop's first provisional patent, No. 10607 dated 23 July 1888, was accepted on 7 December 1888 for "An Improvement in Tyres of Wheels for Bicycles, Tricycles or other Road Cars." This was his first pneumatic tyre patent.³

Thorntons & Co. of Edinburgh, Scotland delivered to Dunlop 2 air tubes and covers on 14 August 1888. These covers were used for Johnnie Dunlop's first pneumatic-tyred bicycle. The front wheel of this bicycle is now housed in the Royal Scottish Museum, Edinburgh. The material used on the cover was Gents Yacht Sail Cloth. This was the fourth experiment with pneumatic tyres. The fitting of these tyres took place late October or early November—wheel size was 28 in. front and 34 in. rear. The bicycle was made by Edlin & Co., Belfast with a weight of 27 lbs. 2 oz., and Johnnie Dunlop was 10 to 11 years of age when he rode it.¹

Just before the Christmas holidays, Mr. Walter Edlin rode Johnnie's pneumatic bicycle over the Shore Road which, in winter, was one of the roughest roads in Belfast. During the run the tyres were tested for punctures, but none were found. The only mishap was a pinched tube which required some attention. It seems that Mr. Charles Sinclair also rode the bicycle along the Royal Avenue past the bank building and into Donegall Place and back. It was about this time that Mr. Charles Sinclair lent his brother Mr. Finlay Sinclair £100 to help finance the Edlin & Co. business. The loan enabled Charles Sinclair to become one of the first shareholders in the future Pneumatic Tyre Co.⁴ Mr. Finlay Sinclair was a partner in Edlin & Co.

In 1888 Edlin & Co., Belfast, placed the first pneumatic tyre advertisement in the *Irish Cyclist* in the 19 December issue. An advertisement board was fixed to the Garfield Street building which read "The Edlin Sinclair Pneumatic Tyre, First on the Market in 1888."⁴

In early January 1889, after business hours, Edlin and Dunlop designed and made patterns for bicycles and tricycles. These patterns were sent to a Glasgow firm that made malleable steel castings. As soon as these castings were returned, Edlin set to work building 12 bicycles and 6 tricycles. The bicycle forks and frame had to be widened to accommodate the new pneumatic tyre, which was much larger than the solid tyre.¹

Arjay (R. J. Mecredy) travelled to Belfast in February 1889 to see the pneumatic tyre at the works of Edlin & Co. He claimed that he saw a puncture in the tyre—this was refuted by Dunlop. The bicycle which Arjay saw was Johnnie Dunlop's first pneumatic tyred bicycle.¹

Pneumatics were first tested at Ormeau Park, Belfast, and ridden by Mr. W. J. Montgomery the Saturday after the machine was completed on 9 March 1889. Again, Edlin & Co. had built this machine (roadster pattern). Later, Hume ordered another roadster machine, supplied to him towards the end of March 1899.¹ On 18 May, Hume won the first race at the Queens College Sports on pneumatic tyres with a racing machine built by Edlin & Co. The weight of the racing machine was 22–23 lbs. The rear wheel was 30 in. with tangent spokes, and the front wheel 28 in. with direct spokes, geared to 62 in.⁶ Dunlop's own notes state that this bicycle was altered for a 50 mile race and was later lost.¹

J. B. Dunlop met Harvey Du Cros for the first time at the Queens College Sports, Belfast, on 18 May. Harvey Du Cros was to become the chairman of the first trading company of Dunlop, known as Pneumatic Tyre & Booth's Cycle Agency Co. Ltd.³

Mr. Dunlop's own racing bicycle was built about the end of June 1889 and was seen with Dunlop at the Old Timers Meeting in 1918 held at Donnybrook. This machine was built by Edlin & Co., Belfast,³ and is now in the city's Ulster Museum.

Hume was the first to ride pneumatic tyres in England. The event, which took place in Liverpool on 20 July 1889 was the Police Sports held at the Police Athletic Society's Ground at the corner of Shiel Road and Prescot Road, Kensington. The ground has since been built over. After the race, Mr. Hume placed the bicycle on display in a local cycle shop window near Lime Street railway station, Liverpool.

In a short time a large crowd had gathered, and the local police had to be called to clear the area.[1]

At the Highland Games in Belfast, on 31 August 1889, Mr. Bowden and Mr. J. M. Gillies expressed an interest in the marketing of the pneumatic tyre. During September 1889, Mr. Harvey du Cros approached Booth's Brothers with the view of floating a pneumatic tyre company. It was at about this time that Arthur du Cros rode J. B. Dunlop's racer. Pneumatics were only seen on a few occasions in England during the 1889 season.[1]

On 16 November 1889, Dunlop, J. M. Gillies and a Mr. Bowden signed to start the first trading company—Mr. Dunlop taking £500 in cash and £1,500 in shares. This sum was half of a total of £3,000 shares. The balance of Dunlop's shares (£1,500) was shared between Gillies and Bowden. Booth's Brothers joined the company for the sum of £8,000—of this £4,000 was paid in shares and the other half in cash. This was for the purchase of Booth's Cycle Agency, Dublin.[1]

The trading company of Edlin & Co., Belfast, was taken over for the sum of £400. The new company was named Pneumatic Tyre & Booth's Cycle Agency Co. Ltd. and was located at 66 Upper Stephen's Street, Dublin. It was floated on 18 November 1889 for the sum of £25,000, but with only £15,010 being subscribed. Mr. John Griffiths was Secretary and General Manager of the new company, and Mr. Edlin and F. Sinclair of Edlin & Co. went to work there as managers. The first board meeting was held on 30 November, and Harvey du Cros was elected Company Chairman, the other board members being: J. B. Dunlop; Richard Booth of Booth's Brothers; Richard Mecredy, Editor of the *Irish Cyclist*; Frederick W. Wood, Director of Woods, Webb & Co; and John Griffiths, Secretary and General Manager of Booth's Bros.[5]

Before the company was formed, patent agent, Messrs. Haseltine, Lake & Co., made a patent search for any air patents but failed to find Thomson's earlier air patent of 1845. Dunlop always stated that he did not know of Thomson's patent. Haseltine, Lake & Co., report that Dunlop's patent was valid was noted in the prospectus of the founder company, Pneumatic Tyre & Booth's Cycle Agency Co. Ltd.[1]

The board meeting of the founder company met on 12 December 1889 to discuss giving the licence for the fixing of pneumatic tyres to a limited number of firms of the cycle trade. A further board meeting on 27 December resolved to throw open the pneumatic tyre to the trade. The first board meeting of the Pneumatic Tyre Co. at Oriel House reported that F Sinclair had been removed to Dublin and Mr. Edlin's services were also required in Dublin to assist in the manufacture of the pneumatic tyre.[3]

Mr. Osbourne Eden's business had been taken over and he had moved to Garfield Street, Belfast, to manage the old Edlin's Works for the Founder Company.[1]

On 30 September 1890, the disclosure of the Thomson patent occurred, and the happy dream of the Founder Company being the sole patentee disappeared. Dunlop disclosed his knowledge of the Aves leaflet which was passed to him by Mr. Redfern, a London Patent Agent. The leaflet dealt with Thomson's patent. A letter of 11 September 1890, listing Thomson's earlier work and sent to the Founder Company by Dunlop, was kept secret for a time by the company. Eventually, Charles Wheelwright of *Sport and Play* published the details.[3]

By now, T. W. Robertson of Belfast had joined the company and ran the repairs department (tyres) at the old Edlin's headquarters in Garfield Street, Belfast. Harvey du Cros was in Chicago in early January 1891 to set up Dunlop tyre branches, and Alfred Featherstone of Chicago was enlisted to help—this company was known later as the American Dunlop Tyre Co. The Dunlop factory in Coventry was set up by Finlay Sinclair on 10 January 1891.[1]

On 9 March 1891, a patent for a valve by C. H. Woods, Patent No. 4175, was registered. Reports in the *Irish Cyclist* issue of 19 August noted the new valve on the market. The patent was sold to the Pneumatic Tyre & Booth's Cycle Agency Co. Ltd. for £1,000.[3]

The board of the Pneumatic Tyre & Booth's Cycle Agency Co. Ltd. decided to buy the Welch patent, which was the first for detachable pneumatic tyres, on 20 April 1891, paying £5,000 for the British rights. The French patent rights cost £1,500 and the Belgian patent rights, £1,000. The agreement was finally signed on 19 May 1891 between the inventor, Mr. C. K. Welch, and the Founder Company.[3]

Following complaints from the Dublin Corporation, in a letter of 2 July 1891 to the board about the smell from the Dunlop works, the board agreed, at its meeting on 29 July, to transfer tyre manufacture to Coventry, England which, by now, was the centre of the bicycle industry.[3]

In 1891, Mr. A. J. Wilson was sent to London to open the first English Department of the Pneumatic Tyre & Booth's Cycle Agency Co. Ltd. in Farringdon Street, London.[3] At the end of March 1892, Mr. J. B.

Dunlop went to live in Dublin at Leighton, Ailesbury Road.[1]

To market the new detachable tyre, "The Dunlop-Welch" name was adopted and Welch joined the Founder Company in June but, at that time, J. B. Dunlop did not like the idea of sharing the Dunlop trademark with Welch.[3]

J. B. Dunlop bought the T. W. Robertson French and German patent for a detachable tyre from the Pneumatic Tyre Co. and Harvey du Cros on 9 February 1893.[1]

At the fourth Annual Report of the pneumatic Tyre & Booth's Cycle Agency Co. Ltd. in September 1893, the shareholders voted that the Cycle Agency be separated from the company and transferred to the John Griffiths Cycle Corporation Ltd.[2]

On 28 February 1894 the Founder Company's name was changed from Pneumatic Tyre & Booth's Cycle Agency Co. Ltd. to the Pneumatic Tyre Co. Ltd., and the Cycle Agency was transferred to the John Griffiths Corporation.[3]

Mr. C. K. Welch resigned from the Pneumatic Tyre Co. in a letter dated 31 October 1894. He withdrew the resignation shortly afterwards, the board having given Welch assurance that he had never lost their confidence.[3]

1895 saw an important event when Dunlop sent a letter of resignation dated 16 March to the secretary of the Pneumatic Tyre Co. Ltd. This was to take effect from 1 May 1895. The chairman replied to Dunlop on 2 April 1895 that the directors desired the chairman to accept Dunlop's letter as a legal notice and, as such, they inserted it in the minutes. On 1 May the board discussed Dunlop's letter and on 2 May it was accepted.[3] By then Dunlop had sold most of his shares in the company.[1]

On 30 September 1895 the Dunlop Pneumatic Tyre Co. Ltd. was formed from the Pneumatic Tyre Co. Ltd. It is interesting to note that the name Dunlop was included in the title of the company for the first time, and at a time when Dunlop had ceased to be connected with the firm.[3]

Notes

1. Dunlop, John Boyd—Private papers, letters and correspondence (made available by the family and collated by the author).

2. McClintock, Mrs. Jean. *The History of the Pneumatic Tyre*. Crow Street, Dublin: Alex Thom & Co., 1924.

3. Du Cros, Sir Arthur, Bt. *Wheels of Fortune*. London: Chapman & Hall Ltd., 11 Henrietta Street, 1938.

4. Edlin, R. W.—Private family papers, England.

5. Booth, B.—Private family papers, Dublin.

6. Bartleet, H. W. *Bartleet's Bicycle Book*. London: Ed. J. Burrow & Co. Ltd., 43 Kingsway, 1931.

7. Cooke, Jim—Private papers, Dublin.

Albert A. Pope

13. Colonel Pope and the Founding of the U.S. Bicycle Industry

In an article published in *Wheel* magazine of 21 May 1897, Col. Albert A. Pope relates that his "interest in the bicycle commenced in 1854, when [he] was a boy victim of the velocipede. About a dozen years later (1868–69) [he] rode the boneshaker."

As a member of the city council of Newton, Massachusetts, Pope was asked to attend the Philadelphia Centennial Exhibition of 1876. There he saw the new English Ariel and Paragon high-wheel bicycles on exhibition.

As he related in a speech given to the leading bicycle manufacturers who had assembled for the New York Bicycle Show (*Boston Post*, 15 June 1894), Pope "went back again and again to study the exhibit wondering each time if it would ever be possible…to learn to balance…on one of those machines. It seemed…then that one must be an acrobat or gymnast to…[ride] such a steed.

"In May of the following year (1877) Pope saw [his] friend Alfred Chandler riding an imported English bicycle through the highways in and about Boston. Pope frequently followed him with a good horse, but he always got away…It was then that [Pope] began to seriously estimate and realize the value of the bicycle."

In the meantime Pope had invited an English friend, John Harrington, to visit him in Boston. The purpose of this visit was to assist him in constructing a "bicycle." In July of 1877 Pope and Harrington, with the assistance of a local Boston mechanic, set about the task.

Pope's first bicycle was a "cumbersome machine." It weighed over 70 lbs. and was difficult to ride. It took Pope "much of the summer of 1877" to master it. Furthermore it cost $313.

Pope asked Harrington to return to England and procure for him an assortment of bicycles. It would appear that Harrington encountered some difficulties, or that there was a falling out, because Pope finally placed an order for 8 machines through Stoddard, Lovering and Co., a Boston import house.

The bicycles arrived in January 1878, and were displayed by Pope at 45 High Street in Boston. The bicycles were 50 and 52 inches in height and included two Coventry machines, two Duplex Excelsiors, two Singers, and two made by Haynes and Jeffries. (By the way, the first Columbia model made in America was modeled after the Duplex Excelsior.)

Col. Pope teamed up with his cousin Edward (E. W. Pope) who served as bookkeeper, and Will R. Pittman, a veteran of the boneshaker era, who took charge of riding instruction.

"All was noise" in this little shop, and the bicycles were sold out. By 1878, 75 English machines had been imported.

In the summer of 1878, Col. Pope made a trip to Europe "to study the bicycling situation." While in England he attended the Harrowgate Camp for Cycling Men accompanied by J. S. Dean of Boston and Herbert E. Owen, then of Washington, amongst others.

He also contacted several English manufacturing companies which manufactured the critical components, such as steel tubing and bearings. In one case Pope was refused a visit by the factory owner. Not to be deterred, he and his cohorts dressed as workmen and gained access to the plant in question.

Synopsis

This paper is based on information derived from the personal scrapbooks of Col. Albert A. Pope, founder of the Pope Manufacturing Company, maker of the Columbia bicycle and various other brands, and traces the founding of the American bicycle industry and specifically of the Pope Manufacturing Company.

The purpose of this trip was obvious. Upon his return to Boston, Pope began to seek out a suitable company to manufacture the first mass-produced American bicycle.

Let's be clear, however: American carriage makers had fabricated velocipedes and boneshakers for many years, but no one had ever succeeded in mass producing a precision engineered machine such as those imported from England.

Pope contracted the Weed Sewing Machine Company of Hartford, Connecticut (which he eventually took over), and in November 1878 began to manufacture his first 50 machines. He was able to price them at $90, $22.50 less than the imported English variety. As I mentioned before, they were a knock-off of the English high-wheeler, the Duplex Excelsior.

Before entering the bicycle business Pope had been engaged in the sale of various patented products, and was therefore aware of the importance of patents. He was also aware that previous efforts to promote the boneshaker had been stifled by writs of injunction against unlicensed fabricators or by excessive licensing fees, usually $25 per cycle or sometimes much more.

Pope became aware of the 1866 Lallement patent and, being convinced that the patent could withstand "attack," set about plotting its acquisition. Pope first applied for and was granted a license from the Lallement patent owners, Richardson and McKee of Boston. This was not an easy task, since they had already agreed to license Cunningham, Heath & Co., a rival firm who were also importing English bicycles. Col. Pope approached Richardson and McKee and made them *an offer they could not refuse*. They notified Cunningham, Heath that their "option had expired," and issued a license to Pope. Cunningham, Heath of course was not going to take this lying down. The result was that Richardson and McKee, to strike a compromise, licensed both Pope and Cunningham, Heath to manufacture under the Lallement patent in the United States.

Pope however was not satisfied. He knew that a half interest in the patent was owned by a Vermont company, the Montpelier Mfg. Co., a carriage maker in Montpelier. He also knew that the owners of this company would not be adverse to selling their half interest.

Pope lured Richardson and McKee into selling him half of their half interest, or a one-quarter interest, by offering a sum greater than the asking price of the Vermont partners. He knew Richardson and McKee would turn around and buy out the Vermonters using these proceeds. He timed his move carefully.

After completing the purchase, Pope rushed to the train station and took the night train to Montpelier. A meeting had been arranged for the next morning during which Pope acquired the Vermont partners' interest, and thereby took control of the patent. This was in the nick of time since, soon after, a letter arrived from Richardson and McKee "who had sought to outwit him" with their purchase offer.

With full control of the patent, Pope squeezed out Richardson and McKee and set about his mission to create the modern American bicycle industry.

Although it might seem that the road was now clear, Pope realized that much had to be done to overcome the anti-bicycle prejudice of the American public, and to create an orderly climate to permit his and other companies to make the type of long-term investments needed to produce the metals and components to manufacture bicycles equal in quality to the English, ... and ... to realize his dream of making the Pope-Columbia bicycle the "Standard of the World."

Pope's first move was to secure the services of a prominent patent attorney, Charles E. Pratt of Boston. Under Pratt's guidance the Pope Company assembled an impressive array of patents on every conceivable aspect of the manufacture of bicycles.

These patents were aggressively defended but not with the purpose of stifling competition. On the contrary, Pope proceeded to grant licenses to his competition, and reduced the licensing fee from $25 to $10 per bicycle. The first licenses were granted to the Western Toy Company, the St. Nicholas Toy Co., Mr. Thomas B. Jeffrey and R. Philip Gormully (later forming the company Gormully and Jeffrey), and of course Cunningham, Heath.

Probably the most notable defense of the patent was in 1881, in the case of *Pope Manufacturing vs. McKee and Harrington*. McKee and Harrington were manufacturing bicycles without a license in open defiance of Pope. In their attempt to discredit the Lallement patent, they placed advertisements in Europe, principally France, offering "healthy" rewards for any evidence that the pedal had been adapted to the velocipede before 1866, and even called Lallement himself to testify in New York, hoping to discredit him. One must also assume they contacted Michaux, since it was common knowledge at that time that Michaux had been the pioneer of bicycling in France. Evidently Michaux either refused to cooperate, or could not offer any evidence even to support his contention that the pedal was not a new invention, but was "100 years old." None of the defense efforts bore fruit, and McKee and Harrington agreed to stop making bicycles!

As an aside, it is interesting to note that Pope later states in an interview published in the *Boston Post*, 23 October 1899, that Lallement actually built Michaux's first bicycles.

Pope put the income from the Lallement patent licensing fees to good work. He imported the best cycling literature from England, and along with the advertising literature from all his competitors, distributed it throughout the land. He commissioned Charles Pratt to write *American Bicycler* in 1879, the first American book on the high wheeler. He then established a periodical dedicated to cycling, called *The Wheelmen*, funding the $60,000 of start-up costs, and assisted in the founding of an association of cyclists named the League of American Wheelmen.

One of his more creative schemes was to induce a small group of wheelmen to willfully violate the New York City ordinance forbidding bicycle riding in Central Park. Pope paid for the defense of these cyclists who, of course, were promptly arrested. This ploy was repeated, or threatened, across the country. The result was that many parks were opened to cyclists, most notably Central Park in New York, South Park in Chicago, and Fairmount Park in Philadelphia. Pope also began to tour the country delivering speeches to business groups urging that attention be given to the betterment of American roads. This in fact became his *cause célèbre*.

Of course there was much more to come in the ensuing years in terms of innovations. Pope introduced or expanded on the use of new marketing ploys such as installment sales, fashion design prizes, art competitions, sporting events, theft and accident insurance, as well as rewards for the return of stolen Columbias, and of course, the "Columbia warrantee," or guarantee of satisfaction. He was a firm believer in advertising, and established a large in-house advertising department under the direction of S. S. McLure (who later became editor of *The Wheelman* and subsequently *McLure's* magazine).

Hartford

He also introduced new technological developments: a tube mill built in partnership with Dr. Mannesman of Germany; the Columbia Ball Bearing, a single row adjustable ball bearing; he designed and had Otis build for the Hartford Plant the first industrial elevator; Edison, the first electrified continuous production assembly line in America (visited and admired by Henry Ford); and many others.

Eventually Pope realized his dream of competing with the English industry. He succeeded not only in exporting his cycles to England, France, and Germany, but also collaborated with the Clément Company in France, assisting them in modernizing their manufacturing and bicycle design. By 1890, when a ladies "safety" model was introduced, the Pope Manufacturing Company had become the largest producer of bicycles. At its peak the company had a daily output of 600 bicycles, one bicycle a minute, 38,000 employees, 3,800 agents, and over 18 acres of manufacturing surface.

The final chapter in this saga is of course the introduction in May 1897 of the Columbia Motor Car. Pope elected to produce an electric vehicle to give it a "wider appeal." He was convinced that an electric vehicle designed for the general public could eventually, like the bicycle, be produced for a much lower cost once mass production began. He was also appalled by the noise, smell, and confusion caused by the combustion-engine motor cars he witnessed

Fig. 13.1. Built in 1897 by the renowned architects Peabody & Stearns, the Pope building in Boston is a classic example of "Renaissance Revival."

on the Champs Elysees and other European thoroughfares during his frequent visits there.

Westfield

His interest in the motor car and declining profits in the manufacture of the bicycle led Pope in 1899 to merge his bicycle, tube, and tire operations with those of A. G. Spaulding and 40 other leading manufacturers to form the American Bicycle Company known as the "Bicycle Trust." While this entity was in existence, it had an installed capacity of 1,200,000 bicycles per year.

The bicycle boom was over, however, and this trust could not stem the tide of red ink. Nor could it kindle the same interest as the motor car. This, of course, led to Pope's creation of the Automobile Trust, backed by William C. Whitney, P. A. B. Widener, and Thomas Fortune Ryan, amongst others, that eventually secured the patent on the internal combustion engine, the Seaton Patent. This in turn led to the famous patent infringement case against a former bicycle mechanic who had applied for a license to manufacture, and having been turned down, decided to proceed without a license. The patent was at first upheld, but the bicycle mechanic appealed and won. The bicycle mechanic was named Henry Ford. The rest is history.

Bibliography

Bearings, Chicago, IL (19 Jan. 1894).

Boston Post, Boston, MA (15 Jan. 1894, 30 June 1895, 23 Oct. 1899).

Cycle Age & Trade Review (21 Sept. 1899).

Cycling, Philadelphia, PA (5 Jan. 1894).

Home Journal, Boston, MA (15 April 1899).

New York Tribune, New York, NY (28 July 1895, 29 Sept. 1899, 24 Oct. 1899).

Profitable Investing, Boston, MA (15 Aug. 1892).

Saturday Evening Gazette, Boston (3 July 1897).

Table Talk, Philadelphia, PA (July 1895).

The Amersegment Gazette, Cleveland, OH (17 Nov. 1894).

The American Athlete, Philadelphia, PA (19 Jan. 1894).

The Bicycling World, Boston, MA (18 June 1897, 3 Aug. 1899, 24 Aug. 1899, 25 Jan. 1900).

The Carriage Journal, Chicago, IL (Nov. 1894).

The Equity, Chicago, IL (27 Oct. 1894, 27 July 1895).

The Wheel, NY (23 Nov. 1894, 21 May 1897, 4 Jan. 1900, 11 Jan. 1900).

The American Wheelman, NY (13 Jan. 1894, 22 Nov. 1894).

The Wheelman (May 1994).

Andrew Millward

14. The Founding of the Hercules Cycle & Motor Co. Ltd.

The following is a brief examination of the origins of the largest producer of bicycles in Britain prior to 1939—the Hercules Cycle & Motor Co. Ltd. Perhaps most notable about the company was its emergence long after the pioneer phase of the cycle industry, and over a decade after the "boom" of the 1890s. The facts surrounding this growth speak for themselves (Table 14.1).

What is extraordinary is the neglect of this phenomenal company by historians of cycling. Looking through the popular histories of British cycling in the past 30 years, the neglect is outstanding; Woodforde,[1] McGurn,[2] Ritchie,[3] and Beeley[4] can muster not even half a dozen references between them. Oddy[5] has drawn attention to the impact on cycling history of the research efforts of writers who are primarily object-oriented, or uncritically utilise for their research mainly secondary works written by such writers.[6] The overlooking of the Hercules phenomenon would offer few surprises from this perspective; throughout the period in question, the Hercules bicycle was built for a mass market, surviving in substantial quantities, and the company made no novel innovations in design,[7] thus enabling it to fail two key criteria—perceived rarity, and novelty essential to attract the attention of the collector historian. Instead inter-war cycling in such accounts is full of references to the so-called "Classic Lightweights" produced by famed builders such as F. H. Grubb, Maurice Selbach, F. W. Evans, Claud Butler, and others whose combined total annual output was unlikely to have surpassed a month's production from the Hercules factory.

The only work to examine the cycle industry in the inter-war years with a more scholarly eye is Hudson,[8] whose thesis on the industry devotes a chapter to the period. Here we are made aware of the Hercules phenomena in the broad perspective, and its overall contribution to the cycle industry's growth and progress. However, it soon became apparent in following up the basic references and in uncovering new source material that something was not entirely satisfactory in the received accounts of the self-made and heroic Crane brothers, Edmund and Harry, who brought bicycles and cycling within the financial means of the working man and woman. Firstly

Table 14.1. Hercules Cycle & Motor Co. Ltd.—Output and Growth Measures

1910:	Entered business to produce a bicycle to be sold at a price in reach of everyone
1922:	Manufacturing 700 machines/week in a small factory
1923:	2,000/week capacity
1924:	5,000/week capacity
1925:	15–20,000/week following extension to 11 acres of factory
1928:	Hercules' total annual output 300,000 bicycles
1933:	Total production 3 million bicycles
1939:	Total production 6 million (i.e., average production of ½ million per year)

Sources: *The Motor Cycle & Cycle Trader*, 25 January 1929, p. 68; *Birmingham Post*, 3 February 1939, and *Hercules Cycle* Magazine (1934)

received accounts were based on only a limited amount of material regurgitating the same story, little of the historical record of the company survived through the years,[9] and an approach from a surviving member of the family for information revealed little had been kept which would throw light on the company's activities during its early years.[10] Particular care was taken, therefore, during the search through cycle trade literature of this period, to note any references to the company in the early stages of its development.

The search quickly threw up some inconsistencies; the first concerned the year of the company's foundation in 1910. The local directory corroborated this date,[11] but a later source suggested that this was not the year that the founders first became associated with the cycle industry. In 1928, in giving evidence to the Standing Committee on Merchandise Marks appointed by the Board of Trade, Edmund Crane admitted to 27 years experience in the cycle industry, implying an involvement of almost a decade prior to the often-cited foundation date.[12] Therefore in examining periodicals, the search for references was brought forward to see if earlier references could be located to the Cranes' business activities.

It was in this context that a second inconsistency arose. In an interview with the local press in 1933, Edmund Crane referred to his father having been a farmer and having been bankrupt; the bankruptcy and the ensuing destitution experienced by the family provided the spur to Edmund opening up a cottage business, which grew to the giant business which, by this time, had reached an output of 3 million cycles, and was providing Edmund and his brother Henry with a combined annual income of £60,000.[13] However, with the appearance as early as 1895 of references to a Crane associated with the cycle trade in the Birmingham area, and in the course of examining the next 15 years of the cycle trade press, a picture of the activities of the family who came to be called the "notorious Cranes" emerged. This paper is intended not just to explain why the origins of such a major company should have remained so obscure for so long, but also to outline the significance of this episode for our understanding of the cycle trade in this period.

In the slump following the boom period of the late 1890s, the industry, despite the reluctance of many of the larger firms, recognised that price falls were necessary, and with one or two exceptions began to manufacture second-grade machines, sometimes under different names.[14] However few embraced the ideas of those commentators who suggested bringing prices down to bring bicycles within the scope of lower income groups.[15] Indeed the price cuts in 1897 by Rudge-Whitworth[16] and in 1904 by Swift Cycle Co. Ltd. (to less than £8)[17] created unrest in the trade. However, cheaper bicycles emerged through a number of outlets: local assemblers using low overheads to keep prices down; cooperative societies and private clubs giving an effective discount through dividends to its members[18]; and through a number of companies who were referred to in the trade as "price-cutters." The activities of these "cutters" was carefully monitored in the trade mainly through the medium of the trade associations representing manufacturers and agents, but particularly through the cycle trade press. The mainstream "price-cutters" tended to market machines for the "own name" or "own transfer" market, i.e., to agents or distributors at trade prices. This proved to be a successful outlet, and some established companies began to enter this market. By 1905 this was a growth area which gradually absorbed much of the business of the smaller assemblers. Evidence for this is provided by the Eadie-BSA merger which was intended to rationalise the fittings trade, and the almost immediate move ca. 1907–08 to manufacture complete cycles for the "own name" trade,[19] and in 1909 to manufacture complete cycles with the "B.S.A." trademark for general sale.

Although price cutting remained an issue, the emergence of a number of firms providing low-priced machines undoubtedly widened the market for cycles and proved popular with agents who could market their own lines alongside those makes for which they had the agency. Being in

Fig. 14.1. The Petros Model D roadster.

receipt of advertising revenue from these firms and not wishing to alienate their main readership, the cycling press began to warm to some of the leading firms, and some of the firms when visited received favourable reports.[20]

However, the price-cutting firms depended on high turnover, and with so many firms able to enter the field it became increasingly difficult to maintain margins without cutting costs and thus prices. For some companies in this position, the temptation began to present itself of selling machines through channels outside the agency system or selling direct to the public. This was frowned upon by the cycle trade in general. Firstly it threatened the position of the agent; the decision by Rudge-Whitworth to adopt a depot system for distributing created an outcry, despite their maintenance of an extensive agency system. Also selling direct to the public represented a breach of trade agreements where trade terms (i.e., discount on price of materials, components, and so on) obtained from supplier firms.

Among the new entrants to the "own transfer" and low-price machine producers was the Petros Motor & Cycle Co. in 1904.[21] The owner Edith Maude Crane was only nominally in charge; the main business was conducted by her husband, Edward John Crane, from 58 Caroline Street, and then later from Allcock Street, Birmingham. Crane had been bankrupted about 1899 not through farming, but as a cycle factory.[22] It is possible that he had been noted in the trade press as early as 1895 in connection with placing paragraph adverts offering known-make cycles for sale in Cork, Ireland.[23]

No references were noted about the company in the early years, but by 1906 their products were noted for their good value ranging from £2 16s 0d for the Model C Roadster to £3 10s 0d for the Model B Roadster (Fig. 14.1).[24] By the following year adverts were appearing more frequently in the trade press describing "Petros Cycles" as "Entirely British Made" (Figs. 14.2 and 14.3),[25] and for £1 16s 6d a bicycle could be bought (without tyres), albeit to a basic specification (Fig. 14.4).[26] However, later in the year

Fig. 14.2. Petros Cycles advertisement.

began the first of a series of episodes which were to lead to major confrontation with the trade.

Complaints were first received concerning Petros Cycles being sold to "outsiders" on the same terms as bona fide cycle agents, the evidence being adverts for Petros cycles appearing in *The Cabinet Maker* and *Household Furnisher*, clear evidence of the company's attempt to widen its market.[27] This was not in breach of any agreement, since the Petros Motor & Cycle Co. was not a member of the Cycle & Allied Trades Association (C&ATA) and were thus beyond its control. However, cycle manufacturers through their association had already taken pre-emptive action by placing an advert in the *Daily Mail*, making the general point to the public that purchasing from such an outlet (although not specifying any particular manufacturer) rendered any manufacturers' guarantee worthless.[28] But the warning appeared to be ineffective given that in the following year, 1908, Petros cycles were exhibited at the Stanley Show[29] and had moved to Bromley Street in Birmingham, perhaps an indication of expansionary activity in the business.[30]

The second wave of complaints concerned the association of machines made by the company appearing in various "auction" sales. This was a way of selling direct to the public under the guise of selling off the bankrupt or outdated stock of some imaginary company. These tactics were not unique to the cycle trade,[31] but arguably they were more prevalent in it. The danger auctions posed was to the agents in whose locality they took place, since many potential customers might be lost through sales of cycles at very low prices. Although the trade press argued that auctions were basically fraudulent,[32] it was actually recognised that they were within the law.

The frequency of auction sales grew rapidly during the years 1908–09. A number of price-cutting firms became involved, and the trade press was quick to expose those connected with the business in the hope that this would discredit them in the trade as a whole. The New Imperial Cycle Co.[33] and the Merlin Cycle Co. were both revealed by the press as being associated with auction sales, the latter company even being associated with supplying machines for auctions in Holland.[34] However, while these firms appear to have modified their policy following their exposure, the Petros Motor & Cycle Co. continued to deny any association with auction sales. Eventually

Fig. 14.3. Petros Cycles advertisement stressing British manufacture.

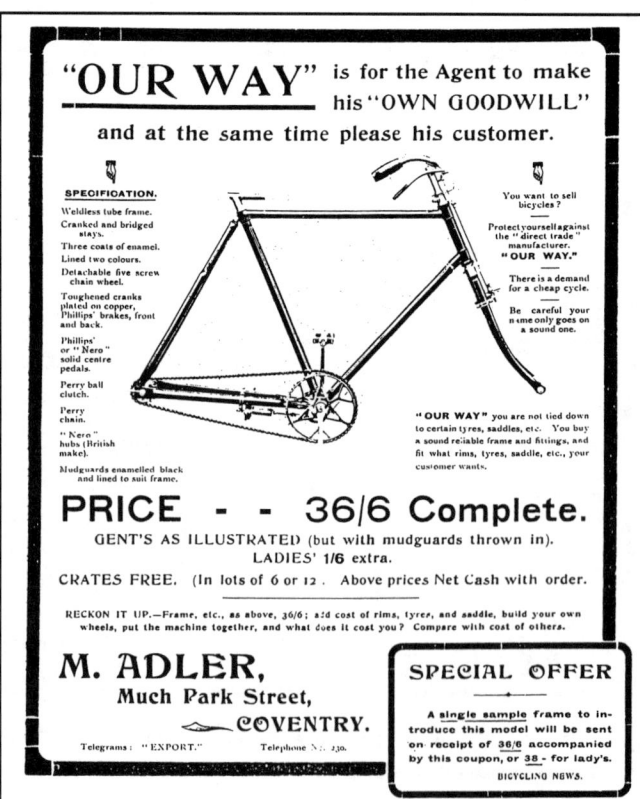

Fig. 14.4. Advertisement showing that a bicycle could be bought without tyres.

The Cycle Trader exposed the extent to which they were involved,[35] but the Petros Company remained unrepentant. For months after their connection was established in the cycle trade press, the company provided cycles for auction under the names, "Fabriken Cycle Co., Birmingham," "The Stagg Cycle Co.," Birmingham,[36] "Royal Cycle Co.,"[37] and "Rival."[38]

The trade, recognising that there was no legal sanction available to stop the auction sales, nevertheless responded with a series of actions. Companies supplying components such as speed gears refused to supply them,[39] and the cycle trade papers refused to take adverts for the Petros concern.[40] However, most importantly, the agents entered into a policy of taking direct action against the organisers of the auctions, aided and abetted by the trade associations who saw auction sales as being to blame for the gloomy start to the 1909 season,[41] and the trade papers who took a partisan view in reporting the breaking and disruption of auctions by local dealers.

The agents' tactics were to intercept handbills sent out to advertise the auction, and for as many local agents to turn up on the day of the sale to heckle and disrupt the auction. In the course of such events tempers frayed, and in due course there were legal actions involving assault, libel, and misrepresentation.[42] *The Cycle and Motor Trades Review* rallied to the support of the agents in these cases by instituting an Auction Writs Defence "shilling fund," requesting 1 shilling from each member to raise money to cover legal costs of defending agents in court[43] and to pay fines where necessary.[44]

In fact the strategy of libelling and then losing in court actually proved effective. Since only damages and no costs were incurred, The C&ATA and *The Cycle & Motor Trades Review* were able to raise 10 actions of slander (9 cases to 1 case respectively), losing one for £10 damages in court and settling out of court for the other actions for a total of £200 to Mrs. Crane.[45] However, since in most cases the auctions had been disrupted without satisfactory sales, the Petros Company began to suffer deterioration in turnover and soon insolvency. Although the Petros concern was divided into 3 departments, the wholesale and retail departments were clearly not as important as the auction department.[46] Due to the high rate of return of unsold bicycles from the auctions and the incurring of legal costs in the various court actions, Edith Maud Crane declared herself and the Petros Motor & Cycle Co. bankrupt in 1910.[47]

The episode was far from concluded. The extent of the outstanding liabilities drew the attention of creditors to question the operation of the business, particularly when Maud Crane decided to sell off machines to her husband and two sons in 1909 shortly before declaring herself bankrupt. This issue was raised by the auditor who concluded that the machines had been sold at below cost price. The matter was thought to be fraudulent, and in 1911 the two sons and their father were brought to trial on charges of conspiracy to defraud the creditors of the company. The outcome was a guilty verdict and Edward John Crane (50 years of age) was sentenced to 10 months' imprisonment, and his sons, Edmund Frank (24 years) and Harry Arthur (22 years) were respectively sentenced to 9 and 6 months' imprisonment, with hard labour.

It is perhaps, in these circumstances, hardly surprising that the two brothers should seek to draw a veil over this episode in their early involvement in the cycle trade, even though their subsequent appeal against conviction proved successful.[48] In 1910 the brothers announced the formation of the Hercules Cycle & Motor Co. Ltd., much to the initial scepticism

Fig. 14.5. Advertisement showing that the Hercules bicycle was affordable for buyer and agent alike.

if not scorn of the cycling trade press,[49] but there was to be ultimate success.

What significance does this episode have for the later development of the cycle trade? The episode did prompt some reflection on the part of the cycle trade press immediately following the convictions of the Cranes. Most obvious was the opportunity it provided to demonstrate cooperation in fighting a threat to their interest, and added conviction to the views of those who wanted stronger institutions to defend the interests of manufacturer and distributor alike from what were perceived as the unscrupulous. The cycle trade press had generally done much to support agents, expressing its attitude to auction breaking almost as a sport, on one occasion even publishing a group photo of "auction breakers" at Llangefni.[50] It was not slow to point out the hard lessons, however. The support had not been as solid for the "shilling fund" as was originally hoped,[51] and in revealing that a considerable number of members of the trade association had supplied the creditors of the Petros concern with goods,[52] thus pointed to the need for more effective action in strengthening the trade association's powers, and culminated in the revival of the Stop-List to enforce trade agreements between members by the cooperation of the manufacturers' association.

The press also recognised that innovation had a role to play by manufacturers who were blamed for allowing bicycle design to be come stabilised, and thus allowing the "cutter" to move in. It was noticeable throughout the early years of the century that the cycle trade press looked to innovations that might revive the established firms. Rather tellingly they were quick to alert the trade to the opportunities presented by "X" frames and spring frames to revive sales, but frowned on cottered frames because it was felt that they would make it easy for anybody to assemble a bicycle with a spanner and screwdriver.

Finally there was a recognition that there was a growing demand for cycles which the "price-cutting" firms were identifying, and the large firms were failing to supply. The scale of the Petros concern revealed a turnover of £27,821 in the year ending 4 July 1910, and the sale of 4,644 machines through the auction department alone (although 6,764 were returned unsold).[53] In addition the business employed 42 girl clerks to send out 30–40,000 circulars a day.[54] While referring to the Cranes as a "notorious company," an editorial in *Bicycling News & Motor Review* admits in relation to the type of bicycle sold "that there was a ready market for them, and it is impossible to disguise the fact that this class of bicycle is rather eagerly snapped up as 'cheap lines' by a certain class of agent."[55] The Hercules Cycle & Motor Co. Ltd., like the Petros company which preceded it, deliberately targeted this market and achieved a breakthrough in the years following World War I (Fig. 14.5).

Notes

1. Woodforde, J. *The Story of the Bicycle*. London: Routledge & Kegan Paul, 1970.

2. McGurn, J. *On Your Bicycle. An Illustrated History of Cycling*. London: John Murray, 1987.

3. Ritchie, A. *King of the Road. An Illustrated History of Cycling*. London: Wildwood House, 1975.

4. Beeley, S. *A History of Bicycles*. London: Studio Editions, 1992.

5. Oddy, N. "Kirkpatrick MacMillan, the Inventor of the Bicycle or the Invention of Cycling History," *Proceedings of the 1st International Cycling History Conference*, 30–31 May 1990, pp. 27–28.

6. Caunter's two-volume analysis of the collection of cycles in the Science Museum, London, is a much-cited work of this style of author. See Caunter C. F., *Cycles. Historical Review* (London: HMSO, 1955 (reprinted 1972)) and *Cycles. Handbook of the Collection*. Part II. Descriptive catalogue (London: HMSO, 1958).

7. Significantly Beeley, S. (1992), op. cit., mentions Hercules in connection with the novel glass fibre cycle frame it exhibited at the 1954 Earls Court Show (pp. 135–36), but makes no reference to its contribution to inter-war cycling.

8. Hudson, N. B. *The Growth and Structure of the Bicycle Industry* (unpublished thesis), MSc. (Econ.), London University, 1960, pp. 120–65.

9. See *Future. The Magazine of Industry*, no. 5 (1947): 39–46.

10. Author's correspondence with J. Vickers.

11. *Kelly's Directory of Birmingham* (various years 1900–20).

12. *Hardwareman & Ironmonger's Chronicle*, 29 March 1928.

13. *Birmingham Gazette*, 21 April 1933.

14. Some examples—Fred Hopper produced "London" cycles sold to the trade at £2 19s 6d, *The Cycle & Motor Trades Review*, 9 Aug. 1906, pp. 126–29; The Swift Cycle Co. Ltd. marketed "Cheylesmore Cycles," *The Cycle & Motor Trader*, 18 Nov. 1904, p. 624; and Humber Co. Ltd. produced "The Coventry Imperial," *The Cyclist Trade Review*, 12 Jan. 1905, pp. 25–26.

15. *The Statist*, 29 Oct. 1898, p. 648. See also *The Times Financial & Commercial Supplement*, 29 August 1904, p. 129.

16. *The Cycle Trader*, 14 July 1897, p. 47.

17. *The Cyclist Trade Review*, 5 May 1904, pp. 625–26.

18. *The Cycle & Motor Trades Review*, 10 Jan. 1907, p. 25; calculates a return of approx. £1 10s dividend on a £10 machine for a 1s membership ticket of the Society.

19. *The Cycle & Motor Trades Review*, 5 March 1908, p. 221.

20. For example, Wearwell Cycle Co. and Merlin Cycles, *Cycle & Motor Trades Review*, 21 Feb. 1907, p. 190, and Bransom, Kent & Co. Ltd., ibid., 28 May 1908, p. 548.

21. *The Cycle Trader & Review*, 5 May 1911, p. 308.

22. Ibid., 24 March 1911, p. 724.

23. *The Cycle Trader*, 25 Sept. 1895, p. 404. In fact the initials "E. F." not "E. J." are used: Edmund would have been about 7 years old at this time.

24. *The Cycle & Motor Trades Review*, 16 August 1906, p. 162.

25. Advertisement supplement, *Bicycling News & Motor Review*, 13 Feb. 1907; ibid,. 17 April 1907; *The Cycle & Motor Trades Review*, 14 Feb. 1907, advertisement section; ibid., 30 Jan. 1908, advertisement section, p. 34.

26. This price compared favourably to adverts for machines sold without tyres, wheels and saddles for £1 16s 6d from M. Adler of Coventry. See advertisement supplement to *Bicycling News & Motor Review*, 24 June 1908. (Fig. 14.4)

27. *The Cycle & Motor Trades Review*, 27 June 1907, p. 656.

28. *Daily Mail*, 16 May 1907 cited in *The Cycle & Motor Trades Review*, 23 May 1907, p. 508.

29. *The Cycle & Motor Trades Review*, 28 Nov. 1907, p. 549.

30. Ibid., 22 Oct. 1908, advertisement section, pp. 6 and 7.

31. It would appear that the jewellery industry suffered from similar sales, ref Goldsmith's Review article cited in *The Cycle & Motor Trades Review*, 9 June 1910.

32. *The Cycle & Motor Trades Review*, 28 Jan. 1909, p. 8.

33. Ibid., 13 May 1909, p. 536.

34. Ibid., 8 July 1909, pp. 747–49. Following this, Mr. Ivy Rogers, the proprietor, admitted that this policy was to prevent this activity affecting home traders, ibid., 15 July 1909, pp. 771–73.

35. *The Cycle Trader*, 12 March 1909, pp. 747 and 750.

36. *The Cycle & Motor Trades Review*, 18 Feb. 1909, pp. 169–70.

37. Ibid., 7 Oct. 1909, p. 1060; ibid., 16 Dec. 1909, p. 1393.

38. Ibid., 1 Sept. 1910, p. 882.

39. Namely B.S.A., Sturmey-Archer and Armstrong-Triplex. *The Cycle & Motor Trades Review*, 18 March 1909, p. 319, and *The Cycle & Motor Trader*, 12 March 1909, pp. 747 and 750.

40. *The Cycle & Motor Trades Review*, 18 Feb. 1909, pp. 169–70.

41. Ibid., 25 Feb. 1909, p. 208.

42. Ibid., 25 March 1909, p. 357; ibid., 1 April 1909, pp. 50 and 51; ibid., 8 April 1909, pp. 391–92; ibid., 11 Nov. 1909, p. 1214; ibid., 16 Dec. 1909, pp. 1399–1401; *The Cycle & Motor Trader*, 18 March 1910, pp. 1246, 1248 and 1250.

43. *The Cycle & Motor Trades Review*, 10 Feb. 1910, pp 121–22.

44. In the case of the *Royal Cycle Co. vs George Hitchins* the judgement was for the plaintiff who was judged to have been slandered. No costs were granted, but damages of £10 were awarded. *The Cycle & Motor Trades Review*, 23 Dec. 1909, p. 1422.

45. *The Cycle & Motor Trades Review*, 10 March 1910, pp. 236–37.

46. *The Cycle Trader & Review*, 5 May 1911, p. 308.

47. The liabilities of the company amounted to £9,482 and assets worth £1,621. *The Cycle & Motor Trades Review*, 1 Sept. 1910, p. 882.

48. *The Cycle Trader & Review*, 12 May 1911, p. 308. The convictions were quashed owing to the unreliability of evidence relating to the appraisal of the prices for which they had been charged for the cycles.

49. *The Cycle & Motor Trades Review*, 22 Dec. 1910, p. 1307; ibid., 12 Jan. 1911; *The Cycle Trader & Review*, 19 August 1910, p. 814.

50. *The Cycle & Motor Trades Review*, 16 Sept. 1909, p. 1008.

51. *The Cycle & Motor Trades Review*, 10 March 1910, p. 237; ibid., 19 May 1910, p. 510.

52. *The Cycle & Motor Trader*, 14 Oct. 1910, pp. 159 and 166.

53. *The Cycle Trader & Review*, 31 March 1911.

54. *The Cycle & Motor Trades Review*, 1 Sept. 1910, p. 882.

55. *Bicycling News & Motor Review*, 5 April 1911, p. 17.

Ross D. Petty

15. Peddling the Bicycle and the Development of Mass Marketing

Historian David Hounshell (1980; 1984) credits the U.S. bicycle industry as being transitional from armory production techniques to mass-production techniques epitomized by Henry Ford's production of automobiles. He states:

> [P]roduction of the bicycle allowed many bicycle makers to improve current production technology and to introduce entirely new manufacturing techniques which would later become standard in mass-production metalworking industries. In the United States, these changes led almost inexorably to the introduction and soon the mass production and mass consumption of the American "mother cow"—the automobile (1980, p. 175).

He notes that production of Columbia bicycles in 1896 reached 60,000, but Western Wheel Works outstripped its rival by producing 70,000 bikes in that year alone. Ford would not produce more than 70,000 Model T automobiles until 16 years later (Hounshell 1984, p. 224). Since these were only the top 2 of over 300–500 U.S. bicycle producers, making over 1.2 million bicycles per year (automobiles would not top this figure for 20 years (Tedlow 1990, p. 130) and automobile sales would not exceed peak bicycle production until 1920 (Hodges 1994, p. 41), bicycle marketers clearly had their work cut out for them (Harrison 1969, p. 290; Hounshell, 1984, p. 201).

By 1899, the bicycle "boom" had peaked. The Census reported over 1.1 million bicycles, with an aggregate value of over $33 million produced by over 300 firms. Five years later fewer than 250,000 bicycles were produced, and by 1909 only 160,000 machines were built. Domestic consumption of bicycles (production minus exports) declined from $28 million in 1899 to $5.5 million in 1909 (Norris 1990, p. 79; Harrison 1969, pp. 290, 299).

While Hounshell (1980, p. 175) credits the industry with the development of "slick mass-marketing practices" to create this bicycle "boom," his work does not document the industry's contribution to mass marketing, but only to mass production. Despite Steiner's (1978, p.37) estimates that annual U.S. retail sales of bicycles probably exceeded $60 million in the mid-1890s, and Coon's (1948, p. 83) calculation that between 1890 and 1896, Americans spent over $100 million on bicycles, marketing historians (e.g., Tedlow 1990; Fullerton 1988) with a few exceptions (e.g., Wood 1958; Presbrey 1929) generally ignore the marketing innovations of the bicycle industry.

Similarly, most bicycle historians (e.g., Beeley 1992; McGurn 1987; Ritchie 1975) appear to attribute the large sales of the "boom" to technological innovation such as the invention of the diamond-frame safety bicycle (the modern bicycle), the reinvention and development of the pneumatic tire, and dramatic decreases in bicycle weight and price. The average bicycle weighed 42 lbs. and cost $120 in 1890, but weighed only 22 lbs. and cost $45 in 1895 (Trescott 1976, p. 56). Bicycle historians largely ignore the active marketing efforts of bicycle sellers. Two exceptions are Fitzpatrick (1980) and Smith (1972).

> **Synopsis**
>
> While the bicycle industry has been recognized for its contribution to mass production in the late 1800s, it has not been generally recognized for developing mass marketing techniques to sell the bicycles it produced. The bicycle advanced the practice of advertising by developing competitive advertising content, image advertising in posters, research techniques to determine advertising effectiveness, and support for the new media (magazines). The industry also developed new promotional techniques including sponsoring racing teams and obtaining celebrity endorsements. It perfected the trade show and annual model changes. Most significantly, the bicycle of the late 1800s was marketed using segmentation techniques that have been thought to have been developed more recently.

This paper will document the marketing efforts of the U.S. bicycle industry in the late 1890s in an effort to define the industry's contribution to the development of mass marketing. That is not to say that the bicycle industry wholly created modern mass marketing. The bicycle did benefit from prior efforts to sell other durable products such as sewing machines and farm machinery. These industries had developed the concept of installment sales which the bicycle industry adopted.

Furthermore, the industry was not innovative in establishing new channels of distribution. Rather, until bicycles were requested by the new channels—large department stores and mail order sellers—bicycles were sold through independent agents at uniform prices, regardless of shipping costs (McGurn 1987, p. 69). Smith (1972, p. 10) describes this practice as innovative: "Pope became the founder of marketing techniques that saw their grandest flowering in the sales of automobiles." However, McKenderick, Brewer & Plumb (1982) document that uniform pricing was well established in 18th-century England.

Regardless of whether this uniform pricing idea was new to the U.S., the bicycle was the first expensive, durable luxury item to be mass marketed throughout the country. Bicycle marketers excelled in three areas: advertising, promotion, and segmentation. Each will be examined in turn.

Advertising

Estimates of amounts spent for bicycle advertising range from Bates' incredible estimate of $1 billion in 1897 (1902, p. 241) to Steiner's calculation (based in part on Presbrey's higher estimates of $6–9 million) of $4–6 million per year for the manufacturers and another $1 million for retailers (1978, p. 37). This would result in an advertising to sales ratio of 6–10%.

Presbrey (1929, p.363) notes that in 1897, bicycle advertising accounted for 10% of all magazine advertising spending. He further cites a 1898 tally of over 2,500 advertisers in national magazines finding that 5% were bicycle advertisers. Similarly, Sherman (1900, p. 20) found that individual bicycle advertisements peaked in *Harper's* magazine in 1896, when they also accounted for 5% of all advertising. Thus, this one item, the bicycle, accounted for 5% of magazine advertising placements, but an even higher proportion of magazine income because the size of bicycle advertisements tended to be larger than average.

Advertising commentators also describe the support the bicycle industry gave to the "new media" of the day, magazines in terms of pages rather than placements. Presbrey (1929, p. 410) notes that in the early 1890s, the Pope Manufacturing Company used large format ads, quarter page, and occasional full page ads, in magazines for its Columbia brand bicycles. He adds (p. 412) that 12 pages of bicycle advertisements in a magazine with 60 pages for all other product advertising was common in the mid-1890s. Bates (1902, p. 241) claims that in the days of the bicycle "boom," magazines and high-grade weeklies carried more bicycle business than anything else. He notes that one issue of McClure's magazine contained forty and one quarter pages of advertising devoted to bicycles and bicycle-sundries. Presbrey (1929, p. 410) concludes: "Especially is the development of magazine advertising indebted to the bicycle, for the bicycle gave the magazine a measure of recognition as a medium which encouraged the use of large space there and more frequent insertion by advertisers in general."

This advertiser support helped convert old magazines and create numerous new magazines that were no longer financed primarily by subscribers, but rather by advertisers (Goodrum & Dalrymple 1990, p. 31). This was the beginning of advertising-financed media seeking mass circulation in order to please its mass advertisers.

With bicycle marketers and others spending vast sums on advertising branded products in magazines, the question then arises, was this advertising effective in producing new sales? In the case of bicycles, the dramatic increase in sales through the "boom" of the 1890s would appear to support the effectiveness of bicycle advertising. Coons (1948, pp. 84–85) notes the hysteria of other merchants during this period who proclaimed that their sales were devastated by the bicycle. For example, barbers complained that their customers, rather than getting a shave and going out, would ride their bikes instead: "when a man skips a shave today, we can't sell him two shaves tomorrow."

Presbrey (1929, p. 413) notes the growth of advertising expenditures of a single firm—Monarch Bicycles. In its first year, 1893, Monarch spent a few thousand dollars and sold 1,200 bicycles. The next year, it spent $20,000 and sold 5,000 bicycles. In 1895, $75,000 worth of advertising sold 20,000 bicycles and in 1896, $125,000 was spent to sell 50,000 bikes. Monarch's advertising outlays were modest compared to the market leader. Pope

Fig. 15.1. Advertisements showing two different street addresses for the Pope Manufacturing Company.

Manufacturing spent more than one half million dollars in advertising in 1896 (Anonymous 1897, p. 277).

However, if bicycle advertising was so effective, why did the "boom" end at the turn of the century? Steiner (1978) and Bates (1902) suggest that the newly formed bicycle trust cut advertising, which at least partially caused a decline in sales. However, there is a chicken and egg problem here. The bicycle trust cut advertising because bicycles were in over supply, so the decline in sales probably began before the decrease in advertising expenditures. Steiner (1978) also suggests it was inevitable that the bicycle be replaced by the car, but automobile sales did not overtake bicycle sales until 1913 (Hodges 1994, p. 41). The mystery of why "the market for bicycles simply vanished" (Hounshell 1984, p. 193) cannot be definitively resolved.

There is other evidence of the effectiveness of bicycle advertising besides the correlation between increased advertising expenditures and increased sales. Colonel Albert Pope may have been the first manufacturer to devise a research methodology for monitoring advertising effectiveness:

> I remember we adopted the method of giving a different store number in each advertisement, so that a great many people thought we owned both sides of the street for a mile. For several years, we kept this account and it satisfied us finally that the best and highest priced mediums were the ones for us to stick with (Anonymous 1897, p. 277).

Fig. 15.1 evidences this system by showing two Columbia ads listing different street addresses.

Bicycle advertising's effectiveness also appears related to two marketing innovations—its competitiveness, and imagery. Wood (1958, p. 276) explains why bicycle advertising was uniquely competitive:

> Bicycle advertising was pumping just as hard as the bicycle factories and the bicycle riders themselves. This was a new kind of advertising. It was noticeably different in many ways from other kinds of advertising. Many of the large regular advertisers had the field to themselves. It was Pears and Ivory soap, James Pyle's, Pearline, and Sapolio. Their advertising was not competitive....[E]ach had a virtual monopoly. In contrast, bicycle advertising was strongly competitive. It was not for a low-priced article which cost little to make and was quickly consumed, making for constant repeat purchases. It was for an item of comparatively complex manufacture, expensive, and durable. The advertising was competitive. It was for a completely new product, it was based on new appeals, and offered new enticements.

The competitiveness of bicycle advertising was derived in part from technical claims of mechanical and engineering features which served as basis of comparison between brands for consumers (Presbrey 1929, p. 412). Hotchkiss (1938, p. 211) notes:

> The first great industry to show the effects of national advertising was the bicycle industry. Beginning in the 80s and continuing through the 90s, the magazines, newspapers, and posters heralded each improvement in construction, and gave the arguments of rival manufacturers. On the surface it was a competitive struggle for the choice of the buyer; in reality it was a continuous education regarding the benefits of this new method of locomotion.

While so called "reason why" advertising was commonly used in 18th-century England (McKenderick, Brewer & Plumb 1982, ch. 4), bicycle advertising advanced this practice through the use of direct, albeit implied references to competitors. Bates

(1902, p. 240) notes that advertising for Victor brand bicycles often implicitly alluded to arch-rival, Columbia. In one ad, referring to a Victor innovation adapted by Columbia, the headline read: "Men originate; Apes imitate." A second ad, referring to Columbia's new racing model with blue wheel rims, stated: "We have no rims of cerulean hue, but we continue to get there—with both feet too."

Stanley Ulanoff (1975) notes that article, comparative advertising used to be commonplace, but until the 1960s was virtually unused in the U.S. and condemned by industry self-regulation. Perhaps this "taboo" on comparative advertising is related to earlier criticism of bicycle advertising for being too competitive. Bates (1896, p. 431) argued:

> I believe that it is a mistake to make attacks on other bicycles. I believe that attacks should not be answered—at least not directly—unless they are of such a character that they can be answered through a court of law....Let the other fellow talk about you all he pleases; let him spend all the money he wants to in advertising you. The more he talks, the more people will know about your product. He is helping people to the knowledge that you are on earth and doing business; he is telling people very plainly that you amount to enough to worry him considerably.

At the same time that bicycle advertising was often competitive, other bicycle advertising emphasized image:

> In physical development of the advertisement the bicycle manufacturer took the lead. In art and typography and copy he made contributions which gave advertising as a whole a new attractiveness. The first American advertisers to use the art poster and the first to engage artists like Maxfield Parrish to do advertising work, the bicycle manufacturers worked an improvement in the art of advertising which by itself not only made their publicity more resultful but gave other manufacturers a new view of the dignity of advertising quite different from the impression created by the long era of patent-medicine leadership (Presbrey 1929, p. 412).

In fact, the bicycle industry was recognized as a leader in the use of artistic posters in advertising (Margolin, Brichta & Brichta 1979, p. 43; Margolin 1975, p. 43). Bicycle advertising posters were

Fig. 15.2 and Fig. 15.3. Posters for Sirius and Déesse bicycles, equating the bicycle with the image of flight.

produced throughout the world by the leading poster artists of the day (Rennert 1973; Weill 1985).

One example of the promotion of poster art to sell bicycles was the 1895 poster art contest held by the Pope Manufacturing Company. Prizes included a Columbia bicycle valued at $100 for 4th place, and the same bicycle with cash for the top 3 artists. The first place prize of $250 plus a bicycle was awarded to renowned poster artist, Maxfield Parrish. Over 600 posters were submitted to this contest by over 400 artists. Many of these submissions were placed on exhibition in Boston, where more than 15,000 people reportedly viewed the show. The exhibition then was displayed in other major cities throughout the country (Pope Manufacturing Co. 1896).

In contrast to technical claims about the quality of construction or components in "competitive advertising," several pictorial themes and artistic styles emerge in bicycle poster advertising. First, the bicycle is often equated with the image of flight and light weight as the posters for Sirius and Deesse bicycles (Figs. 15.2 and 15.3) illustrate. Birds or fast running dogs are often shown in bicycle poster advertising as symbols of both of these images (Sanders 1991, p. 131; Rennert 1973, p. 75). Barnicoat (1972, p. 163) suggests that such posters are early examples of the artistic style now called "surrealism," which was popular in the 1920s. Both of these posters also show a scantily-clad woman or perhaps goddesses in an apparent effort to relate the bicycle to ancient classical Greece as well as attract the notice of male potential purchasers. As Nick Sanders (1991, p. 130) states:

> It would seem that [bicycle poster artists] who depict scantily clad and sometimes nude women, were not only contrasting the softness of female beauty to the hardness of the machine itself, but had realised that revealing more of the woman's body commanded a greater attraction to their posters and thus a greater visibility to the product or event they were advertising. The effectiveness of this approach foreshadowed the continued exploitation of women in advertising, resulting in today's maxim "sex sells."

In contrast, the poster for American Crescent (Fig. 15.4) shows an attractive woman, but more fully

Fig. 15.4. Poster for American Crescent, in Art-Nouveau style.

Fig. 15.5. Realistic poster illustration for Humber.

dressed in an Art Nouveau style. The image suggests effortless speed even though the woman is merely holding, not riding, the bicycle. The last example, a poster for Humber bicycles (Fig. 15.5), later acquired by Raleigh, shows a realistic scene with a "new woman" of the 1890s leading a ride and beckoning to her companions, at least one of which is male, to catch her. Again the ride seems to be effortless on her part, no doubt because of the quality of her bicycle.

Bicycle posters also portrayed the relationship between the bicycle and preceding modes of transportation. Gallo (1974, p. 94) suggests that the poster for Peugeot bicycles (Fig 15.6) shows the bicycle to be "as noble a steed as the horse." However, the bicycle in the picture appears in a subservient position to the horse, and is being held by a lower ranking soldier who is handing a message to his superior officer mounted on the horse. The poster may be appealing to members of the middle class who aspire to upper class status, or may be showing how the practical bicycle has largely replaced the horse, which is now only used occasionally as a symbolic means of transportation.

A poster for Terrot cycles and automobiles suggests that the train too is outmoded as a means of transportation. A taunting "new woman" expends little effort to keep ahead of a furiously steaming locomotive. Nick Sanders (1991, p. 129) also notes that the woman controls the bicycle with one hand in the center of the handlebars, showing great ease of handling. Similarly, Fig. 15.5 shows that the Humber bicycle can be easily controlled with one hand.

The images presented by these and numerous other bicycle poster advertisements may still be deemed "competitive" in the sense that they all suggest no effort is needed to "fly" on the advertised brand of bicycle. Some posters explicitly show other bicycles or horses and trains to be outmoded. However, the image advertisement presents its selling message to the emotions of the viewer, in contrast to the written message to technical superiority presented to the reader's analytical intellect.

The contrast between these two types of bicycle advertising, not only in the industry, but often the same company, may have contributed to the famous advertising debate in the early 20th century. Proponents such as Albert Lasker and Claude Hopkins argued that advertising should be "salesmanship in print," and therefore should adopt "reason why" copy. Others, such as Clowery Chapman, advocated that advertising was "persuasive art; mental images, not rational arguments, cause the prospective customer to buy" (Lears 1988, p. 258).

According to Lears (1988, p. 260), by 1925 "reason why" and atmosphere advertising converged. Both could co-exist in the same advertisement or in different campaigns for the same product. The example he provides is 1925 corset advertising, but bicycle advertising suggests that these two types of advertising coexisted even before the debate that distinguished them.

Promotion

In addition to advertising, the bicycle industry used other methods of promoting its wares. Some activities of the bicycle industry promoted the activity of cycling generally. Albert Pope, founder of the American bicycle industry and the Columbia brand of bicycles, promoted cycling in many ways. He helped to start both local cycling clubs as well as the League of American Wheelmen, the first and still continuing national organization of bicyclists. He fought legal restrictions of bicycling and lobbied extensively for improved roads. He also financed bicycle magazines and books (McGurn 1987).

The bicycle industry also developed techniques for promoting individual brands. The advertising technique of claiming members of royalty using the advertised product dates back at least to 18th-century

Fig. 15.6. Illustration from Peugeot poster, about 1890.

England (McKenderick, Brewer & Plumb 1982). Bicycle manufacturers adopted this practice, particularly in Europe where members of royalty became interested in the fad of the wheel. Bicycle marketers also improved this practice by not merely referring to royal users in advertising, but by obtaining actual advertising endorsements in the form of specific quotations of royalty. Turner (1965, p. 104) describes endorsements of two princes, including one whose endorsement was in French, in an advertisement that was otherwise in English.

Bicycle companies also hired famous cycling athletes to promote their products. Albert Pope hired Will Pitman, noted velocipedist (a velocipede was the earliest form of pedal-operated bicycle) to demonstrate his 1878 Columbia high-wheel bicycle. Interest was so strong that Pitman was arrested in New York City for causing a disturbance. Pope enjoyed free publicity as the New York newspapers debated the fairness of this arrest (McGurn 1987, p. 68). Pitman went on that year to win the first 1-mile bicycle race ever run in this country (Smith 1972, p. 144). Needless to say, he was riding a Columbia.

Similarly, cycling champion A. A. Zimmerman was sponsored in 1892 by Raleigh bicycles when he became world champion. Raleigh riders won no less than 2,300 racing prizes, as the advertisement in Fig.

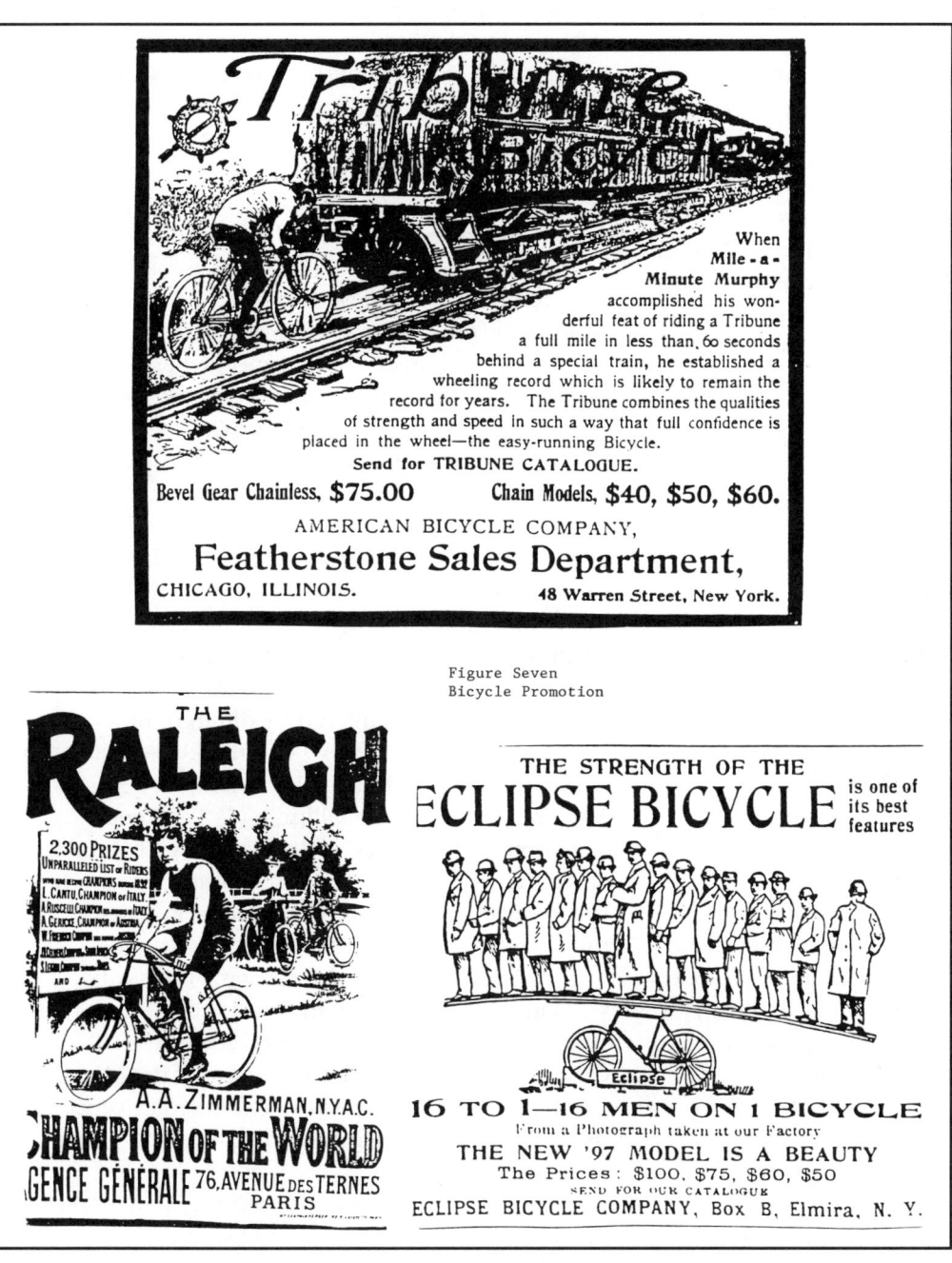

Fig. 15.7. Bicycle promotion.

15.7 shows (Bowden 1975, pp. 18–19). In 1899, C. W. Murphy, noted bicycle racer, became "Mile-a-Minute" Murphy as he became the first person to travel 60 miles per hour under his own power while "drafting" behind a locomotive (Smith 1972, p. 138). Tribune Bicycles, of course, featured this feat in their advertising (Fig. 15.7). Lastly, the simple stunt of placing 16 men on a bicycle to show its strength also is illustrated in Fig. 15.7.

The practice of linking bicycle advertising to the performance of bicycle racers was commonplace. Remington Arms advertised that the winner of the Irvington-Milburn Road Race had used one of its "scientifically constructed" bicycles. Waltham Manufacturing proclaimed that famous racer, Walter Sanger, rode one of their bicycles, neglecting to inform anyone that he was paid by Waltham to do so (Smith 1972, p. 34). Jim Fitzpatrick (1980, p. 47) quotes from the *Austral Wheel* to note:

> ...when a champion pulls down a record the credit of his victory is claimed by the builder of his machine, the maker of his tyres, the patentee of his saddle, and the manufacturer of his chain. Then the oil with which the chain was lubricated, the toe-clips which kept his feet on the pedals, the shoes he wore, the training oil used by him, the soap he patronized, and the pills which set his liver right, all have a share in the victory. The man himself is little else but a pedalling advertisement.

Another interesting aspect of bicycle promotion was the evolution of the annual trade show and annual model changes. The first cycle trade show in the U.S. was held in 1883 in Springfield, Massachusetts (Smith 1972, p. 31). This was preceded by the Stanley Show in England, established in 1878 (Beeley 1992, p. 79). In the U.S., annual shows began in 1891, and by 1894 big exhibitions were held in both Chicago and New York. These shows peaked in 1896 with over 225 exhibitors in Chicago and over 400 in New York. Many famous people and lots of fanfare accompanied them (Smith 1972).

Although Smith (1972, p. 19) claims that planned obsolescence originated with the bicycle industry, in fact McCormick developed annual model changes for expensive, durable products in the 1840s (Hounshell 1984, p. 159). Furthermore, periodic "fashion" changes for less expensive products dates back at least to the 1700s (McKenderick, Brewer & Plumb 1982).

A key difference appears to be that McCormick's product changes were primarily motivated by experimentation and competitive pressures. While this was likely true for the early years of the bicycle industry, once the safety bicycle was perfected and pneumatic tires adopted, annual model changes appeared to contain little innovation, despite promotional claims to the contrary. According to Smith (1972, p. 19), both the *New York Times* and the *New York Journal* accused the industry of making minor stylistic changes that served no useful purpose other than increasing sales.

Thus, while McCormick originated annual model changes, the bicycle industry may claim the dubious distinction of originating the specious or stylistic model change. Hounshell (1984, p. 186) asserts that Henry Ford's gross over-production made stylistic annual changes a necessary marketing strategy, but the bicycle industry clearly first adopted the annual model change as a marketing strategy.

Market Segmentation

Tedlow (1990) asserts that there are three phases in American marketing history. The first "fragmentation" characterized the early 1800s when markets were local and low volume because transportation costs were high. After the 1880s, some industries passed into phase two, market unification where dominant firms unified the national market under one or more existing brands. Clearly the U.S. bicycle industry led by a handful of large firms fits this characterization.

According to Tedlow (1990), phase three, segmentation, did not begin for automobiles until the 1920s, and for most other products, such as soft drinks, not until after WWII. This phase still enjoys high volume marketing at a national level, but employs demographic and psychographic segmentation to create divisions in the national market that can be targeted by different firms.

Other authors believe that market segmentation began before this century. For example, McKenderick, Brewer & Plumb (1982) argue segmentation occurred in 18th-century England. Hollander & Germain (1992) present examples of youth-based segmentation occurring in the 1880s in this country.

This paper also disagrees with Tedlow by showing that the bicycle industry followed segmentation strategies beginning in the 1870s. Contrary to Henry Ford's marketing of the Model T as a universal car, bicycles were marketed to various discrete segments defined by usage, price, gender, and image/lifestyle.

Functional and youth-based segmentation in the bicycle industry first became obvious in the days of the high wheeler. Generally speaking, only young fairly athletic men would pedal perched precariously upon a penny farthing. The industry developed all sorts of tricycles for women and risk-averse men. Even with the dominance of the safety bicycle by 1890, different models were marketed to different segments such as racers, tourists, and women.

Furthermore, during the bicycle boom, specialized bicycles were made for even narrower functional segments. Bicycle advertising and catalogs also touted delivery bicycles for carrying and delivering items such as mail, and even a Yukon bicycle for use in the cold wilderness of Alaska during the gold rush.

Price segmentation was commonplace. Albert Pope, founder of the company that produced and sold Columbia bicycles, did not want to tarnish Columbia's premium image with lower priced bicycles. He secretly acquired the Hartford Bicycle Company in 1890, nominally run by his cousin George Pope, to produce mid-priced bicycles. The connection between Columbia and Hartford bicycles was kept quiet until 1895 when the two became officially affiliated (Hounshell 1984, pp. 202–203).

Tedlow (1990, p. 6) states that "value pricing" is one example of modern segmentation. In the 1890s, one value-priced marketer was the Chester Bicycle Company of Indiana. Chester claimed it could sell $100 bicycles for $85 because it did not sponsor a racing team (which it asserted amounted to $10 of the price of other bicycles), did not pay high salaries or commissions, and did not advertise widely. This "low overhead" strategy appears consistent with "value pricing" strategies of today.

As noted above, segmentation based on gender became commonplace in the days of the high-wheel bicycle. It continued with safety bicycles. By 1896, every third bicycle that was ordered was an open frame women's model (Beeley 1992, p 74). This women's model still exists today. Yet gender segmentation started in the 1870s, when a woman's velocipede was marketed which featured skirt protectors over the spoke wheels and both pedals on one side for side-saddle riding (Ritchie 1972, p. 150).

Gender segmentation for bicycles also is apparent in poster advertising. The Humber ad (Fig. 15.5) and the Terrot ad clearly are attempting not to appeal to women generally, but rather to the "new women" who were asserting their right to equality, to travel freely, and to vote. Many other ads contain a similar appeal (Rennert 1973, pp. 22, 30, 41, 45, 47, 51, 64, 70). Other ads directed at women show closer companionship with men on bicycles (Rennert 1973, pp. 32, 61, 73, 81; Gallo 1974, p. 94) or even a family relationship (Rennert 1973, p. 18). Edward Penfield's poster for Stearns bicycles shows a woman coasting on a bicycle with the headline: "Ride a Stearns and be content" (Margolin 1975, p. 43). It is not clear whether this should encourage the new woman, or keep her in her place.

Other psychographic or lifestyle appeals concern bicycling as an activity attractive to beautiful women (Fig. 15.4; Rennert 1973, p. 55), and an activity of the well-to-do (Rennert 1973, pp. 23, 31, 36) or as an equalizer within society as the Peugeot ad in Fig. 15.6 suggests. Indeed in 18th-century England, many products were sold to the middle class by appealing to their desire to emulate the rich (McKenderick, Brewer & Plumb 1982). In contrast, bicycle advertising extended this technique by showing middle-class cyclists in advertising. Instead of appealing to the desire to be rich, bicycle marketers appeared to believe that members of the middle class would recognize and accept the value of their own class status. Of course such advertising also appeals to those aspiring to join the middle class.

Conclusion

The bicycle industry in the 19th century was characterized by mass production, production as a second line by other manufacturing firms, and by small scale assembly and production of components. Marketing strategies developed to stimulate demand for all of these producers. National advertising in magazines promoted competitive qualities and images of major brands. Racing teams and celebrity endorsements further stimulated sales. Segmentation was practiced, both temporarily with annual stylistic model changes for those who "must have the latest wheel," and demographically by appealing to people with different bicycling interests, different sensitivities to price, and different self-images to which marketers appealed. Many of the so-called "modern" marketing techniques were used to sell bicycles 100 years ago.

References

Anonymous, "Advertising 'The Columbia'," *Profitable Advertising*, 7(8) (1897): 275–278.

Barnicoat, John. *A Concise History of the Poster*. New York: Harry N. Abrams, Inc., 1972.

Bates, Charles Austin. "The Rise and Fall of Bicycle Advertising" in *The Art and Literature of Business*. New York: Bates Advertising Company, 1902, vol. 4, pp. 239–43.

———. *Good Advertising*. New York: Holmes Publishing Co., 1896.

Beeley, Serena. *A History of Bicycles: From Hobby Horse to Mountain Bike*. Secacus NJ: Wellfleet Books, 1992.

Bowden, Gregory Houston. *The Story of Raleigh Cycle*. London: W. H. Allen, 1975.

Coons, Hannibal, "Bicycles Built for All," *Holiday* 4(1) (1948): 83.

Fitzpatrick, Jim. *The Bicycle and the Bush: Man and Machine in Rural Australia*. Melbourne: Oxford University Press. 1980.

Fullerton, Ronald A., "How Modern is Modern Marketing? Marketing Evolution and the Myth of the 'Production Era'," *Journal of Marketing* 52 (January), 108–25.

Gallo, Max. *The Poster in History*. New York: American Heritage Publishing Co., Inc., 1974.

Goodrum, Charles and Helen Dalrymple. *Advertising in America: The First Two Hundred Years*. New York: Harry N. Adams, Inc., 1990.

Harrison, A. E., "The Competitiveness of the British Cycle Industry, 1890–1914," *Economic History Review*, 2nd ser., 22 (1969): 235–303.

Hodges, Karl. (1994), "Did the Emergence of the Automobile End the Bicycle Boom?" in *Cycle History: Proceedings of the 4th International Cycle History Conference*. San Francisco: Bicycle Books, 39–42.

Hollander, Stanley C. and Richard Germain. *Was There A Pepsi Generation Before Pepsi Discovered It?* Lincolnwood, Il: NTC Business Books, 1992.

Hotchkiss, George Burton. *Milestones of Marketing*. New York: The Macmillan Co., 1938.

Hounshell, David A. *From the American System to Mass Production*, 1800–1932. Baltimore, Md: Johns Hopkins University Press, 1984.

———. "The Bicycle and Technology in Late Nineteenth Century America," in *Transport Technology and Social Change*, Per Sörbom, ed. Stockholm: Tekniska Museet, (1980): 173–185.

Lears, T. J. Jackson. (1988), "The Rise of American Advertising," in *American Media: The Wilson Quarterly Reader*. Washington, D.C.: The Wilson Center Press (1988): 255–270.

Margolin, Victor, Ira Brichta, and Vivian Brichta. *The Promise and the Product: 200 Years of American Advertising Posters*. New York: Macmillan Publishing Co., Inc., 1979.

Margolin, Victor. *American Poster Renaissance*. New York: Watson-Guptill Publications, 1975.

McGurn, James. *On Your Bicycle*. New York: Facts on File, Inc., 1987.

McKenderick, Neil, John Brewer and J. H. Plumb. *The Birth of a Consumer Society: The Commercialization of Eighteenth-Century England*. London: Europa Publications Ltd., 1982.

Norris, James D. *Advertising and Transformation of American Society: 1865–1920*. New York: Greenwood Press, 1990.

Pope Manufacturing Co. *Exhibition of Columbia Bicycle Art Poster Designs*. Boston: Pope Manufacturing Co., 1896.

Presbrey, Frank S. *The History and Development of Advertising*. New York: Doubleday & Co., Inc., 1929.

Rennert, Jack. *100 Years of Bicycle Posters*. New York: Harper & Row, Publishers, Inc., 1973.

Ritchie, Andrew. *King of the Road*. London: Wildwood House, 1975.

Sanders, Nick. *Bicycle: The Image & the Dream*. Great Britain: Red Bus Publishing, 1991.

Sherman, Sidney A. "Advertising in the United States," *Quarterly Publications of the American Statistical Association* 7 (December) (1900): 120–163.

Smith, Robert A. *A Social History of the Bicycle*. New York: American Heritage Press, 1972.

Steiner, Robert L. "Learning from the Past—Brand Advertising and the Great Bicycle Craze of the 1890s," in *Proceedings of the Annual Conference of the American Academy of Advertising: Advances in Advertising Research and Marketing* (1978): 35–40.

Tedlow, Richard S. *New and Improved: The Story of Mass Marketing in America*. New York: Basic Books, 1990.

Trescott, Martha Moore, "The Bicycle, A Technical Precursor of the Automobile," *Business and Economic History* 5 (2nd series) (1976): 51–75.

Turner, E.S. *The Shocking History of Advertising*. Harmondsworth, England: Penguin Books, Ltd., 1965.

Ulanoff, Stanley M.. *Comparison Advertising: An Historical Retrospective*. Marketing Science Institute Working Paper, (February, 1975).

Weill, Alain. *The Poster: A Worldwide Survey and History*. Boston: G. K. Hall & Co.

Wood, James Playsted. *The Story of Advertising*. New York: The Ronald Press Company, 1958.

Nadine Besse and André Vant

16. A New View of Late 19th-Century Cycle Publicity Posters

Bicycle publicity posters were produced in great numbers at the end of the 19th century, mainly between 1892 and 1896. Some were signed by recognised artists and are valued as works of art. Though mass-produced, they have a place in the history of art, and are not devoid of social significance. Of course, they are also prized for the cycle information they carry.

Posters as Industrial Archives

Industrial archives are either difficult to consult or nonexistent. Sales catalogues and publicity posters are our main source of information. There is easy access in France to the collections of the Cabinet des Recueils at the Bibliothèque Nationale, the Musée de la Publicité, the Musée des Arts Decoratifs, and especially the Bibliothèque Forney. The Musée d'Art et d'Industrie of Saint-Etienne also has an important collection of 150 posters and 50 doubles.[1]

The recent computer filing of this collection, along with the other collections in the museum, drew my attention to the specific interest of these posters as cycle information. (I was helped by Samya Imboul in classing them according to themes.)[2]

Posters as Information

Publicity posters are valuable as industrial archives, giving trade names, graphic peculiarities, trademarks, addresses of head offices, factories, and wholesale depots, sometimes even giving pictures of the plants themselves. Changes in the names of the printers are interesting too. Indications on industrial registration can also be used as dating elements.

Factory Historical Documents: Trademarks and Their Different Styles

Solar Symbols: Some firms had a fad for certain written or graphic themes, but all used yellow strategically, which is apparently recognisable as a typical cycling colour. Why this colour? No one knows. Perhaps the wheel and its spokes (les rayons = the rays) evoke the sun. Yellow was often the background colour of trademarks. Some firms added the initials of the founders to make their trademarks more distinctive.

Withworth showed a black hand on a yellow background; Fernand Clément & Cie, a yellow clover leaf on the background of a cycle wheel; Société des Vélocipèdes Clément & Cie: a cockerel on a wheel; Strock & Cie: an "S" in the middle of a wheel.

Other solar or zodiacal symbols appeared in trademarks: the moon, stars, lions. They were often repeated in posters, the moon with Venus, goddess of

Fig. 16.1. Rudge. La Déesse poster.

love (Rudge, "La déesse"; Clément & Cie; and others). A moonbeam pointing to the Milky Way showed the cyclist's ideal destiny. The Rouxel & Dubois poster was characteristic.

Other symbols: The terrestrial globe expressed the worldwide commercial ambitions of the maker. The cockerel, a symbol of vigilance during the French revolution, with the usual nationalist wordplay on the Latin origin, vindicated the French origin of the bicycle. The horse as emblem is halfway between these two, but is somewhat contradictory.

Adopted Names

Some trade names play on their symbolic value: Kosmos suggests supra-terrestrial elevation and performance; Gladiator—strength, endurance, though the trademark was a horseman on a terrestial globe; Libérator—lightness and freedom (with wings); Phébus—solar-cycle analogy (in classical legends, Phébus was the equivalent of Apollo); Déesse—the Goddess—being of course the bicycle itself. The trademark included a quarter moon and stars with obvious biblical implications; Diamant—beauty, strength, luxury, durability, and sparkle; La Française and La Métropole—the figure of a woman bedecked in red, white and blue to underline the French character of the make.

Other makers preferred to give their bicycles names from the natural world suggesting performance: Papillon—the lightness of flight, nimbleness; Ouragan—the irresitible strength of nature; La Guèpe—as light as a butterfly but with more purpose and sureness of aim; Falcon—which soars and never misses its prey.

Publicity Tactics

Trade names and trademarks are not the only distinctive traits of publicity posters. Many poster designers followed favourite themes, sometimes seduction (Withworth), or gracefulness or universality (Rouxel & Dubois). This depended on the goods proposed and on the supposed personality of the buyers (the depiction of cyclists gives useful hints on dress at the time).

Underlining national or local origin was part of the effort to boost the goods offered for sale. Some brands, for instance, La Française or La Métropole, stated this quite openly. Others added some graphic element to their trade name to invite local trade, for instance Décauville and its profile of a robust smith, or the bicycle amusingly pictured as fresh-grown farm produce carted off to market by a stereotyped buxom country girl.

Even printed commercial information about the designers enhanced the reputation and importance of firms. Posters were also issued by trade syndicates to promote the trade as a whole.

Bicycle Accessories

Following the main builders, the makers of bicycle accessories participated in the same way. Sometimes, it was the other way round: highly acclaimed

Fig. 16.2. Rouxel & Dubois poster.

accessories contributed to the reputation of the bicycle itself.

Tyres: Tyres played an essential part in the fame of bicycles from 1890 onwards, and there were posters that promoted tyres. For instance, one showed a burly policeman wondering what had caused a crowd around a bicycle with Kosmos tyres. The idea that air, that embodiment of freedom, was trapped in a tyre, seemed the acme of modern progress. "G & J" tyres, described as the "kings of clincher tyres," were depicted drawing the admiration of pretty girls. Stella tyres were shown giving wings to a legless cripple.

Other Accessories: La Fucosine—"no more punctured tyres with Focusine," a patent self-obturer. L'Electroléine, with its impressive pseudo-scientific name, was a new grade of lamp petrol lengthily described as a "scientific discovery." Even under its public pleasure-park approach, this poster appealed to the general interest in practical science fostered by 19th-century popularising in science magazines. The poster for Christy bicycle saddles is characteristic. On a yellow background, a girl proffered in her right hand an "anatomic and hygienic" saddle with the drawing of a feminine pelvis correctly seated, and in her left hand the drawing of the "old harmful unhygienic and distorting" system, with reference to old-fashioned feminine stays, since discarded by women.

Status Symbols: There was frequent reference to the horse, sometimes as a thing of the past. The motto was then, "leave the horse of flesh and blood to the past, use the modern steel horse." But the image of the horse as a strong status symbol was used more often to suggest elegance, social rank, and distinction. The new cycling vocabulary owed a lot to the equine world: saddle, manège, "velodrome" from "hippodrome," and others. However, reference to the horse could be used both ways, and there was matter for a study of changes in its meaning and usage as the years passed by.

After the stir caused by the Paris-Brest-Paris race of 1891, victories in racing events promoted bicycle sales. In spite of the high social standing of the army at the time, the use of the bicycle for military purposes was far less effective as a publicity theme: the greater attraction was enjoyment over utility. In the last decade of the century, the bicycle was essentially an instrument of pleasure.

In posters, generally speaking, the bicycle was not pictured in detail, and one would have had difficulty seeing the difference between one make and another. What counted and attracted the eye was the graphic makeup and decor around the bicycle, which was being promoted as a somewhat abstract and glorified silhouette. In these posters, style and graphic treatment were expected to stimulate the buyer more than technical information.

Specific Graphic Themes

Nevertheless, though the general style of these posters, with their large chronolithographic format, belongs to the society and tastes of the time, they do express themes specific to the cycling world. The intermingling of these two elements contributes to their quality.

Fig. 16.3. Cycles Papillon poster.

Major Cycle Themes

The theme of airborne flight, with its implication of lightness and speed, was mentioned by Philippe Gaboriau at the 2nd Conference on Cycle History at Saint-Etienne in 1991, in his study of Maurice Leblanc's novel, *Nous Avons des Ailes*. Today's illustrations show the same notion depicted by wings, flowing hair, and draperies.

The combined man-machine graphic theme needs full treatment, with due attention to cycling literature. Baudry de Saunier examined "the spanner in one hand and the scalpel in the other" idea in the chapters he devoted to the physiological analysis of the cyclist, embodiment of a new "half-flesh/half-steel" race of men where there was no separation between man and machine.[3] Poster designers deliberately pictured the new revolutionary hybrid creature.

The equine theme was often linked with that of elegance and attractiveness. The more general themes of pleasure, happiness, and the carefree love of life were often specifically related to the practise of cycling. Keizo Kobayashi did say, in his book on cycle history, 1816–70, that cycling had made him discover the pleasure of life.

The theme of the discovery of the French countryside by means of the bicycle, treated in the cycle-touring literature and magazines of the time, subtly and discreetly pervaded the graphics of posters, especially after 1902.

Unusual Publicity Themes Treated Originally

Attractiveness and Longing

A well-used theme explored aspects of longing centred on the bicycle, often combined with horse and horseman. The man/bicycle/Sagittarius theme was strongly modelled on its attractive, elegant equine counterpart, and inspired scenes of amorous flight and abduction. The allusion to the story of the

Left: Fig. 16.4. New Howe Co. Ltd. poster.

Below: Fig. 16.5 Liberator poster.

Sabine women is evident, and the swish of rubber tyres echoed the thud of hooves.

Women

Women were pictured, with a touch of erotic suggestiveness, as the goddesses of this revolutionary conquest of liberty, having had access to greater freedom and pleasure thanks to the bicycle. They were shown as mother-goddesses bedecked with an extraordinary mixture of all sorts of ancient Greek, Roman, Celtic, or Northern mythological attributes, apparently to fix the bicycle theme in the historical heritage of humanity. As warrior goddesses, weapons in hands and brandishing the flag of modern progress, they were like Mariannes on the barricades.

More particularly, a lady was shown astride a bicycle to show its compliance, riding ease, comfort, and safety, or she held it up to the sky like a heavenly offering. She was often more than a mere way of enhancing the bicycle—she could be its personification, its imaginary incarnation. The Dayton poster, on the theme of St. Anthony's temptation somewhat irreverently treated, passed easily in a period of relaxed social censorship.

In a scene of celestial sublimation, a goddess, carried skyward in her flowing robes, crowned a levitating cycling champion with glory. The cyclist himself was never winged, the bicycle only rarely. Its stark geometry was set off by the comely shape of the woman carrying it away up to the heavens in a flurry of windblown robes (Strock). The idea was that woman was the muse of the new art of cycling.

Graphism and Message

Cycle posters, like any others, embodied all the artistic achievements of past and present. The relation between the rigourously modern lines of the bicycle and the decor in which it was set, was significant in art history then and now.

There was an analogic transposition of the notions of modernity and lightness through the depiction of woman and her attributes, and the graphic, geometric, and abstract expression of aerial

Fig. 16.6. Delizy & Poiret poster.

lightness. But this type of expression was too modern to be understood by the usual public. So, to carry its message, posters relied on the social code of the day, expressed smilingly or lyrically, with a fillip of what was considered "good French wit."

The period characteristics of these posters appear strong when you compare them to the posters of the 1920s. The latter rediscover the notion of speed, expressed in a different way with new techniques, showing the modernisation of industry and society during the 1914–18 war effort, thus renewing the graphic rendering of the bicycle.

Notes

1. Bibliographical indications: The exhibition organised from 31 May to 23 September 1979 at the Musée de l'Affiche et de la Publicité, in Paris, showed the public the diversity, breadth, and thematic richness of cycle poster production. The introduction to the catalogue, by Geneviève Gaetan-Picon, dwelt on all these themes, but also encouraged readers to study further.

   Alfred Lemercier, published by Charles Lorilleux & Cie, both characteristic late 19th-century lithographers, introduced newer and more economical techniques for the reproduction of chromolithographic posters. In Lemercier's words, "Chromolithography is forging ahead apace. Steam printing presses are being built in every country. Never has this wonderful technique given a living to so many artists and workmen. The artistic poster, until now unknown, is carrying the day. Cheret, that great artist, produces surprising effects with the simplest of means. We can soberly say that many of these posters are masterpieces of art worthy of museum status. Other artists have adopted this medium, and modern machinery has allowed the most living talents to adorn our walls, instead of the childish posters of yesteryears."

Further Reading

Bayard, Emile. *L'Illustration et les Illustrateurs*. Paris: Editions Delagrave, 1897.

Lemercier, Alfred. *La Lithographie Française de 1796 à 1896*. Paris: Charles Lorilleux & Cie, 1899.

Barnicoat, John. *Histoire concise de l'affiche*. Paris: Hachette, 1972.

Arwas, Victor. *Affiches et gravures de la Belle Epoque*. Paris: Flammarion, 1978.

Musée de l'Affiche, Paris. Catalogue de l'exposition, *La Petite Reine: Le Vélo en Affiches à la fin du 19ème siècle*. 1979.

Gallo, Max. *The Poster in History*. New York: American Heritage, 1972.

Freeman, Larry. *Victorian Poster, American Life*. Watkins, 1969.

Metzl, Ervine. *The Poster, its History and its Art*. New York: Watson-Guptill, 1967.

Minguet, Philippe. *L'Affiche en Wallonie*, exposition catalogue. Liège, 1980.

Weill, Alain. *L'Affiche dans le monde*. Paris: Somogy, 1984.

Hillier, Bevis. *L'histoire de l'affiche*. Paris: Fayard, 1970.

Osterwalder, Marcus. *Dictionnaire des illustrateurs (caricaturistes et affichistes) 1800–1914*. Ides Callendes.

Jullian, Philippe. *Les symbolistes*. Ides Callendes.

2. Note on the filing of cycle posters at the Musée d'Art et d'Industrie de Saint-Etienne.

A filing slip is established for each poster with the following designations: filing and study number; trademark of announcing firm; date or estimated date; main titles; other mentions; names of printer, editor, draughtsman; library wetstamp (when it exists); fiscal stamps; dimensions (height and breadth); general description (including key words for computer filing); state of item (need for restoration, framing, and so on); origin of item; how and when acquired; photos (amateur and professional); expositions; publications; insurance value.

A pre-restoration photo is taken and added to the file. A professional photo is taken after restoration. The photo can be filed in the databank for eventual publication.

3. Baudry de Saunier, L. *Ma Petite Bicyclette, sa pratique*. Paris: Flammarion, 1925.

Volker Briese

17. From Cycling Lanes to Compulsory Bike Path: Bicycle Path Construction in Germany, 1897–1940

In 1990, Burkhard Horn wrote the thesis, "Vom Niedergang eines Massenverkehrsmittels—zur Geschichte der Städtischen Radverkehrsplanung"[1] at the University of Kassel. In this work he analyses the bicycle problem, among other issues. His work is based mostly on the interpretation of specialist magazines for town and transport planning, as well as on scientific literature on transport. Literature on the general and technical history of the bicycle and cycle sport is found in bike-sport magazines, and biographical materials and archives. While scientific literature on transport (which hardly ever considers organisations and institutions connected with the bicycle scene) sometimes slightly affects the social and political sphere of transport technology, literature on cycling as a sport hardly ever influences transport technology and planning.

Radmarkt as Source

The magazine *Radmarkt*,[2] which I have chosen as my main source, takes a position in the middle. Since the first issue in 1886, *Radmarkt* has been published regularly, at the peak of the bicycle market even weekly, featuring up to 200 pages. No other German magazine in this field gives such continuous up-to-date information on the trade and industry, technical aspects, and social framework of the bicycle scene. We can deduct from *Radmarkt*'s work that the subjects it has dealt with have had an important place in social debate. The editorial section of the magazine, originally conceived for commercial advertisements, includes very committed articles, though politically restrained. It often took positions in favour of specific interests, though, specially favouring either the official German professional body of the bicycle trader's union, or the bicycle industry. However, it kept a visible distance from bicycle sport associations, which produced their own publications, always friendly towards bicycle traders and manufacturers. Nevertheless, *Radmarkt* reported on these associations, and they were able to publicise their position via the magazine.

Radmarkt has generally distanced itself from politics, except for the period under the NS Regime, when it followed the general propaganda guidelines of the time. In the controversy between bicycle and motor vehicle users, *Radmarkt* has generally taken a neutral position. This is apparent from its adoption shortly after the turn of the century of the name *Radmarkt und das Motorfahrzeug*.[3] Its publishing company, Gundlach Biclefeld, thereby acknowledged the interest the bicycle trade and industry sector had in the motor vehicle industry. This move was a good example of the thinking at the time. Most bicycle associations were not against motor vehicles; this can be seen by the extension of other association names in the 1920s (e.g., "Arbeiter-Rad- und Kraftfahrerbund 'Solidarität'"[4] or "Deutscher Rad- und Motorfahrer-Verband 'Concordia'"[5]). *Radmarkt* therefore gives good insight into the problem of bicycle paths at the time. Often articles were published by the magazine verbatim, declarations by organisations and unions, leaving statements of primary sources intact.

Thesis

It is often stated in today's scientific literature on transport that cyclists in Germany were, as early as 1890, demanding separate cycling facilities for reasons of safety. This is repeatedly said without evidence and seemingly without further verification.

If sources of the time are examined, other motives are found: the initial concepts for bicycle lanes were aimed at creating more comfortable and easier paths to drive; roads were designed for equestrians, carriages, and carts.

Even the separation of the means of transport was not a main concept. Special lanes for bicycles on roads were not seen as important. Only at the end of the 1920s was the safety of bicycle riders taken as an argument for the construction of cycle paths. This became the main reason for the construction of bicycle paths, and finally for their legal enforcement by ordering cyclists to use them.

Government and city authorities were convinced during the period of the motor vehicle expansion to spend large amounts of money on the construction of roads and even motorways (especially after 1933, during the expansion for military use). These activities were partly fostered by cyclists and their societies; however, construction of bicycle paths was very limited, except in some cities, and was often financed by the bicycle users themselves. At the end of the 1920s, mass construction of paths really started, when bicycles were beginning to create disturbances in the fast traffic flow of motor vehicles. At the time, there were 12 million cyclists compared with fewer than 1 million cars. Mass construction of bicycle paths started in Germany only when the state supplied the means for it as a move to create employment, and for the state of emergency.

Bicycle path construction was hailed in a propaganda move as a feat in favour of cyclists. This compensated the bulk of the population for the government's massive fostering of motorcar transport.

It is still an exception to find the original paths and cycle-track networks built for cyclists. Nevertheless, or perhaps particularly for this reason, the 1926 legal obligation to use these paths exists (as long as they are available, regardless of their condition). The strict enforcement of this decree can be regarded as proof of the central motive for the construction of these paths: the free circulation of motor vehicles on roads.

From the Cycling Lanes to the Compulsory Bike Path

The first demand for paths specially designed for cyclists was justified on the grounds of the difficulties encountered riding on pavements conceived for heavy vehicles. For the most part, these roads were built with large stones, because small ones could not resist the weight of heavy carts. The lighter bicycles needed a much cheaper road surface, more comfortable to ride on. Futhermore, the conditions of unpaved roads caused terrible dust clouds in dry weather, from contemporary reports.

In 1901, again there were demands for a special road section designed for cyclists, to foster bicycle tourism. At the same time there were requests from the cycle industry for the wellbeing and health of the public. Notice that this was not a request for separate roads for cyclists, but for the assignment of a section of roads to cyclists, later called "Radfahrstreifen"[6] in Germany. The bicycle is regarded as "something between a pedestrian and a carriage," for which an adequate lane had to be created. Because arterial routes out of cities were specially difficult to use by cyclists, bicycle tourism declined. The market suffered the consequences, as fewer bikes were bought. Road surfaces cracked under the weight of heavy vehicles, and horse droppings made them slippery, creating a potential danger for cyclists. The argument for safety took on a very different perspective.

The first lanes for cyclists were created in Bremen, Hamburg, Hannover, Lübek, and Magdeburg. There is no intention here to discuss which city first introduced these lanes, but sources indicate Bremen as the pioneer, where special lanes for cyclists have existed since 1897. These were 2.5 m wide, 2-way sections in the middle of the road, consisting of coal cinders or copper dross. At the turn of the century, the bicycle was the fastest road vehicle, and their circulation was consequently not obstructed by slower carts. After 1910, lanes were transferred to the side of the roads. From the 1920s, arguments between police and cyclists began to emerge as roads were paved with asphalt; these were more comfortable to ride on than the cycle lanes, which were susceptible to weather conditions and wear. Cyclists preferred to use the streets which had been asphalted for motor vehicles.

Since the construction of different methods for each category user emerged, a mentality of assignment and possession appeared: this began with the creation of special pavements for pedestrians (called "Bürgersteige"). As the cyclist in Bremen did not accept the often flooded and dangerously damaged lanes, the city built tar-asphalted lanes from 1930. In Bremen some private cycle paths existed that could only be used by riders paying an annual fee: however, the bulk of cycle lane construction was carried by the city. A similar situation, where the city installed and financed cycle lanes, was Hamburg. In 1899, 250,000 Marks were spent for the construction of paths in and around the city. Until 1919, the expenditure rose to up to 2 million Marks.

A very different situation was to be found in Lübek, where from 1900 cycle owners bore the costs of path construction. Numberplates were issued for bicycles upon receipt of payment. With the help of these payments, the cycle path network was completed before the beginning of WWI. In 1919, most citizens voted for the removal of the tax as the repairs for war damage were much cheaper than the 25,000 Marks received from the levy on cyclists. As the bicycle was a necessary means of transport, the citizenship regarded this "special tax" as an injustice. The obligation to carry a numberplate (originally evidence of having paid) remained in force though. By using numberplates, it was simpler to control cyclists' behaviour.

In Hannover, the construction of bicycle paths began with the creation of a cycle promenade through the city's forest Eilenriede. The disintegrating cyclist's association "Radfahr-Renn-Verein" donated 20,000 Marks to the town council of Hannover for the construction of bicycle paths. A yearly tax of 1 Mark for the use of these paths was imposed to preserve their condition.

In 1936, *Radmarkt* praised Hannover for its cycle lane construction, declaring it exemplary. For 35 years all new roads were as a norm built with reserved lanes for cyclists. In total there were 120 km of lanes by 1936: another 80 km could be added if considering surrounding areas. All new construction or restoration of roads included cycle lanes as a norm.

The city most noted for the early construction of cycle lanes was Magdeburg. This was probably also a consequence of the long serving municipal architectural counsellor, Dipl. Ing. Henneking. He was the pope of cyclepath constructors in the 1920s and a public personality in this area. In 1898, the "Magdeburger Verein für Radfahrwege e.V."[7] was founded, an organisation which controlled the installation of cycle tracks in Magdeburg and the surrounding territory in cooperation with city authorities. For a long time the civil engineering and garden authorities worked under the supervision of Henneking. To him we owe a very clear description of the "Magdeburger Vereins für Radfahrwege"[7] and its work. He described it as follows: "It was an association of businessmen and civil servants; among them some were municipal or elected city officers who had some influence over the administration of the city. Every morning before the beginning of the office or business activities, the members rode with their bikes through the wide and pretty park of Magdeburg to places outside the city, drank their morning coffee, and went if possible swimming in the Elbe river. They returned after 1 or 1½ hours back to their daily work, refreshed from their time in the beautiful countryside, cycling and swimming in the river. These men understood that if cycling was to be a complete pleasure and relaxing activity, suitable paths had to be created."

The municipal authorities constructed cycle paths in the city; the association, those leading to the suburbs. Magdeburg's solution to the creation of cycle lanes was a simple one: it was made possible by installing kerbstones to create lanes on one or both sides of the street. This concept was introduced in the "Richtlinien für die Schaffung von Radfahrwegen"[8] of the "Studiengesellschaft für Automobilstraßenbau"[9] (STUFA) issued in spring 1927. These guidelines were very influential in the policy of cycle lane construction. The Magdeburger association evolved from 500 members at the time of its foundation to 49,000 members in 1927. In 1929, the network of bicycle paths amounted to 400 km. A major portion was financed by the association itself, for which it spent "hundreds of thousands of goldmarks."

Initially the construction of paths was financed by the association alone, but it didn't take long before resources of municipal authorities were used. Large sums were also donated by rich and enthusiastic members of the organisation.

In 1919, i.e., after WWI, the initiative was undertaken by the "Deutscher Radfahrerbund."[10] They demanded the construction of cycle paths as part of the state of emergency. In their declaration we find among other issues the following: "The bicycle is today much less a leisure vehicle than a necessary means of transport…which the state and the community cannot give up. The state and municipal authorities cannot and should not watch the actual situation impassively. Traffic is being strongly delayed by wrecked log roads and paved streets as well as by country roads where cycling is difficult. The amount of damage to cycles and tyres is increasing. The increased difficulty of circulation wastes many hours of workers' productivity, a waste that is nowadays not necessary. Accidents are increasing to a worrying extent too."

It is not clear in this description if the accidents were caused by collisions with other vehicles (particularly motor vehicles), other bicycles, or were simply falls. Countrywide statistics of accidents show pedestrians as the main victims of motor vehicles, while bicycle accidents amount to only around 11%, a low figure given the number of bicycles circulating at the time. Fostering bicycle tourism demanded the installation of bicycle lanes at least on one side of roads, by removing bumps and grass humps.

Even in 1926–27, the already mentioned (and by then retired) municipal architectural counsellor of Magdeburg, Dr. Dipl. Ing. Henneking, wrote in an edition of a booklet by the "Verein Deutscher Fahrrad-Industrieller"[11] an article entitled "Bicycle Traffic: Its Economic Importance and the Construction of Cycle Paths." He argues particularly for a solution to strongly increased bicycle traffic in cities and the countryside. STUFA[9] declared that the solution to the bicycle traffic problem lay in the creation of cycle lanes, which should be constructed according to local conditions, and the design of bicycles (part of the already mentioned guidelines[8] publicised in "Verkehrregelung").[12]

The motive for intervention was the increased number of cyclists: it was necessary to secure unhindered and smooth cycle traffic, and free the streets for motor vehicles at the same time. While earlier the independent cycle path was a standard provision, STUFA declared it necessary only in certain conditions. It was required only if it was not possible to build a special lane on the streets for reasons of cost, space, or other reasonable considerations. Still, in 1927, the argument for cycle paths was for the comfort of cyclists, as the following quotation demonstrates: "As long as the road is built with noiseless pavement, asphalt, tar, concrete, or wood, the installment of special cycle lanes on the roadside is generally not essential."

Henneking for his part recognised the dangers to cyclists by motor vehicles: "The stronger motor vehicle traffic develops in the highways, the more dangerous the riding of bicycles on these roads will be." High speeds by cars made them dangerous to cyclists, who should avoid them by using cycle paths: "The creation of specially conceived paths for bicycles is the only real solution to the yearly increasingly difficult problem of creating safe traffic conditions for cycles and pedestrians on the highways. These paths should be separated from the actual road."

"Will the Cyclist Leave the Street?" was the title of an article in 1928. Here for the first time there is a clear argument "that something has to happen soon if we want to avoid an increase in accidents. These are already routine today. This is necessary if we don't want the strong increase in motor vehicle circulation in Germany to create unstoppable developments."

The original motive for the paths changed: no more were comfort and good road surfaces the main issue. The paths now functioned to take cyclists off the street. The following years of cycle-path construction showed little concern for the quality of the surface. Even the original concept and value of cycle paths changed; the German name was reduced from "Radfahrweg" to "Fahradweg," and later to today's short "Radweg."[13] More often, this new terminology was used in publications of the "Reichsgemeinschaft für Radfahrwegebau."[14] This was the result of the preference given to motor vehicle transport by the NS Regime, giving bicycles a secondary position.

Discipline through the Legal Enforcement of Cycle Paths

The traffic regulations of 1934, issued first in Prussia and then in the whole of the country, were concerned with the problem of disciplining cyclists.

In 1926–27, there already existed an obligation to use bicycle paths in the "Verordnung für den Kraftfahrzeugverkehr." This was no problem at the time for most cyclists, as bicycle paths were not available in most cities, and those that existed were there to improve cycle circulation. They offered a better surface than the streets, but when the street already had a good surface for bicycles, no lanes or paths were built for them.

The legal obligation to use bicycle paths existed in most countries already, but the year 1934 marked the beginning of the enforcement of this rule as a disciplinary instrument against cyclists.

On 1 October 1934, the "Reichs-Straßen-Verkehrs-Ordnung" (R.St.V.O.) came into force. In Article 26, the obligation to use specially conceived paths, therefore also cycle paths, was formulated and propagated: "If a street is conceived for specific types of traffic (footpath, bicycle path, riding path), is the circulation of this traffic limited to the section of the street reserved for it?"

The Use of Cycle Paths: The First Obligation of Cyclists

Sections of the R.St.V.O. are repeatedly published as suggestions in the "Verkehrssicherheit für Radfahrer."[15] The first rule was that bicycles have to possess brakes (rear tyre brakes are enough), bell, rear reflector or red lamp, and a lamp, which should not dazzle other people. To this rule was added in 1935: "Always use existing bicycle paths!" In 1936, this is called "the important rules of behaviour: 1. Cyclists must use the bicycle paths."

This intensive propaganda did not exist before 1934. Cyclists were no longer content to use narrow, delicate (and therefore often defective) paths. They preferred to use the streets for motor vehicles, thereby creating problems with the police.

There was no sign of protest by the bicycle associations, now either outlawed, or as a political move by the NS Regime, grouped under the name of "Deutscher Radfahrer-Verband."[16]

International Comparison

In conclusion, I would like to compare the history of cycle-path construction in Germany with other countries, using the limited information in my possession. I can do this very superficially, as I don't have detailed studies. Maybe my statements will induce scholars to check their validity though studies of these countries.

The idea of bicycle paths did not originate in Germany. Robert R. Smith reports in his book, *A Social History of Bicycles*, of several finished and planned projects for bicycle paths before the turn of the century. The difference lies in demand—these were principally for improved streets and highways. At the time, bicycle paths were used nearly exclusively for leisure trips. While at the turn of the century bicycles in Europe changed from being a sport and leisure vehicle of the rich to a means of transport for an increasing proportion of the population, Americans had already abandoned the bicycle for the motor vehicle. "The bicycle craze" was over. *Radmarkt* reports that although 1.5 million bicycles were bought every year, especially by children and sportsmen, no more bicycle paths were constructed except in some cities in the east.

The first initiatives for bicycle paths in Germany were similar to those in other countries. However, German motives for the construction of paths, especially in the 30s, were different from reasons given in other countries, from the information available. For example, neither in Holland or Denmark was the demand for bicycle paths connected to the fostering of motor vehicle transport. Maybe this is the reason why in these two countries cycle paths remained preserved after WWII, instead of being destroyed, as they were in Germany until the late 70s, to allow for car parking. It sounds more believable that in other countries paths were really built for the comfort and safety of cyclists. The motive to free the roads from bicycles to leave them to motorcar transport seems to have been a secondary reason.

The original demand in 1897 in Germany for bicycle paths praised foreign countries and specially the Belgians for their example in building them. In 1936, an exhibition was held with the slogan "Germany needs bicycle paths!" This was organised by the NSDAP, the "Hauptamt für Volkswohlfahrt"[17] and the "Reichsgemeinschaft für Radwegebau."[14] Belgium and Denmark were used as examples to show how far behind Germany was in the construction of bicycle paths. However, the real drive for construction of paths came to Denmark in the 30s. Henneking showed photographs from Copenhagen depicting streets dominated by cyclists, but not streets with separate sections for motor vehicles and bicycles.

In a report in 1920 by *Radmarkt*, "Eine Nation auf Rädern,"[18] Charles Paul Engel describes the world of cycling in Holland in rosy colours: "The increasing use of bicycles naturally created the desire for good bicycle roads. We have to thank the efforts of the Algemeene Nederlandsche Wielrijders Bond for the extensive network of good bicycle roads that exist along the main highways of the country. There are equally good bicycle roads leaving the highways into all remote places." Holland is the only country to do so much in this respect. The author calls the paths roads because they were much better than the narrower simple paths of Germany. These roads were built by the government, strongly fostering the already wide use of bicycles.

A later report shows a less euphoric picture as it declares that bicycles in small towns are used because tramways or omnibuses hardly exist. The main causes are the one-family houses in small cities of only 75–100,000 inhabitants, reaching a diameter of 6–8 km, which makes public transport unprofitable. This report also mentions a tax for bicycles of 2.50 fl., through which the state collected 7,500,000 fl. Foreigners cycling for more than 3 months in the country had to pay the tax. In Brabant and Limburg there was also a provincial street tax. However, bicycle lanes, called "Rijwielpad," constructed with this money were very good: "In each street there is at least one, but generally at each side, a specially designed 'klinker' or 'platten' pavement."[19]

There are no numbers available, but it was affirmed "that in Holland accidents fell to a minimum through the exemplary construction of these paths." Henneking, however, gave as reason for the low casualties in 1927 the greater discipline by cyclists in Holland, and he was the last person anybody could accuse of being against bicycle paths: "No cyclist (in

127

Amsterdam, where from the photographs we know that there were no cycle lanes, V.B.) would cause disturbance by riding excessively fast. There is at all levels a clear understanding of the necessity to accept traffic discipline."

During the 1930s, countries other than Belgium, Holland, and Denmark adopted the policy of constructing bicycle paths: France, England, and Switzerland built them intensively. If Germany was a leader in the construction of paths, as *Radmarkt* affirms, it cannot be proven, even though at the time the dimension of the works was very important. In England narrow paths like the German ones were built. The following is reported: There the cyclist was against the construction of cycle paths, "without being able to give any sound reason, maybe only the obstinacy not to touch anything in the established order."

Notes

1. "From the Downfall of a Mass Means of Transport—The History of Bicycle-Path Planning in Towns."
2. Bicycle Market.
3. The Bicycle Market and the Motor Vehicle.
4. Workers Union of Bicycle and Motor Vehicle Users "Solidarity."
5. German Union of Bicycle and Motor Vehicle Drivers "Concordia."
6. Bicycle lanes.
7. Magdeburg's Cycle Path Association, Inc.
8. Guidelines for the Creation of Bicycle Paths.
9. Study Group for Motorcar Road Construction.
10. German Cyclist Union.
11. Association of German Bicycle Manufacturers.
12. Traffic Regulation.
13. "Bicycle-riding-path"/"bicycle-path"/"bike-path."
14. Reich's Association for the Construction of Bicycle Paths.
15. Traffic Safety for Cyclists.
16. German Bicycle Association.
17. Central Office of Popular Welfare.
18. A Nation on Tyres.
19. Brick or concrete-tile pavement.

18. Cycling or Roller Skating: The Resistible Rise of Personal Mobility

Hans-Erhard Lessing

Two-wheeled personal transport owed its origin to ice skating having become popular during the minor "ice age" at the turn of the 19th century. Yet it is still unclear why, after the short boom of 1817–19, the running machines or velocipedes disappeared from the newspapers for nearly 50 years. While one reason certainly was the fascination for the upcoming railways, another might have been that the mobile avant-garde were afraid of balancing on large wheels and switched to roller skating. For instance, inventors in the 1820s created all kinds of miniaturised 2-wheelers, resembling roller skates but called velocipedes. A model of mutual interaction is proposed where advances in the learning curve for balancing in one mode of mobility benefitted the other one. This nicely fits the rise of the front-pedal velocipede of 1866 after an American, James Plimpton, turned his roller-skate patent of 1863 into a worldwide rink business, and taught the American public to get along with both feet off the ground. The front-pedal velocipede, a batchelor machine, was in turn discarded after 2 years in favour of the more social roller skating on covered skating rinks, which took hold even in Europe.

One of the questions in cycling history for which we have no satisfactory answer is: why did it take nearly 70 years to make cycling popular among both sexes—from the velocipedes of 1817 to the safety bicycles in the late 1880s. Looking at the machines alone we cannot tell the reason, and the usual argument is the bad condition of the roads. But this is not quite true since there were indeed some good roads—especially in France—built for the military or the ruling nobility. Thus most news on German velocipede rides centered around the so-called "Kunststrassen," i.e., artificial roads that usually connected the ruler's castle with his summer residence, like Mannheim with Schwetzingen, or Berlin with Potsdam.

A much stronger argument is that legislation turned against velocipede riding, at least in England, Germany, and Italy, either to satisfy enraged citizens and carters, as was the case in England according to Davies,[1] or for political reasons as in Germany, where sportive activities of students, like draisine riding, were regarded as subversive and therefore forbidden.[2] But after a while, this prosecution must have faded away, since we have evidence of velocipede riding in the years afterwards: in Germany there was a comeback of draisines in 1833 as children's vehicles,[3] and one source[4] mentions draisine activities in Dresden in 1843. Alex Clark wrote to the *English Mechanic*[5] in 1835 that a 2-wheeled velocipede was manufactured in London. While newspapers and magazines turned their

Fig. 18.1. Detail from a leaflet announcing roller skate run in 1790 (Schweizerisches Sportmuseum, Basel).

attention to the railways, we should not infer from the lack of velocipede news that velocipedes no longer existed.

From the earlier conferences, you know that my argument has been that the fear of balancing on two wheels kept the general public from adopting the 2-wheeler. Ice skaters were prepared to take on the challenge of balancing and this was a daring minority then—at least in England, France, and Germany, in contrast to the Netherlands. As a consequence, amateur mechanics everywhere returned to 3- or 4-wheeled constructions to provide the stability the public wanted. Meanwhile I looked into the history of roller skating and found some stunning coincidences, based on which I propose a new view of the history of personal mobility.

Ice Skating—Where It All Began

Around the turn of the 19th century, there must have been a minor ice age with strong winters, e.g., the Thames was frozen in 1788–89 and 1813–14, enabling skating on it.[6] Ice skating had long been a means of travel and transport in the Netherlands with its many canals, and we have a report of Dutch women skating to a distant marketplace while balancing milk vessels on their heads and knitting wool simultaneously.[7] Gender roles were different in neighbouring countries, with skating as a pastime. In France and Germany, only male skaters were allowed. Women skating was regarded as indecent—women were shifted around on stool sleds by the men.[7] When describing the new running machines of Karl von Drais, his contemporaries used the metaphor "skating on the road"; and indeed the ergonomics of his 3- or 4-wheeled ladies' rikscha (as we would call it today) is nothing more than a chair shifted around on the road.

Roller Skating

The roller skate is definitely older than the single-track velocipede. Its beginnings were presumably the need to bring ice skating on stage rather than the unrealistic desire to continue ice skating on the road in summer. The first recorded event on stage appears to have been at London's Drury Lane during a play by Tom Hood in 1743, which I have not yet been able to verify.[8] Scarce mentions are "a pair of skaites contrived to run on small metallic wheels" demonstrated indoors by John Joseph Merlin sometime between the years 1761 and 1772,[8] and "patins a terre" invented by Maximilian Lodewijk van Lede according to the 1790 edition of the Gothaic Almanac.[9]

The first picture we have is on a leaflet announcing a 3-mile run between The Hague and Scheveningen judged to be completed in 5 to 6 minutes. The soldier of the Swiss Guard was reportedly hindered by the many spectators, and the roller skates so unknown that they were exhibited afterwards in the inn "Den Orangen Jäger."[10] Anyhow, his roller skates were 2-wheel in-line skates, as we would call them today. Karl von Drais was then the tender age of 5, but of course these could have inspired his single-track invention of 1817 if he had had access to the leaflet or other literature, which we don't know.

Inspiration the other way round is more distinct. Soon after the velocipede boom since 1817, the first patents on roller skates appeared: 1819, *a brevet* without picture on a *patin* (roller skate) by the Parisian mechanic Petibled with the text: "Description of skates destined to perform in a room everything that skaters can do on the ice with ordinary skates." According to Ginzrot[7] these were 3-wheeled (1 front, 2 back) and were demonstrated outdoors in Paris. In 1823, the next patent went to Robert John Tyers, fruit merchant on Picadilly Square for his Volito; I know only the German description: "Vorrichtung zum Schnellaufen," that is, provision for fast walking, with 5 wheels in line. And in 1825, an anonymous article published in *English Mechanic* showed a velocipede which was nothing but a roller skate for one foot only while the other one was free to touch secure ground; as such it is also an archetype of a boy's scooter. In 1828, Jean Garcin obtained the brevet "for a mechanism called cingar (anagram of Garcin) for skating in all seasons *on a prepared floor*."[10] So the majority of these patents still tried to imitate an ice skate using small wheels that were unsuitable for outdoor conditions. How many users there were is unknown.

The Mobile Avant-Garde

Jean Garcin appears to be a protagonist of a social group that I would call "the mobile avant-garde." We know he was an ice skater and manufacturer of skates initially, since in 1813 he wrote a booklet on ice skating.[11] Ice skating was really something special in France, with a hierarchy of masters evolving who wore a special costume, *le gilet rouge*, the red collar; Garcin was called a *gilet-rouge*.

Then in 1818, he demonstrated the draisines in the Luxemburg Gardens of Paris, hired them out, and gave driving lessons in several places.[12] Ten years later he switched to roller skating. Here was somebody who switched from one mode of mobility to the other in due time, and the social group to which he catered which was willing to pay for the fun of mobility must have followed this change, too.

It is not known when French women were emancipated from the stool sled on the ice. It is also not known if the rikscha-type velocipede was a success among mobile couples in 1818. It appears that the velocipede turned out to be a batchelor machine, something for daring young men, except for rare references to Johnson's lady's velocipede. Anyhow, in 1853 we find a picture showing a man and a woman roller-skating together, in a French book on ice skating.[13] Mobile fun on roller skates had become much more social than velocipede riding.

What had happened? The breakthrough was due to a stage event again: in 1849, Meyerbeer's opera *Le Prophète* showed a simulated ice-skating scene on roller skates built by Legrand, and was a huge success throughout Europe. Roller skating took off everywhere, e.g., in Berlin, where a beer hall had waitresses on roller skates.

Still the simulation of figure skating on ice—which was then a true revolution—through roller skating was more than imperfect. None of the proliferating roller-skate designs could be guided in curves except at the expense of enormous friction and exertion. This problem was solved in 1863 by James Plimpton, an American mechanic who became a multimillionaire by exploiting his patent. His "rocking" roller skate had two parallel sets of wheels, one under the ball and one under the heel of the foot, working on rubber springs. When the skater pressed or leaned on one side of his foot, the front and hind wheels on that side came closer together and allowed a curved line. In the same year, Plimpton started his business of licensing skating rinks and leasing (never selling) his roller skates in his new Plimpton building in New York. It became a worldwide monopoly on roller skating and skating rinks—the start of a significant part of American culture that still exists even in small towns today where teenagers date. In 1865, the first European skating rink in London's Crystal Palace was opened.

Why not Cycle with the Feet Off the Ground?

By 1866, the balancing skills on four small wheels under each foot were already widespread, and we all know that Pierre Lallement obtained a U.S. patent in that year on the old velocipede, but now with cranks on the front wheel. This meant a very critical initial phase to gain momentum and lift the feet off secure ground to put them onto the cranks. It took the German inventor Karl Benz two weeks to teach himself riding. Several removable contraptions were developed to keep the velocipede upright. It is my point that the boneshaker was not pure chance, but only understandable with the rise of roller-skating skills.

Interestingly enough, in the U.S. boneshakers were hired out initially on indoor skating rinks[14] so nobody felt the need to buy the costly machine since an entrance fee had to be paid anyhow. Only in

A VELOCIPEDE.

Sir,—The above is the drawing of a Velocipede, intended to be fixed on one foot, when the *velocipedestrian* pushes himself away with the other. As the wheels are about six inches in diameter, it may be used on any road tolerably smooth; and as the foot is brought near the ground, and is supported by the strap, A, it will not wrench or fatigue the ancle, as the common skates do; the whole body, too, will be as much at liberty as in walking.

The patent "Land-skate" has the wheels directly under the foot, and, from their being so small, it can only be used on a boarded floor, or a place equally smooth.

I am, Sir,
Your obedient servant,
* * * * *

Fig. 18.2. Velocipede to stand on (from Mechanics Magazine, 1825).

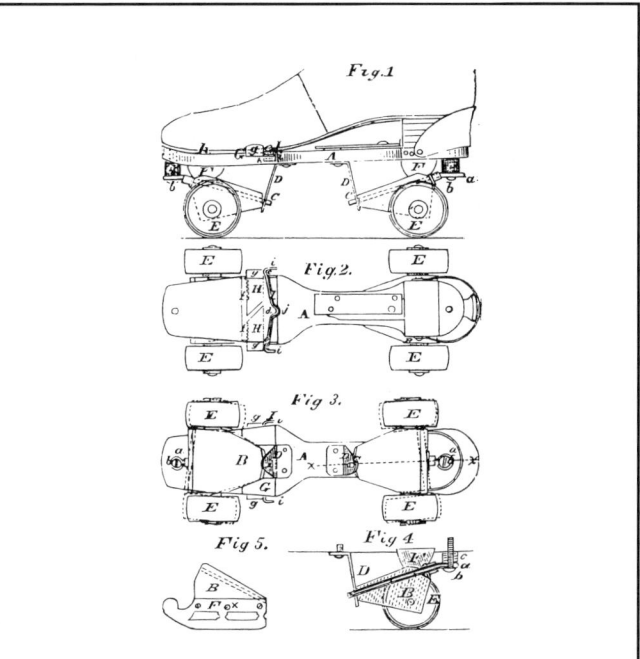

Fig. 18.3. James Plimpton's patent drawing, 1863.

December 1868, reports began about outdoor activities, and then the boom set in. In Vienna the riding school was indoors, too. In Paris boneshaker fans profited from the new macadam boulevards constructed by Haussmann. Despite some initial fanfare and separate driving schools, women apparently did not join in in large numbers. The forged frames were heavy and the rides very strenuous—no wonder that outdoor distance riders were slower (40 miles in 15 hours) than those on the lighter draisines had been (27 miles in 7 hours). By 1869, Maurer added a roller-skating room to his enterprise. Once more cycling turned out to be a batchelor's pastime, whereas roller skating became the social event for both genders even in Europe, with rink owners organising masquerades and other get-together events. It comes as no surprise that boneshaker cycling was throttled by roller skating even before the onset of the Franco-Prussian war in 1870. A French author wrote in his roller-skating book[15]: "Roller skating is in fashion. It has replaced advantageously the velocipede."

The Give-and-Take between Cycling and Roller Skating

Needless to say, skating rinks continued to expand on the continent. Again the Grand-Bi proved to be a batchelor's machine and a stunt accessory on skating rinks. Presumably skating rinks worldwide formed the stage for the famous trick rider Nick Kaufmann.

From what has been said, I have assembled preliminary gender statistics that can be merely qualitative. The resistible rise of cycling appears to be a one-sided batchelor affair until the 1890s when women jumped onto safety bicycles. Roller skating profitted early in the 1820s from the hobby horse, but due to its two-gender openness, throttled boneshaker cycling in 1870. Cycling profitted from roller skating in 1866, and stifled indoor roller skating in the 1890s when the rinks in London and Berlin closed down. Its rebirth in 1907 as an outdoor activity.

Notes

1. Thomas Stephens Davies. "On the Velocipede," May 1837, lecture manuscript, reprinted in *The Boneshaker*, no. 108 and 111 (1985–86).

2. H. E. Lessing. "Karl von Drais' Two-Wheeler—What We Know," *Proceedings of the 1st International Cycle History Conference*. San Francisco: Bicycle Books, 1990, p. 5.

3. Karl v. Drais, letter reprinted in M. Rauck, K. F. Drais von Sauerbronn. Erfinder und Unternehmer (vol. 24 of Beiträge zur Wirtschafts-und Sozialgeschichte). Franz-Steiner-Verlag, Stuttgart, 1983.

4. Paula v. Bülow. *Aus verklungenen Tagen*. Leipzig, 1924, p. 15.

5. *Mechanics Magazine*, London, vol. 23, no. 633 (23 September 1835): 32.

6. N. N.. "Frostiana or a history of the river Thames in a frozen state…to which is added: The Art of Skating." London, 1814.

7. J. C. Ginzrot. *Die Wagen und Fahrwerke der verschiedenen Völker des Mittelalters*. Munich 1830, reprint 1979 by Olms Presse, Hildesheim-New York, vol. 3, p. 328.

8. Greater London Council (ed.). *John Joseph Merlin—The Ingenious Mechanick*, catalog, 1985.

9. *Gothaischer Hofkalender 1790*. Gotha 1790, p. 36.

10. Sam Neveu. "Les origines du roller-skate" in: Schweizerisches Sportmuseum Basel (ed), Schweizer Beiträge zur Sportgeschichte, Band 2/1990, pp. 30–55.

11. Jean Garcin. Le vrai. *Patineur ou Principes sur L'Art de patiner avec Grace*. Paris, 1813.

12. Keizo Kobayashi. *Histoire du Vélocipede de Drais a Michaux 1817-1870—Mythes et réalités*. Tokyo: Bicycle Culture Center, 1994.

13. Paulin-Desormeaux. "Patinage et Récréations sur la Glace…" *Encyclopédie-Roret*, Paris (undated, but 1853).

14. Norman L. Dunham, "The Bicycle Era in American History," unpublished thesis. Harvard University, 1956.

15. H. Mouhot, *La Rinkomanie*. Paris, undated (1876).

Les Bowerman

19. Clubs—Their Part in the Study of Cycle and Cycling History

The *Oxford English Dictionary*[1] gives some 16 main uses of the word "club." The sense of a number of people who meet habitually for a common purpose is primarily an English concept dating back to the 17th century. The earliest connotations were of meetings for drinking, gaming, socialising, or discussing politics, i.e., the gentlemen's clubs, many of which still survive in London. The sense of persons combining to pursue some common object such as chess, cricket, or natural history is more an 18th-century development. When bicycling as an activity grew up around 1870, it lent itself admirably to the club concept—with socialising and sporting as common objectives.

The Liverpool Velocipede Club was in existence by March 1868, according to a quoted testimonial in Lightwood,[2] and there was a velocipede club in Carpentras near Avignon in France by March the following year. Both are mentioned in my own local *Surrey Comet* newspaper.[3] There may have been others. The best known of these very early clubs was the Pickwick Bicycle Club formed at Hackney, East London, on 22 June 1870, so named because the novelist Charles Dickens, author inter alia of *The Pickwick Papers*, had died only a fortnight earlier. This club still exists, but mainly as a dining club with some bicycle interest.

I am at present running a column in *News & Views*, one of the periodicals of the Veteran-Cycle Club, about early cycling clubs, and it appears that the earliest surviving one, in the UK at least, is the Peterborough Cycling Club founded in 1874. (Albeit of the same town, this club is not to be confused with the Peterborough Vintage C.C. which hosted this year's IVCA Rally. I would, incidentally, be pleased to hear details of any overseas cycling clubs which have existed continuously for 100 years or more.

All that is merely by way of setting the scene. The purpose of this paper is not to give a history of early cycling clubs so much as to examine the part which clubs have played in the study of cycle and cycling history. It seems to me that there are two main ways in which this has been done. The first is that some of the early clubs have left papers, records, or archives which are invaluable in understanding the personalities involved, their activities, the machines they used, and the atmosphere in which they existed. Information about what they may have left is very sparse, and there is no record of what is where. I gather that a cache of such material has recently surfaced for the London-based Amateur Bicycle Club of the 1870s, and that we may some time hear from Nick Clayton, inaugurator of these conferences, about the ABC. I believe Lorne Shields of Canada has similar material for the Surrey B.C., another 1870s club. Over and above that I know not.

There is now, of course, a repository for such material, namely the National Cycling Archive, of which Andrew Millward is secretary. Perhaps greater publicity leading to greater public knowledge of the archive is required. I would earnestly request that

---

Synopsis

Bicycle clubs have been in existence since 1868. Club archives, journals, and published histories are essential sources for the study of cycle and cycling history. The first club for devotees of old cycles was formed at Coventry in 1951. The first one specifically formed to study cycle and cycling history was the (Southern) Veteran-Cycle Club in 1955. The American Wheelmen followed in 1967, and the International Veteran-Cycle Association in 1985. Each of the latter three organizations publish journals containing invaluable articles on cycle and cycling history.

anyone with knowledge of such material should make its existence known to Andrew as a matter of urgency. The problem is that club minute books and other records are frequently handed from one club secretary to the succeeding one, no record is made of what exists, and the books just disappear from view or, even worse, are thrown away by somebody with no interest in history. If it is considered that the average tenure of office of a club secretary is perhaps five years, the material is likely to have passed through some twenty pairs of hands in the case of a centenarian club.

Club magazines have always been a feature of cycling clubs. They of course, unlike the primary records such as minute books, have had print runs varying with the size of the club membership, as a result of which many have survived as a lively insight into cycling club life. Often a wealthy and/or enthusiastic member has had his collection of "club mags" bound, which increases the survival rate. My own collection of bound club magazines includes a run of *Stanley Gazettes* from 1897 to 1906, the *London Bicycle Club Gazette* from 1880 to 1904, and the *North Road Gazette* from 1903 to 1928.

Grassroots cycling clubs also often contribute to the study of history by the publication of their own histories. Considering that such studies are for the most part prepared by amateurs who would often prefer to be out on their bicycles, the quality has been remarkably good. Of my list of 45 English centenarian clubs, only 8 have published such histories and that does not include the Pickwick. They are the Hastings & St. Leonards C.C. (founded October 1876),[4] the Anfield B.C. (March 1879),[5] the Manchester Wheelers' Club (1883),[6] the North Road C.C. (October 1885),[7] the Catford C.C. (April 1886),[8] the Shaftesbury C.C. (1888),[9] the De Laune C.C. (1889),[10] and the Yorkshire Road Club (1891).[11] There may be others. Some have published notes at various stages, sometimes on dinner menus on the occasion of 50 or 60 year anniversaries. The Polytechnic C.C. (1878) and the Bath Road Club (1886) are examples falling into this category. I confess to knowing little about the position regarding overseas clubs save that the Véloce Club de Cholet in France (1888)[12] has published a centenary history. From that it appears there are several French clubs with a history of more than 100 years. I should be pleased to learn details of them and/or to see any history they may have published.

The earliest published history is that of the Pickwick B.C.,[13] which I excluded above on the grounds that it lapsed as a cycling club many years ago. The history was published in 1904 when the club was 34 years of age. The "History Sub-Committee" says in its Introduction that:

> This book, if published, will undoubtedly be of considerable value to all who have an interest in the sport, for it is well known that the Pickwick Bicycle Club was closely identified in the early days with all the important events that marked the rise and progress of cycling.

The Pickwick has thus played a unique double role in cycling history—it was one of the first to make

Fig. 19.1. An early club, the Guildford C.C. (founded 1877) at camp in 1886. The trophy is the "Anchor" shield, now owned by the British Cycling Federation.

cycling history, and it was the first to publish a cycling club history.

The other main way in which clubs have played a part in the study of cycle and cycling history is when they have been formed for the purpose of reviving (and hopefully recording and publishing) memories of earlier days, or for the specific purposes of studying and publishing historical matters, or of encouraging the preservation and displaying of old machines.

With its long history of clubs of all sorts, it is not surprising that the UK has led in this field. My knowledge is thus principally of such matters in this country, but I would again welcome any information from overseas which would help complete the picture.

Let us cast from our minds to start with the "Fellowship of Ancient Cycles" formed by H. W. ("Sammy") Bartleet in 1925, since this existed only in his mind (see *Bartleet's Bicycle Book*[14] published in 1931 and recently reprinted by the Veteran-Cycle Club).

We will go, then, straight to the Fellowship of Old Time Cyclists of which the organisation mentioned in my previous paragraph was undoubtedly a spoof. The FOTC was formed in 1916 (surprisingly in the middle of the Great or First World War) originally for men born in 1872 or earlier (i.e., at least 44 years of age at the time) who had ridden the ordinary or high bicycle before 1890. Later the 1872 requirement was dropped, and riders of the tricycle included. An annual meet and ride to Ripley, the "Mecca of all good cyclists,"[15] in Surrey, was held attracting large attendances. It provided a link to keep alive memories of the unique early days. As to its part in the study of history, that is perhaps marginal save that many column inches were devoted in the cycling press each year to reporting details of the personalities involved in the meet. Given the qualifications for membership, the end was inevitable, and in fact finality was reached when the last member died on 31 August 1971.

Although various individuals, notably Bartleet mentioned above and Godwin Southon of Shalford near Guildford, had amassed collections of old cycles, the first club for those interested in such machines seems to have been, appropriately enough, the Coventry Veteran-Cycle Club which was formed in May 1951. The main objective, it appears, was to ride and display old cycles. There was a close association with the Bartleet collection, by then owned by the City of Coventry.

On October 20, 1952, or in 1953, depending on which account you read,[16] the Peterborough Vintage Cycle Club was formed, and originally centred around the collection of 140 machines owned by Cyril Mundy. Its aim, as noted by Cliff Denton in his brief history of the club in the programme for this year's International Rally mentioned earlier, is "to restore, show, and ride cycles of pre-1935 manufacture." By 1955 there was a similar club at Bawtry.

At this stage enter the brothers Derek and John Roberts. Enthused by a visit to a collection of old cycles at Diamond End near Luton, they wrote to the cycling press suggesting the formation of a society to cater for those who were interested in "cycles which preceded modern ones."[17] This resulted in the setting up in 1955 of the Southern Veteran-Cycle Club. Because they did not envisage that it would have any particular geographical base, they originally intended to call it the Veteran-Cycle Club by analogy with the Veteran Car Club formed a few years earlier, but added "Southern" for fear of appearing to impinge on the domain of the three existing locally based clubs. The objective has always been "to stimulate an interest in old cycles and cycling history." It was never envisaged that ownership of machines was necessary, interest in the subject always being held to be sufficient. No cut-off date was ever set, thus avoiding the pitfalls which such an artificial deadline causes. History does not of course finish at any particular date, as these conferences clearly appreciate. The word "Southern" in the name was dropped in 1987. Without a date limit or restriction on machines, the club is very broad church, the common thread holding the membership (now over 1,600) together being perhaps the history of development of cycle design and use over the whole period.

In October the same year (1955), Derek Roberts called a meeting of the above four clubs at which he proposed that they be amalgamated into one National VCC, and that that body shoud take over and publish the SVCC's periodical *The Boneshaker*. The three locally based clubs rejected that, preferring their independence, but they liked the idea of association. Thus the National Association of Veteran-Cycle Clubs (NAVCC) was formed "to co-ordinate the work of the constituent clubs, to publicise the veteran-cycle movement, and to help form clubs where needed."[18]

The SVCC affiliated but left in 1959, rejoined in 1960, and lapsed in 1971. Feelings still sometimes run very strongly about these matters in the UK, and I therefore have to be careful not to tread on any corns, but the problem was that those running the SVCC at the time found it frustrating trying to cooperate with a body which, at that time (I do not speak of the present), disregarded its own rules and sometimes could not say what those rules were. This difference in outlook may have reflected the fact that the local clubs were based largely on an individual's own collection of machines and the display of them, whereas the very much larger (S)VCC was based in historic research and publication, and always had a strong tradition of sociable riding deriving from its connection with the cycling clubs.

In 1965, Derek Roberts created yet another organisation for those keenly interested in the past. The Fellowship of Cycling Old-Timers, with worldwide membership like the (S)VCC and the American Wheelmen (mentioned in the next paragraph), is effectively a successor to the FOTC mentioned earlier, of which Derek Roberts, although not qualifying as a member, was the last secretary. The new fellowship is for anybody over 50 years of age who is or has been a cyclist. Its principal activity is the quarterly magazine, *Fellowship News*, which publishes a mixture of members' reminiscences, historical articles, and much else. There have been 118 issues, nowadays running to approximately 100 pages. Bound and indexed volumes may be borrowed by members from the FCOT archivist.

Another major development in the study of cycle and cycling history occurred on 15 October 1967, when, taking inspiration from the SVCC, the American Wheelman was formed to "keep alive the heritage of American cycling, to promote restoration and riding of early cycles, and to encourage cycling as part of modern living."[19] Full membership is restricted to riders of high bicycles or solid-tyred safeties. There is thus emphasis on the earlier machines.

We then come right down to May 1985 when, at an international rally at Aegerital in Switzerland with drive from Bernard Barbeau, the decision was taken to form an International Veteran-Cycle Association, the principal purpose of which in practice is to decide the location of the main international rally for forthcoming years. It includes both affiliated clubs and individual members. For the past three years, a twice-yearly magazine, now named *The International Veteran Cycle*, has been published under the editorship of Walter Ulreich. Although largely devoted to association business, each issue has contained at least one useful and well-researched historical article.

There are other small veteran-cycle clubs both overseas and here in the UK, all of relatively recent formation. Of the UK ones, both the Desford Lane Pedallers and Bygone Bykes Yorkshire have had some effect beyond their immediate locality. The latter, in particular, publishes a journal known as *The Spokesman*, which has contained matter of interest to cycle historians. It is, perhaps, a pity that such matter has not appeared in a publication with wider circulation.

So what part *have* the veteran cycle clubs played in the study of cycle and cycling history? All have served to foster enthusiasm for the subject, encouraging their members to look out for old machines, which as often as not might otherwise have been destroyed. A certain amount of largely superficial research normally follows, and often restoration, although as Nicholas Oddy argued at the Neckarsulm Conference, many if not most machines

Fig. 19.2. Cover of the Summer 1994 issue of The Boneshaker, the first periodical devoted to cycle history.

would be better from the historical point of view left unrestored. With the smaller local clubs, the benefit of any research is usually lost as any findings are not published. The great benefit deriving from the local clubs, and this is reflected in their objectives, is that the machines are displayed and demonstrated to the public, thus disseminating knowledge of the past, which is presumably the purpose of history.

The (S)VCC has taken cycle history very much further than that. From the start 39 years ago, it has published a magazine (originally quarterly but now four-monthly) devoted almost entirely to cycle history. As most will know, it is named for better or for worse *The Boneshaker*. It was the first cycle history periodical to be published, and issue No. 135 has recently appeared. It is comprehensively indexed (by myself, Derek Roberts' early indexes having been discontinued due to lack of sales), and forms the most comprehensive bank of published cycle history matter available. Its particular value from an academic point of view is that the pages are open to criticism, with the result that assertions can be and are tested. It is a prerequisite for persons set upon writing books on cycling history to first see if their subject has been treated in *The Boneshaker*. Over the years, several have rushed in without taking this precaution, and have finished with egg on their faces. There is no time in this paper to detail the contents over the years, except to instance the slaying of the myth of H. J. Lawson's claimed 1873 safety bicycle, the dissemination to a wide readership of Jacques Seray's demolition of the supposed 18th-century bicycle of the gentleman who turned out not to be the Comte de Sivrac, and the only comprehensive account of the development of the tricycle. There is a strong international flavour. The present print run is 1,200.

The (S)VCC also adds to the sum of published cycle history by means of its (now) bi-monthly *News & Views* magazine. Originally intended for topical and ephemeral matters, it has always had a strong historical content, usually of items insufficiently learned or esoteric to make the pages of *The Boneshaker*. For example, a recent query as to whether the wartime BSA folders really were "Parabikes" led to the publication of contemporary flight records. Debate is sometimes forceful, as in current academic argument over the respective merits of Michaux and Lallement in the development of the bicycle. Like *The Boneshaker*, it is indexed.

The six-monthly *Wheelmen* magazine, first published in 1971 and now up to issue No. 44 is the other main cycling history periodical (the *International Veteran Cycle* has yet to establish a firm reputation). A quality product, it contains a mix of Wheelmen club matter and learned historical articles of great interest. To instance only two, there are items on the Wright brothers' origins as bicycle manufacturers, and on early women cyclists. One slight caveat is that neither criticism nor corrections appear, as a result of which he who asserts first always carries the day. An index is provided retrospectively, like the VCC publications.

An academic who is a notable contributor to these conferences, and who in reality knows better, has claimed that the VCC is just a collectors' club. I hope I have gone some way towards showing that by virtue of its unrestrictive objectives specifically mentioning history and its publications, the VCC is, perhaps more than any other, a cycle history club, which is in no way to decry the contribution to cycle history made by others.

To a certain extent these cycle history conferences, the brainchild of Nick Clayton, the present editor of *The Boneshaker*, have taken on a role previously performed by the VCC and the Wheelmen, but that is clearly to the common good as we now have a live forum with more contribution than ever before from academia/the groves of academe. Even here, I suggest, at risk of being howled down, that the clubs have a part to play—namely that their members with pooled and long practical experience of actually using cycles across the whole spectrum of history, and with the detailed knowledge of their machines which come from repairing and restoring them, are able to bring matters back down to earth when academics take off into the ether, as they have been known to do when making a particularly esoteric or provocative point. Perhaps it is safest if I say no more.

Notes

1. *Oxford English Dictionary*, 1971 ed.
2. *The Cyclist's Touring Club, being The Romance of Fifty Years' Cycling*. James T. Lightwood (1928), 17.
3. *The Surrey Comet* columns entitled "Metropolitan Gossip" in issue of 30 January 1869 and "Miscellaneous Intelligence" in issue of 20 March 1869.

4. *Eighty Years Awheel, a Record of the Hastings and St. Leonard Cycling and Athletic Club from 1876 to 1956.* J. K. Southerden (1962).

5. *The Black Anfielders, being the story of the Anfield Bicycle Club 1879–1955* (1956), and Centenary Edition (1979).

6. *A History of the Manchester Wheelers Club (formerly Manchester Athletic Bicycle Club).* T. M. Barlow and J. Fletcher (1983).

7. *Fifty Years of Road Riding (1885–1935), A History of the North Road Cycling Club, Ltd.* S. H. Moxham.

   The Second Fifty Years of Road Riding (1935–1985), a History of the Second Fifty Years of the North Road Cycling Club. Gates, Lovett, and Sellens.

   Along the Great North and Other Roads, the North Road Cycling Club, 1885–1980. A. B. Smith (1981).

8. *The First Fifty Years of the Catford Cycling Club.* E. J. Southcott (1939).

   The Second Fifty Years of the Catford Cycling Club. R. A. Reynolds (1989).

9. *The First Hundred Years—Shaftesbury Cycling Club, 1888–1988.* Nichol, Beavis, and Jordan.

10. *A Century Awheel, 1889–1989, a History of the De Laune Cycling Club.* Mike Rabbetts.

11. *Yorkshire Road Club, 1891–1991, a History.* Compiled by members and edited by F. Beckwith, M.A. (1991).

12. *Véloce Club de Cholet, 1880–1988.* (1989?).

13. *History of the Pickwick Bicycle Club.* Compiled by The Hon. Mr. Crushton (1905).

14. *Bartleet's Bicycle Book* by H. W. Bartleet (1931), reprinted 1983 by John Pinkerton and 1993 by the Veteran-Cycle Club.

15. An expression attributed to Lord Bury (later the Earl of Albemarle) in *Bicycling News* of 19 February 1887, 313.

16. Mrs. P. Leatherhead, Hon. Secretary of the PVCC, in a booklet on the National Association of Veteran-Cycle Clubs, published July 1963, and Cliff Denton, PVCC Chairman in the Introduction to the Souvenir Programme for the IVCA International Rally, 1994.

17. *Cycling* 20 January 1955, 72 and *The CTC Gazette* February 1955, 37.

18. NAVCC booklet of July 1963 mentioned in (16) above.

19. The Wheelmen Constitution.

Roger Alma

20. Malvern Cycling Club, 1883–1912: Social Class, Motivation, and Leisure Use

This paper is based on the detailed study of a Victorian cycling club in a developing spa town in Worcestershire. It examines the social class of the members and considers their motives for forming the club and for maintaining its active life into the 20th century. Questions of sport, recreation and leisure are addressed. In particular, the paper considers the ways in which the club contributed to the life of the town in providing a focus for a range of leisure activities. Members formed ties within the business community and contributed to local and national politics. As a recreational rather than a sporting club, the Malvern C.C. had a distinctive role to play in the development of cycling, while Malvern cyclists, such as Lady Harberton, Edward Elgar, Charles Santler, and Henry Morgan, found in cycling a stimulus to creativity in the diverse fields of women's emancipation, music, and engineering.

Malvern

In 1801, Great Malvern, in Worcestershire, was a village with a population of 951 inhabitants. By 1851, the population had grown to 3,911, and by 1901 had reached 9,676. The rapid growth, which accelerated after the coming of the railway in 1861, was closely linked to the development of Great Malvern as a spa town, attracting visitors in search of good health from the water cure and recreation from exercise on the Malvern Hills. With increasing numbers of visitors came the need for hotels, schools, banks, shops, and a range of professions and trades. The conveniences of the town and the beauty of the surrounding landscape attracted residents, either in retirement or for the summer season. The railway enabled businessmen to commute to Worcester from Malvern.[1]

Membership

In 1885, two years after the founding of the Malvern Cycling Club, T. H. S. Escott wrote:

> A social movement quite as remarkable as that which has been going forward among the better portion of the English middle class has been taking place, and is

Fig. 20.1. The Malvern Cycling Club, outside The Hundred House, Great Witley, Worcestershire, 19 July 1894.

now steadily progressing on a lower social stratum. This class would have once been called the small shopkeeper class, and its present condition is almost the growth of yesterday...Only the commercial prosperity of England could have generated the new social order from which the chief patrons of theatres and outdoor amusements are drawn.[2]

This observation is reflected in the picture that emerges from a study of the membership of the Malvern C.C. The earliest available membership list, for 1890, shows that ordinary members were drawn almost without exception from the professional and commercial classes, many being Malvern shopkeepers, the group singled out by Escott for its upward mobility and interest in leisure pursuits. Some of those on the 1890 list were founder members, and the membership remained essentially unaltered in character throughout the club's lifetime.

In 1890, there were 57 members in all: 15 honorary members, and 42 ordinary members, including 2 ladies. The honorary members included aristocrats and gentlemen of independent means as well as other leading members of the community. At least 17 members were related and others were closely connected through business or employment: for instance, H. D. Acland and Sir Edmund Lechmere had mutual banking interests[3]; F. A. Love and A. D. Melvin were employed at Madresfield Court by Lord Beauchamp, Love as butler and Melvin as estate clerk; T. Armstrong, organist at Newland, had ties with the Madresfield estate through the Beauchamp Charity; H. J. Lewis took over J. H. Baker's building firm after Baker's tragic early death in 1890[4]; John Hamsher, James Alexander Jones, and the Santler brothers, Charles and Walter, were in the cycle trade and supplied members with their machines[5]; in 1899, Henry Jones was buried by J. J. Towndrow,[6] one of whose occupations was undertaker; and without doubt there were many other ways in which business was facilitated by membership of the club, whose activities were reported in the local papers by W. H. Melhuish and later, H. R. Vine-Stevens.[7]

The first cycling club in Malvern preceded the Malvern C.C. by some years. Founded in 1876, the Western Ramblers Bicycle Club was one of the earliest in the country. Its members took part in cycle races and the club's first race meeting was held on the Worcester B.C.'s bicycle path in Worcester in 1880. J. B. Tierney, of Malvern, who won the 12-hour Amateur Championships in Edinburgh in June 1880, competed. In 1880 and 1882, members attended the Midland Meet at Leamington Spa. I can offer no explanation for the disappearance of the Western Ramblers, which coincided with, but was not necessarily caused by, the appearance of the Malvern Cycling Club.[8]

The Malvern C.C.'s first run was on Saturday, 11 March 1883, starting at 4:30 in the afternoon and covering some 20 miles. Eighteen riders assembled, including Rev. C. E. Ranken (President), F. Davis (Bicycling Captain), A. E. Gwynn (Tricycling Captain), and H. J. Bridgewater (Secretary).[9] Ranken was a remarkable man of great gifts and enthusiasms. An ardent cyclist, founder-member of the Malvern Club, and a consul of the Cyclists' Touring Club, he was also a notable chess player, becoming president of both Malvern and Worcester chess clubs and representing the county. When he died in 1905, in his 78th year, he was still a much loved vice-president of the cycling club. Unable to join the regular club runs in his old age, he nevertheless continued to take exercise on his tricycle "almost to the last." Ranken, and men like him, gave continuity and stability to the club over the years of its existence.[10]

Motivation

There seem to be 3 levels of motivation that might be considered: the motivation that leads individuals to take up cycling; the motivation that leads individuals to combine in cycling clubs and organisations; and the motivation of a social class in using cycling to define itself and to make a contribution to society as a whole.

Individual Motivation

Cycling in the 1870s and 1880s offered a new and exciting athletic challenge, in mastering the machines, in competition, and in tests of skill and endurance. It also opened up the countryside for exploration, giving mobility and freedom to a generation with increasing leisure time and self-confidence. For women, in particular, cycling was an important means towards emancipation. For the urban middle classes, access to the landscape on little-used roads was an ideal opportunity for exercise and recreation, as well as for visiting places of interest. The rapid evolution of the cycle itself became a subject of great interest to cyclists, who were eager to take advantage of the latest technology, and who responded promptly to innovation. The bicycle and tricycle also became convenient, practical, and effective means of transport.

Group Motivation

The Victorian cycling clubs offered companionship, instruction in cycling, access to information about cycling, and access to a range of social activities: they served as a means of promoting cycling as a respectable pastime for men and women anxious not to compromise their social standing; they organised racing, social riding, and touring; and they acted as pressure groups to facilitate cycling by advocating better roads, road signs, maps, accommodation for tourists, and information about services.

Class Motivation

In considering this aspect, I am indebted to Peter Bailey's *Leisure and Class in Victorian England* (1978). Bailey argues that:

> During the industrial revolution…leisure disappeared under an avalanche of work. When it re-emerged it had not only been reduced but relocated in the life-space, forming a separate and self-contained sector in an increasingly compartmentalised way of life.

For the emerging middle-class men and their families in an increasingly urban context,

> …leisure provided an opportunity to confirm and consolidate their social standing….Building a community was a task which went hand in hand with the confirmation of class identity, and helped determine the shape and nature of middle-class leisure in a changing environment….The solitary family was inadequate for social fulfilment and the middle class…had to build its secondary associations to combat the strains of the new environment. For recreation these might take the form of private house or garden parties among business associates or the extended family, but a major agent of regeneration was certainly the formally constituted club or society. These voluntary associations embraced a wide range of activities: sports, amateur soldiering, literary and scientific education and debate, the definition and promotion of professional interests, and the pursuit of reform—all, in varying degrees, performed an important social function….By such means did the mid-Victorian middle classes sustain communities of interest which overcame the barriers of a cellular urban society.[11]

It is possible to see this process at work in the Malvern Cycling Club, many of the members also being connected with other voluntary associations of the kind listed above.

What motives underlay the founding of the early cycling clubs? In the 1870s, the motivation was complex. Peterborough Amateur Bicycle Club, for example, was formed in 1874 as part of a nation-wide movement whose aim was "to associate the principal amateur bicycle riders in Great Britain together." The objects of the Peterborough Club were "to unite bicyclists in the city and neighbourhood, to get up races, to provide prizes and to arrange excursions."[12] The club was therefore formed as part of a national network with an interest both in sport and recreation, while the word "unite" reflects a degree of interest in self-protection and good public relations. In 1877, in Hampshire, the *Christchurch Times* reported that:

> Bicycle clubs are now established in most of the large towns throughout the county: their object is to train members in the art of bicycle riding, to see that offences against the public are not wantonly committed by careless and indiscreet riding, and also to protect the members from the stupid treatment they sometimes receive from pedestrians, drivers and others, by whom their lives are occasionally imperiled.[13]

Similar concerns can be found in a *Berrows Worcestershire Journal* article of May 1877 in which the reasons for the formation of the Worcester B.C. were set out.[14] An interesting mixture of public concern and self-interest is evident. Those able to afford cycles were from a social group concerned with its public image. Law-abiding and respectable, they exercised discipline in their conduct, and sought respect from others, to allow them to use the roads freely and in safety. On a ride to Evesham in June

Fig. 20.2. Clarendon School, North Malvern. The three Miss Flints, who founded the school in 1898, encouraged their young ladies to ride cycles.

1877, the members of the Worcester Bicycle Club were carefully drilled:

> The captain, on the way, drilled the members, by sounding the bugle for mounting, dismounting, single-file, double-file, which was carried out very well indeed, considering that the club is in its infancy, the dismounting being particularly well done...

The ride had its lighter side, however:

> On the return journey several members picked up glowworms and put them in front of their hats, the effect being very novel.[15]

Once formed, clubs worked to ensure that their members could enjoy cycling without hindrance. Articles in local and national papers had the objects of publicising the activities of the club in order to recruit more members, and of informing and educating the general public. Campaigning for cyclists' rights and well-maintained roads were further preoccupations, along with erecting road signs and danger boards. The C.T.C. was closely associated with such activities. A number of the Malvern C.C. members also belonged to the C.T.C., ensuring that pressure was kept up locally.[16] They subscribed to the Road Improvement Association, "formed for enlightening the much-enduring British rate-payers as to the best systems of road repair;"[17] they published articles and letters on road conditions in local papers;[18] they entertained local roadmen to teas;[19] they contributed to the construction of the new Jubilee Drive on the Malvern Hills, now one of the most beautiful of local roads;[20] and they paid for the erection of danger boards.[21] Lord Beauchamp and Sir Edmund Lechmere, M.P., carried considerable local influence. After 1888, Lord Beauchamp was a member of the County Council. It is clear that they were encouraged to use their influence. In 1885, for example, at the Malvern Cycling Club annual dinner, Ranken "hoped Sir Edmund...would in the next session help to give a county government measure, which would place the roads under the control of local bodies. He trusted too that something would be done for opening parks to cyclists (Applause)."[22]

It would be wrong to infer that cyclists in the 1880s were motivated in exactly the same way as those in the previous decade. In Malvern, as elsewhere, the public were much better informed about cycling than before. The early accounts of the club's activities, and comments by members in the local press, suggest a more relaxed and less defensive attitude; however, in broad terms it is reasonable to assume a degree of continuity. Echoes of the motives expressed by the first cyclists can be found in a speech made by the Malvern Cycling Club captain, John Need, at the annual dinner in 1905, by which time active club membership was beginning to wane. He said there was much less need for a club than in earlier years, as "many of the obstacles that formerly confronted devotees of cycling had disappeared, and the necessity for combination was not therefore so great."[23]

Malvern C.C. seems to have been formed as a social club, for recreation rather than racing, though in 1883, members did compete in races, with some success. Their reason for withdrawing from racing is in itself instructive. Having won prizes at the Great Western Railway Widows and Orphans Fund fete in Malvern in 1883, several entered the following year. Over the winter, there had been discussion of the possibilities of laying a cinder racing path in Malvern, but on the day of the races, on an indifferent grass track, competitors in associated running events were identified as professionals. Their presence compromised the amateur standing of all competitors at the fete, so, on the advice of NCU officials, the Malvern riders withdrew from the contest. They never raced again, and the idea for the track sank without trace. Social standing and membership of the club depended on amateur status.[24]

Malvern C.C. members responded to the challenge of long distance cycling. The Worcester Tricycle Club made it a matter of honour to undertake one long ride a year, and three Malvern club members may have been inspired by this when they rode the 125 miles from Malvern to Bournemouth in 24 hours in June 1883. Setting out on Saturday evening, on their "Royal Mail" bicycles, they survived a thunderstorm on the Cotswolds between Cheltenham and Cirencester, and rode on through Swindon, Marlborough, Salisbury, and Christchurch to arrive in Bournemouth with a few minutes in hand. They returned by train on Monday with an excursion party from Malvern.[25] Until well into the first decade of the 20th century, members went on tours at Easter and Whitsun.[26] The club published touring hints in its handbook, and kept a collection of road maps for members' use.

The greatest long-distance cyclist of the Malvern club, and perhaps of his generation, was Harold Freeman, a man of infinite leisure, and the epitome of the English sporting gentleman. Born in 1850, he earned athletic honours at Oxford, and played international rugby football for England from 1872 to 1874. He was an expert at squash racquets, fives, hockey, and tennis, and played cricket for

Hertfordshire between 1877 and 1884. In that year he began his habitual practice of spending each winter in Switzerland. He was founder of the Davos tobogganing club and president for 30 years. He commenced cycling in 1869 on a "bone-shaker," "from which he ascended to the ordinary," progressing through the whole history of the development of the cycle, "ultimately descending to the safety, after a little experimenting with geared front drivers." As a committed tourist, he rode throughout the summer months. From 1877 he kept an accurate record of mileage, noting distances and road conditions on a pad during his journeys, and transcribing the information into a series of leather-bound volumes. He first exceeded 10,000 miles in a year in 1895, and by the time of his death, which came in 1916, shortly after his only son was killed in action in WWI, Freeman had covered over a quarter of a million miles on 11 different machines, his longest ride being 173.5 miles in 24 hours. His charts were published in *Cycling* annually. In 1915, his 65th year, he covered 12,579 miles. He was the last president of the Malvern Cycling Club. His life well illustrates many of the various appeals of cycling to his contemporaries: the physical challenge; the love of sport and recreation; the organising skills; the technical interest in the development of machines, of which he built up quite a collection; the systematic and careful recording of mileage, which he made use of in his *Cyclists' Guide and Route Book* (1898); the companionship, with members of the Malvern club and his touring companions, particularly T. W. Weeding, who wrote his obituary in *Cycling*; and an interest in wildflowers and architecture.[27]

In 1879, G. J. Romanes had written in *Nineteenth Century*:

> Recreation is, or ought to be, not a pastime entered upon for the sake of pleasure which it affords, but an act of duty undertaken for the sake of the subsequent power it generates, and the subsequent profit which it ensures.[28]

Fortunately, if they came across this pompous nonsense, the members of Malvern Cycling Club ignored it. They had the good sense to enjoy their cycling for its own sake and for the pleasant social activities which became associated with it. Peter Bailey argues that:

> ...the middle class, as the most substantial beneficiaries of the new bonus (of leisure), were themselves uneasy about the potentially corrupting effects of leisure on the internal disciplines of their own class.[29]

It is possible to find evidence which might support Bailey's case, and even to hear echoes of the kinds of argument that were put forward by Romanes, in the record of the Malvern Cycling Club, but I think it would be wrong to give too much emphasis to such evidence.

I do not see unease in the positive way in which Ranken, a clergyman, spoke at the 1889 dinner of the recreative benefits of cycling:

> Now he had reached the years of maturity he liked to ride quietly and take his wife with him, and enjoy the fresh air and beauties of nature. His idea of the purpose of a cycling club was to enable its members to escape from the bustle and excitement of every day life into the calm and solitude of the countryside. (Applause).[30]

The profit motive can be found in a speech given by G. H. Williamson, Mayor of Worcester, and an industrialist of some standing, at the 1895 dinner. Noting that the club did much to promote good fellowship, he commented that he had "thoroughly enjoyed cycling among the beautiful lanes of Worcestershire." He added, however, that:

> ...this kind of riding was an educational as well as a healthful exercise, and tended to a wholesome mind. Cycling had also introduced into the country an important industry in which millions sterling were invested and thousands of persons had found employment.[31]

He had been an honorary member of the club since its foundation and his brother was an active member of the Worcester T.C. Evidently it helped the image of the pastime and of club members if pleasure could be seen to go hand in hand with other benefits, such as good health and prosperity, but the overall impression from reading about the activities of the members is one of relaxed enjoyment, fellowship, and good fun.

Good humour, self-confidence, and absence of cant can be found in an instructive exchange of letters in the *Malvern Advertiser* in 1889. "A Blue-ribboned Cyclist" had written objecting to the cycling club "apparently sanctioning hotels, by making them invariably their starting point on the way home," and to riding on Sundays. A vigorous defence was made. Arthur Melvin replied that:

> The Malvern C.C., as a club, has no more concern either directly or indirectly with the promotion of

temperance or Sunday observance principles than it has with the propagation of Buddhism or the Lost Tribes theory; it is simply an association for the promotion of cycling, and its arrangements are naturally made with a view of promoting such recreation in a manner which may be most convenient to its members.

A second barrel was fired by the club captain, David Coldwell, a local chemist, and the correspondence closed.[32]

The sociable nature of the club, and of the local cycling community as a whole, is indicated by the number of runs arranged in conjunction with other clubs in the district. Outings were made to places of interest, such as the village of Ripple, where, while the club went to view the misericords in the church, three members left in charge of the machines organised an impromptu athletic match for the village children. The unusual spectacle of a cycling club in this "remote" village brought out the entire population, and as the local paper concluded in its report:

> Altogether, the visit of the Malvern Cycling Club will be reckoned a memorable one for the villagers—a day to reckon the age of their children from.[33]

It was 1887. The village was a mile from the main road between Worcester and Gloucester. Such visits were characteristic of other local clubs, too. For instance, in 1889 the Worcester T.C. rode to Castlemorton Common to watch a display of shelling practice by the artillery, and in the same year they visited the salt baths at Droitwich. In 1891 they attended an organ recital at Newland Church, given by Mr. Armstrong, of the Malvern C.C. The Malvern Club took its cue from their Worcester friends in establishing a photographic section and in taking a first-aid course from Dr. Dixey, an honorary member.[34]

In its social life, Malvern C.C. made a considerable contribution to the entertainments of the town and to local charities. After the 1889 annual dinner for the 56 members and their guests, others arrived, and 200 people enjoyed the dancing in Malvern Assembly Rooms.[35] Two years later the club organised a fancy dress ball at the Assembly Rooms, the proceeds to go to Malvern Rural Hospital. Costumes could be hired from an enterprising club member, Caleb Foxwell, a Malvern draper. The public were admitted to view from 9 to 11 o'clock. The *Malvern Advertiser* recorded that "a ball of this particular character had not been held in Malvern for several years."[36] Victoria's Golden Jubilee was celebrated with a cycle meet.[37] The Diamond Jubilee celebrations involved a parade of decorated cycles with cyclists in ornamental and fanciful costumes. Thirty-four ladies and 42 gentlemen entered. The ladies' prize, of 3 guineas, went to Miss F. Butler, a district nurse from the Wyche, whose machine had "a framework and canopy of evergreens and flowers; also the words 'Patience and Water Gruel are excellent for Gout'..." Mr John Need, of the Malvern C.C., won the gentlemen's competition, dressed as a cavalier. "Cheers were given for the Queen, Lady Foley, and Dr. Dixey (Chairman of the Urban Council)."[38] Such cycle parades were popular in Malvern well into the 20th century. Cycle gymkhanas were also held. At one in 1899, in aid of North Malvern and Cowleigh Nursing Funds, Viscountess Harberton presented the prizes.[39]

Lady Harberton's name is one to conjure with in the history of women's emancipation. Though not a member of the local cycling club, she had a house in Malvern, and was a familiar figure locally in her cycling costume. A founder member of the Rational Dress Society, she fought uncompromisingly for "a style of dress based on considerations of health, comfort and beauty." Her speeches were reported in Malvern papers, as was the famous case she brought against the landlady of the Hautboy Hotel at Ockham in Surrey who objected to her rational dress and refused to serve her in the coffee lounge. At a Sanitary Institute Conference in Southampton in 1899 she argued that:

> There was no pluck required to wear rational dress. The wearers might be greeted by a few boys who shouted "bloomers," but ladies should do what they believe to be right, no matter what anybody said.[40]

Lady Harberton would no doubt have approved the spirited defence put up by a Miss C. Hilliard in 1899, who was charged with furiously riding a bicycle down Church Street in Malvern. Miss Hilliard's lawyer said his client "admitted riding fast, but she was not riding furiously and she had the machine under full control." Not persuaded, the magistrate fined her 10/- with 5/- costs.[41]

The freedom of dress Lady Harberton fought for, and the independence cycling gave many women, made major contributions to the women's movement. In Malvern, as elsewhere, it is possible to find good evidence for the way in which cycling enhanced women's lives. John Need's sister, before she married, was a gifted amateur landscape painter, and used her cycle to find subjects.[42] The girls of

Clarendon School in North Malvern, started by the three Miss Flints in 1898, were encouraged to cycle for recreation.[43] In 1899, Dora Penny was able to ride the 40 miles from Wolverhampton to visit Edward Elgar at Birchwood, arriving "rather warm and dusty," returning to Worcester to catch the evening train home.[44] Such evidence supports the claim made by Kathleen McCrone that:

> The social impact of the bicycle in the late-nineteenth century is difficult to exaggerate….By enabling women to escape from chaperons and the physical bounds of home, it brought the sexes together on equal terms more completely than any other sport or pastime.

Because of its public nature and wide popularity, cycling focused attention on women's right, desire and need to participate in healthy, outdoor exercise and to play a full part in the life of the nation. The New Woman, pedalling her way to freedom, was a sign of dramatically changing times. Her ability to ride 50 miles a day and repair her own machine belied the traditional image of female helplessness and frailty, and conveyed a new one of strength, vigour, and self-sufficiency. Awheel on the open road, she appeared every inch an independent being who could think, say, and do what she liked, who deserved to be taken seriously, and who rejected sartorial and ideological corsets of the past.[45]

Edward Elgar learnt to cycle in 1900, and very quickly his Royal Sunbeam became essential to his creativity. With his cycling companion, Rose Burley, headmistress of a Malvern private school, he explored the surrounding countryside. She wrote:

> Much of Elgar's music is closely connected with the places we visited for, as we rode, he would often become silent and I knew that some new melody or, more probably, some new piece of orchestral texture, had occurred to him.

The cadence of pedalling, as well as the inspirational quality of the landscape, appear to have contributed to the creative process. Cycling became for Elgar what walking was for Wordsworth—both a necessary recreation and a source of inspiration.[46]

A more practical creativity was found among cycle manufacturers in Malvern. Several club members were cycle agents, their trade no doubt benefiting from the connection. Some, including Charles and Walter Santler, also made cycles. It was an exciting time for anyone with a glimmering of interest in technical matters: the brothers, particularly Charles, were continually experimenting and seeking solutions to a whole range of technical problems. While studying at Birmingham College of Science, he made a freewheel in his spare time, testing its effectiveness by fitting it to the treadle of a small turning lathe. He developed this with the help of a Malvern tailor, John Nicholls, for application to cycles, and they took out a patent in 1884. The patent was allowed to lapse, but Santler could lay claim to being an early pioneer of the free-wheel mechanism, which he fitted to his tricycles in 1885. Santler also developed a bottom-bracket spindle with replaceable cones, and a range of tricycles and bicycles, including a chainless cycle with bevel gears, and one of Harold Freeman's "front-drivers." By 1890 the brothers had designed and built a motor car, experimenting with steam, benzoline, and petrol engines. Their "Malvernia," tested in 1894 at

Fig. 20.3. Advertisement in the Malvern Advertiser, 1 Sept. 1883.

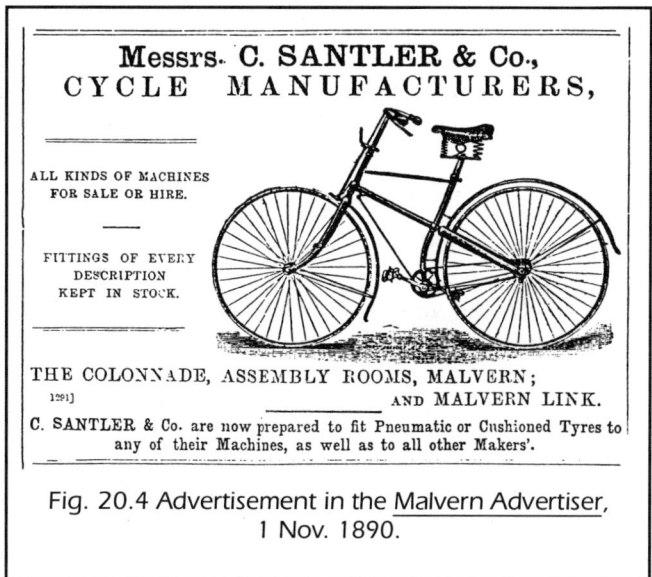

Fig. 20.4 Advertisement in the Malvern Advertiser, 1 Nov. 1890.

Madresfield Court, has been accepted by the Veteran Car Club as the earliest recorded 4-wheeled motor car of British manufacture.[47]

Messrs. Santler and Co. went into the production of motor cars in 1897 and continued as a car manufacturer until 1922, by which time Henry Morgan, their main Malvern competitor, was firmly established as one of the leading manufacturers of sports cars. Cycling had been Morgan's first love, too. He made his first cycle as a student at Crystal Palace Engineering College, where he proved unbeatable in college races. He opened a garage in Malvern in 1906 and within a few years was making his famous 3-wheeler car, the "Runabout."[48]

It was the motor car, of course, that sounded the knell of middle-class clubs like the Malvern C.C. The development of the motor car was even more rapid than that of the cycle, and clearly accelerated its decline as a fashionable mode of transport. In 1905, of the 5 members on the club Whitsun tour, 2 went by motor car.[49] Local cycle manufacturers could not compete in price with mass-produced machines in the first decade of the 20th century. In 1900, a BSA cycle cost 10 guineas: Burgess' "Lighting" on the same advertisement was priced at £13 10s. A Humber at J. A. Jones's shop was also 10 guineas, with "the most perfect free wheel." By 1907, the Humber was priced at 8 guineas, with "easy payments of 9/- a month." After the turn of the century, there were also many secondhand cycles for sale: the bottom had fallen out of the market. Cycle manufacture ceased in Malvern.[50]

In the 1890s, fashionable interest in cycling led to the development of a number of short-lived clubs: Barnards Green C.C., Barnards Green "Swifts" C.C., which became Malvern "Swifts" C.C., "Lightning" C.C. (promoting Arthur Burgess' cycles), Malvern Link C.C., and Wyche C.C. Malvern Cycling Club and the "Swifts" developed ladies" sections in 1898, but neither outlasted the fashion or the century. Both the "Lightning" and the "Swifts" were racing clubs, the "Swifts" holding meetings in Malvern until 1908, the year in which Ernie Payne, of Worcester St. Johns C.C. was a member of the gold-medal pursuit team at the London Olympic Games. His win provided no inspiration in Malvern, for the "Swifts" disappeared in that year.[51]

Club cycling had ceased to hold its appeal. The bicycle became a utilitarian means of transport rather than a fashionable source of recreation. Young men turned to other sports. The members of Malvern Cycling Club were getting old and there was no renewal from their own class. Their interest in civic life gave them little spare time for cycling. Of the 17 members of Malvern Urban District Council in 1900, no less than 6 were Malvern Cycling Club members.[52] The club was finally wound up in 1912, donating its funds to charity.[53] During its lifetime, the club had made a notable contribution to local and national life, forming associations that helped bond the community together, introducing a range of functions and entertainments that gave pleasure to many in the town as well as to themselves, and setting an impressive example of civic leadership.

Bibliography

Alderson, J. D. and Ruston, D. M. *Morgan Sweeps the Board*. Gentry Books, 1978.

Bailey, P. *Leisure and Class in Victorian England*. Routledge & Kegan Paul, 1978.

Brailsford, D. *Sport, Time and Society: The British at Play*. Routledge & Kegan Paul, 1991.

Freeman, H. *Littlebury's Cyclist's Guide and Route Book for the West Midland District*. The Worcester Press, 1898.

McCrone, K. *Sport and the Physical Emancipation of English Women, 1870–1914*. Routledge & Kegan Paul, 1988.

Moore, J. N. *Edward Elgar: a Creative Life*. Oxford University Press, 1987.

Oakley, W. *The Winged Wheel*. C.T.C., 1977.

Smith, B. S. *A History of Malvern* (2nd ed). Alan Sutton, 1978.

Street, R. T. C. *Victorian High Wheelers*. Dorset Publishing Co., 1979.

Sutton, R. A. *"Malvernia": The Origins and History of the First Motor Car built by Charles and Walter Santler*. Michael Sedgwick Memorial Trust, 1987.

Primary Sources

Much of the information comes from bound volumes of the *Malvern Advertiser*, 1876–1902, and of the *Malvern News* of the same period, kept in Malvern Library. Both papers were published weekly. After 1904, the *Malvern Gazette* became the leading local paper, and volumes for 1904 to 1916, and some subsequent years, have been consulted. Additional material comes from Peterborough newspaper articles; early cycling magazines; handbooks of the Malvern Cycling Club kept in Malvern Library; the minute books of the Worcester Tricycle Club and related material kept in Worcester Records Office; and records of the Worcester St. Johns Cycling Club. Information about members of the Malvern Cycling Club comes from the club handbooks for 1890 to 1906, and from *Kelly's Worcestershire Directories* of 1888, 1892, 1900, and 1906.

Notes

1. Smith, B. S., *History Of Malvern*, 1978.

2. Quoted in Bailey, P., *Leisure and Class in Victorian England*, 1978.

3. Sir Edmund Lechmere laid claim to being the first cyclist in Malvern, in a speech at the 1885 annual dinner (*Malvern Advertiser*, 19.12.1885). "Some thirty-five years ago he had a velocipede—a sort of knife-grinding affair in appearance—on which he rode round the hills so often that he was called 'the flying knife-grinder' (laughter). He remembered meeting Dr. Gully one day, who spoke of the capital exercise which these machines supplied to the lower extremities." Dr. Gully was one of those responsible for introducing the "water cure" to Malvern.

4. *Malvern Advertiser*, 15.2.1890.

5. Following criticism of the hill-climbing capabilities of the "Quadrant" in a feature by "Cog" (possibly a cognomen for J. A. Jones) in the *Malvern Advertiser* (2.7.1887), John Hamsher, who sold "Quadrants," wrote to the paper (9.7.1887). Editorial comment noted trade rivalry. A. G. Gwynn, the Malvern C.C. captain, wrote in Hamsher's defence the next week, and after a reply by "Cog," the correspondence closed.

6. *Malvern Advertiser*, 28.10.1899.

7. Members' occupations from *Kelly's Worcestershire Directories*.

8. Information from *Malvern Advertiser*, 31.7.1880, and *Cyclist and Wheel World Annual*, 1884, which gives the honorary secretary as E. J. Bartleet, the captain as E. W. D. Perrins, and the membership as 40. E. W. D. Perrins may be a misprint for C. W. D. Perrins (1864–1958), associated with Lea and Perrins Worcester Sauce and the Royal Worcester Porcelain factory.

9. *Malvern Advertiser*, 17.3.1883.

10. Information from the obituary published in the *Malvern Gazette*, 14.4.1905.

11. Bailey, P., *Leisure and Class in Victorian England*, 1978, pp. 76 and 77.

12. Information from Peterborough Cycling Club centenary programme, 1974.

13. *Christchurch Times*, 11.8.1877, quoted in Street, R. T. C. *Victorian High Wheelers*, 1979.

14. *Berrows Worcestershire Journal*, 12.5.1877.

15. *Berrows Worcestershire Journal*, June 1877.

16. At the 1884 AGM, Ranken advised members to join the CTC.

17. *Malvern Advertiser*, 7.5.1885.

18. e.g., *Malvern Advertiser*, 30.4.1887.

19. 1890 Malvern C.C. handbook.

20. *Malvern Advertiser*, 7.5.1887.

21. Danger boards were erected on Camp Hill and at Little Malvern in 1884. *Malvern Advertiser*, 28.2.1885 (AGM report).

22. *Malvern Advertiser*, 19.12.1885. Sir Edmund was a politician to the last. He died at a constituency meeting in Pershore in December 1894. His last words were, "I'm all right." (*Malvern Advertiser*, 22.12.1894).

23. *Malvern Gazette*, 20.1.1905.

24. Reported in *Malvern Advertiser*, 30.8.1884, and in *The Cyclist*, 27.8.1884. The NCU officials were J. J. Neale, of Bristol, and H. Sturmey, of Birmingham.

25. *Malvern Advertiser*, 7.7.1883. Dennis Brailford, in *Sport, Time and Society: The British at Play* (1991), points out the importance of the 1871 Bank Holiday Act: "The addition of a Monday break on at least three occasions a year gave added recreational force to the already strengthened weekend. More broadly, the 1871 Act presaged the strong leisure growth that was to characterise the whole coming decade." p. 123.

26. The last record tour was to Oxford, Whitsun 1907. CTC members were reminded not to forget their tickets (*Malvern Gazette*, 17.5.1907).

27. Information from *Malvern Gazette*, 5.7.1907, 2.8.1912, 28.2.1913, 21.7.1916 (his obituary); and from *Cycling*, 26.6.1907, and 27.7.1916.

28. Quoted in Bailey, P., *Leisure and Class in Victorian England*, 1978.

29. Ibid.

30. *Malvern Advertiser*, 17.10.1889.
31. *Malvern Advertiser*, 2.2.1895.
32. *Malvern Advertiser*, 13.4.1889 and 20.4.1889.
33. *Malvern Advertiser*, 21.5.1887.
34. Information from Worcester Tricycle Club minute books. Club runs, e.g., *Malvern Advertiser*, 2.5.1885, 26.6.1886. The photographic section was formed in 1893. The first aid classes were organised in 1888. "An ambulance class of nine members has been held under the able and gratuitous instruction of Dr. Dixey. It is hoped that the knowledge gained will be of service to members in assisting not only fellow cyclists, but others." (*Malvern Advertiser*, 3.3.1888). The WTC course of five classes cost members 2/6 in 1887. They took an examination, and the examiner's fee was 3 guineas. In 1892 they purchased an ambulance bag to carry on runs.
35. *Malvern Advertiser*, 19.10.1889.
36. *Malvern Advertiser*, 4.4.1891.
37. *Malvern Advertiser*, 6.6.1887.
38. *Malvern Advertiser*, 26.6.1897.
39. *Malvern Advertiser*, 16.9.1899.
40. *Malvern Advertiser*, 6.9.1899. The general information is from Lady Harberton's obituary, published in the *Malvern Gazette*, 5.5.1911.
41. *Malvern Advertiser*, 4.11.1899.
42. Information from Mrs. Smith, of Malvern, John Need's daughter, who was born in 1899, in conversation in 1986, and from Mr. Dennis Baker, grandson to both John Need and J. H. Baker.
43. *Malvern This Week*, 20.8.1986 (a short-lived local paper).
44. Moore, J. N., *Edward Elgar: A Creative Life*, 1987.
45. McCrone, K. *Sport and the Physical Emancipation of English Women, 1870–1914*, 1988, p. 183.
46. Moore, J. N. Ibid.
47. Information about the Santler brothers comes from a variety of sources. Dr. Alan Sutton's book is the most accessible. Charles Santler made claim to being the first motorist in Malvern in a letter to the *Malvern Gazette*, 19.3.1932. The 1884 free-wheel patent is number 5993. It was described in the *Malvern Advertiser*, 12.9.1885. The spindle is referred to in an article in the *Malvern News*, 16.1.1897. A range of cycles is described in Santlers' 1898 catalogue lent to me by Mr. Edgar Barber, of Malvern. In it are a number of commendations, including reports on machines from Harold Freeman and Henry W. Ravenshaw, a distinguished engineer and one-time member of the Western Ramblers B.C. The *Malvern Advertiser* regularly carried illustrated advertisements for Santlers' cycles. Information about Charles Santler's experimental engines is from a letter to the *Malvern Gazette*, 23.11.35.
48. Information from Alderson, J. D., and Ruston, D. M., *Morgan Sweeps the Board*, 1978.
49. 11 and 12 June 1905. See Oakley, W., *The Winged Wheel* (1977), for an account of the impact of the motor car on cycling, especially on CTC membership. In 1906 the CTC debated admitting motorists as members.
50. Information from advertisements in the *Malvern Advertiser* and *Malvern Gazette*, 1900 to 1910.
51. Information from the Malvern Advertiser, e.g., 6.4.1895, 10.9.1898, 13.5.1899, 6.6.1900, 1.12.1900; and from *Worcester St. Johns C.C., 1888–1988: A History* by R. Alma, published privately for club members.
52. Malvern C.C. members of the MUDC in 1900 were: H. E. Dixey (chairman), H. A. Acworth, A. C. Baker, C. F. Grindrod, G. Howell, and G. P. Yapp. Arthur Wilesmith, whose brother was a Malvern C.C. member, was president of Malvern Link C.C. T. C. Santler was an active MUDC member in later years. Arthur Baldwin, M.P., father of Stanley Baldwin, who became Prime Minister, was president of the Malvern C.C. from 1899 to 1908.
53. *Malvern Gazette*, 31.5.1912: "For the past season or so things have been going a bit slack in the Club; in fact it has existed only in name. I suppose this is due to the fact that cycling is now so general, being indulged in by all classes, young and old, that there is less need for the Club than there was in the early days of cycling, when it had fewer devotees."

Nick Clayton

21. Little and Often— The Records of the Amateur Bicycle Club

On 16 May 1994, Sothebys sold 3 lots which comprised the complete records of the Amateur Bicycle Club from 1871–1903. The hoard consisted of 7 minute books, a quantity of bronze badges, a replica of the Members Gold Challenge Medal, and a quantity of printed and manuscript ephemera including bills, letters, menus, meet cards, rule books, and other items. The collection, under the patronage of Lorne Shields, is destined for Ottawa Museum, and he has kindly allowed copies to be made which it is intended will be available to researchers in England. It is a record of the earliest days of cycling, and will provide a new source for historians interested in the period. As a social document it has particular fascination because the ABC was a highly idiosyncratic club. It was written almost entirely by one man, the man who was Honorary Secretary and Treasurer of the ABC for over thirty years, Henry N. Custance Esq. In effect, it is the story of his adult life.

The first minute book begins on 16 May 1871 with the official founding of the club, and this minute refers to a preliminary meeting which had been held the previous January. Included also is a letter dated 21 January 1870, which speaks of someone who "wishes to join the ABC." This is significant because it is some 5 months before the formation of the Pickwick Bicycle Club on 22 June 1870. The Pickwick is generally held to be the senior English club.

In 1877, *Bicycling News* carried an anonymous article about the Amateur Bicycle Club from information most probably supplied by Custance. It has his style.

> The Club was founded by three or four friends dining together and enjoying themselves over some excellent port wine, whilst discussing a tour taken in 1869 on boneshakers...the Club was speedily formed, early in the year 1871, from gentlemen belonging to the staff of the Middlesex Hospital, the Skating Club and the London Rowing Club.... The ABC always was, and we trust always will be, a club in which gentlemen may seek their recreation and enjoyment. In its numbers the Club is sufficiently large for the encouragement of sociability amongst its fifty or sixty members, who being of equal stations in life, have no difficulty in seeking companions for tours....The qualifications for candidature are perhaps very severe, but at the same time we believe that the executive have been wisely guided in maintaining that every candidate must not only own a

Fig. 21-1. Letter dated 21 January 1871, enclosing the name card of a gentleman who wishes to join the ABC. This letter appears to establish the ABC as the oldest bicycle club in England.

bicycle and prove himself a gentleman to the satisfaction of the Committee, but must also be personally known to both his proposer and seconder.

Today we might consider this policy a trifle snooty, and indeed it appears to have been of mixed benefit to the ABC, for while the line was held for 30 years, the minute books complain constantly of poor attendance at meets and lack of esprit de corps among the members. In the very first month, only May and Custance turned out for the meet at Swiss Cottage. Custance reported "the thinness of attendance at this meet is probably due to the cold N.E. wind that was blowing." By 27 August, "The Captain" (Custance was also Captain as well as Hon. Sec. and Treasurer for the first 4 years) "regrets that more members do not show up at meets."

Because the members were middle class, they all had many other calls on their time. They had a variety of other hobbies: shooting, racquets, yachting, rowing—Custance himself was a keen oarsman. Many had families and country seats which kept them away; most of them also worked very hard. There are minuted apologies from the Rev. Crofton, Club Chaplain, that he was detained by a wedding or a funeral, and Herbert Canning, captain from 1890–96, was neglectful of his captaincy through pressure of work at the British South Africa Company in the City. John Tudor-Frere, the enthusiastic captain from 1875–80 whose country seat was Roydon Hall, Diss, Norfolk, lost interest for some unexplained reason in 1879: it would not seem to have been family ties at that date, for in 1893 he writes to Custance, "I am to leave town next Wednesday. I am to pass the rest of my life at Roydon and sometime in April a girl will marry me."

Despite the regular distribution of printed meet cards, Custance found it necessary to send the following circular to members in June 1872. "Dear Sir, I regret that I should have the occasion to draw the attention of the Committee at their last meeting to the scanty attendances of the several members at the Meets of the Club." This was accompanied by a listing of the 31 members and the number of meets they had attended so far that season.

Various ideas were discussed to overcome this continuing problem, although they never got round to admitting members who actually enjoyed going out cycling and had the time to do so. In 1876, Custance put up a prize for races to take place at the beginning of each meet before setting out on the run. This resulted in some neat little maps being pasted into the minute books, but no noticeable increase in attendances. Six years later in 1882, they agreed to award annual cash prizes to the best attenders; £5.00 for the first, £2.00, and £1.00. This plan too had no effect on turnout, but it gave Custance the additional job of keeping the score. Almost predictably, the man who won first prize every year was the man who thought up the idea, the man who kept the score, Henry N. Custance Esq., Hon. Sec. and Treasurer. It is very odd how this fierce amateur could without qualm pocket £5.00 of his friends' subscription moneys, in some years nearly half the total income of the club, simply for turning up for meets.

His analysis does however provide some interesting statistics. There were about 1,780 attendances at meets over the 30 years; Custance with 593 accounted for nearly one third of them. The next highest with 168 was Tredway Clarke, the captain from 1881–88, and although there were in total about 90 members over the years, the 10 most active accounted for three quarters of all attendances, the other 80 averaging less than 6 rides each.

The Club Championship Gold Medal

The Gold Medal story plays a prominent part in the minute books, and the bronze replica included in the hoard is one of those given to the annual holder.

On 28 January 1874, it was resolved "to expend a sum not exceeding £15 in purchasing a Champion Cup or Medal to be run for by bicyclists...with a view of rendering bicycling more popular with the General Public." Somewhat complicated rules for a contest were drawn up and published in *Bells Life*, and drew a letter from the famous professional John Keen. While signing himself "Yours Obediently" he rather cheekily pointed out that it would be difficult to make a challenge for a medal that had yet to be won, and he proposed some alterations to the rules. The ABC accepted Keen's suggestions and he duly won the race, which was held on 23 November at Lillie Bridge. His share of the gate money was £6.11.0, which he acknowledged with the hope that "at the next competition there will be a larger meeting as it will be better known then." It was a vain hope: there were no challenges the following year, and when the Committee required Keen to walk over on the road, he declined as it was snowing. Instead he signed the minute book, resigning all claims to the medal.

Having taken their medal back, the Committee recycled the 10 Mile Championship Medal to become the Members Gold Challenge Medal. It was initially raced for twice annually, and in later years once annually, over a course most usually from the Lion

Hotel, Barnet to Market Place, St. Neots. The first race in April 1876 was contested by 5 members, but at the second held in August, Custance walked over unopposed. This sad state of affairs was often the case over the next 25 years, although the medal never seems to have lost its importance in the eyes of the members. On 8 June l877, *Bicycling News* featured Custance in a biographical article. His C.V. was padded with the information, "He has also done a little racing, having three times contested the Members Gold Challenge Medal of the ABC and held it from 5 August 1873 until 28 April l877 when Mr. Crofton, who is also a member of the Dark Blue Bicycle Club, deprived him of possession."

The minute books expose this little pork pie. As we have seen, the first race was in 1876, not 1873, and Custance won only the once when he was unopposed. True, Crofton, who was a fair rider, did beat him in 1877, but so did Compton, the only other starter.

The Machines They Rode

There are many references to the machines ridden by members, particularly in the early days. King and Custance began as boneshaker riders, and surprisingly Custance kept his rubber tyred 40-in. Parfrey until March 1876, when he changed it for a 54-in. Keen Eclipse. Similarly Tudor-Frere rode a 38-in. Beck, essentially a boneshaker with fat rubber tyres, until April l876. The Beck brothers, J. & E., were early members of the club, and Beck machines were popular. A run in April 1872 comprised 5 Becks, 3 Keen Bros, and 1 Ariel. Beck stopped manufacturing about 1875 and John Keen received the club favours. There are several reports of visits to Keen's works at Surbiton Hill and later Clapham. In 1878, Custance and Bicknell both had the new 100-spoke Eclipse, although it seems that Keen's machines were as unreliable as most, and his repair service distinctly leisurely.

9 November 1878: "At Streatham Hill the wire thread of his front tyre parted and poked its nose through its rubber sheath…transfixing the fleshy part of its owner's right thigh….In the Falcon Road the Hon. Sec. fortunately overtook the Vet walking along, and told Keen to send and fetch the nag away for repairs speedily. (This of course he did not do for weeks.)"

14 March 1885: "The Hon. Sec. permanently lamed his fiery steed by John Keen out of 'Metal,' by breaking its back just behind the saddle, and sending its rider to earth with a decided bruise of his crupper…it seems more than doubtful whether this celebrated Eclipse can be got ready again (judging by the tardy action so inseparable from John Keen) by Easter."

As the ordinary gives way to the safety, other machines appear. Mr. May is noted on his new Kangaroo on 28 May 1885, and Mr. Innes is riding one as late as June 1888. Herbert Canning, the captain from 1890–96, had a veritable stable of machines, appearing in the course of one year on a geared Facile, a brand new Whippet, and a Humber pneumatic. But what in 1896 was W. F. Adam's "sliding seat Gee"? Whatever it was, he was still riding it in 1898.

We have noted that John Keen appears in these records as supplier of machines to the club, and also as the leading character in the 10 Mile Challenge Medal debacle. The original manuscript letters from him, pasted into the minute books, probably represent the only surviving examples of his hand. They fix the date of his move from Surbiton Hill to Clapham Junction at some time between May and September 1875, and they also give us a flavour of his writing style—literate, respectful, and neat. When a

Fig. 21.2. Drawing of Henry N. Custance, probably done at the ABC dinner, 18 January 1879, by R. Gantony, the club artist.

benefit for Keen was got up in 1885, £5.00 was sent from club funds.

The Amateur Question and the Hampton Court Meets

The amateur question was much discussed in the early days of the sport, and the eponymous ABC had a special interest. In March 1875 they resolved it "desirable that this Club be forward in the organisation of an Association to recognise a certain class of clubs," but as negotiations continued, the ABC moved further and further away from the idea of associating with anyone. An undated letter to Custance from Penrose Hon. Sec. of the Dark Blue Bicycle Club says, "I shall be glad to know what position the ABC will take with regard to the question of association….You and we are more apt to be particular about it than either the Cambridge or the LBC which are more democratic. I think it of great importance that ABC and DBCC should act together on this question, representing, if I may say so, the conservative element of bicycling. I think you and Frere are Oxford men, I should be glad to propose you as honorary members."

The final decision was reached at committee on 11 March 1878. "The ABC are of the unanimous opinion that at the present time the constitution of a Bicycle Union is not desirable or needed."

Predictably the club developed a similar animosity to the annual Hampton Court monster meets. On 11 April 1874, the club met at the Greyhound Hotel, Hampton Court, "with several other clubs, 38 machines in all," and while the others formed a procession around the fountain of Diana, "the ABC elected to look on." In 1876, very reluctantly the ABC did in fact join in. Custance sourly noted in the minutes, "This day's meet was attended by some twelve clubs of which only four could honestly be denominated as being composed exclusively of Gentleman Amateurs, many of the members of the remainder being far below par and in fact no great improvement on the noisy radical mechanics and other republican rascals who put in their noses where least wanted and most objectionable."

Fig. 21.3. Menu and programme cards from ABC annual dinners.

The following February he conveyed the ABC opinion to the editor of *Bicycling News*. "I am instructed to inform you that my committee regard last year's meet of clubs at Hampton Court as having been a success only in point of numbers. As a meeting calculated to advance the character and respectability of bicycling, my committee are unanimously of the opinion that the meeting could not have been a more signal failure, and they will, therefore, not recommend any of our members to aid in repeating such an event." On 29 May 1880, Mr. Compton "amused himself by trotting round by Hampton Court to see the 'Arries' in Monster Meet assembled, found all things much as he had expected."

The Annual Dinner

While the meets of the club received scanty attendances, the AGM and dinner was a popular occasion usually drawing about 30 members and guests. The Hon. Sec. read the accounts of club meets which he records "afforded considerable amusement and hilarity to the meeting." Perhaps it is the fact that they were written to be read aloud which makes the minutes so interesting today. The favourite venue for the dinner was the Egyptian Saloon at the Cafe Monico on Piccadilly Circus where they would usually enjoy a ten-course dinner with elaborate printed menu followed by a programme of recitation and songs.

Meets

The accounts in the minute books tell of who turned up, the state of the roads, where the riders rode to, and of the pub stops, which in accordance with the club toast were "Little and often." Such detailed accounts can become repetitious, but it is from these descriptions that we learn most about the character of Custance and his friends. A middle class Mr. Pooter, he relates with straight face encounters with bucolics, rustics, and urchins, not all of which reflect well upon the club.

20 April 1872: "A member running down a moderately steep hill met a most respectable old farmer to whom he said, 'Good Morning,' to which the bucolic replied, 'Good Morning Sir, lor when I seed you a coming over the hill I took you for a donkey, Hah Hah.' To which the ABC replied, 'Indeed, then I wonder you did not begin to bray.'"

16 August 1873: "At Elmers End some juvenile rustics disporting themselves in the middle of the road retired quickly if not gracefully before the advancing steed, and saluted the Club with 'Wo hoa Wiskers' and 'Wo hoa Fat-un.'"

24 November 1894: "The run was taken into and around Richmond Park where some self important stranger on being passed (on foot with a young friend) let fly at the Hon. Sec. in some very unparliamentary language demanding 'why the — did you not ring your bell Saar?' whereupon the Hon. Sec. gave him fully to understand that his most unparliamentary nomenclature must apply entirely to himself and referred him to the footpath (Saar) as being his proper ground."

There is an implication in the reports that the ABC members could, if they only wanted to, outride all they met on the road, and yet we know that the best amateur riders like Whiting, Causton, and Keith-Falconer chose to join other clubs. The ABC stalwarts continued their sparsely attended meets, and it was perhaps just this exclusivity which

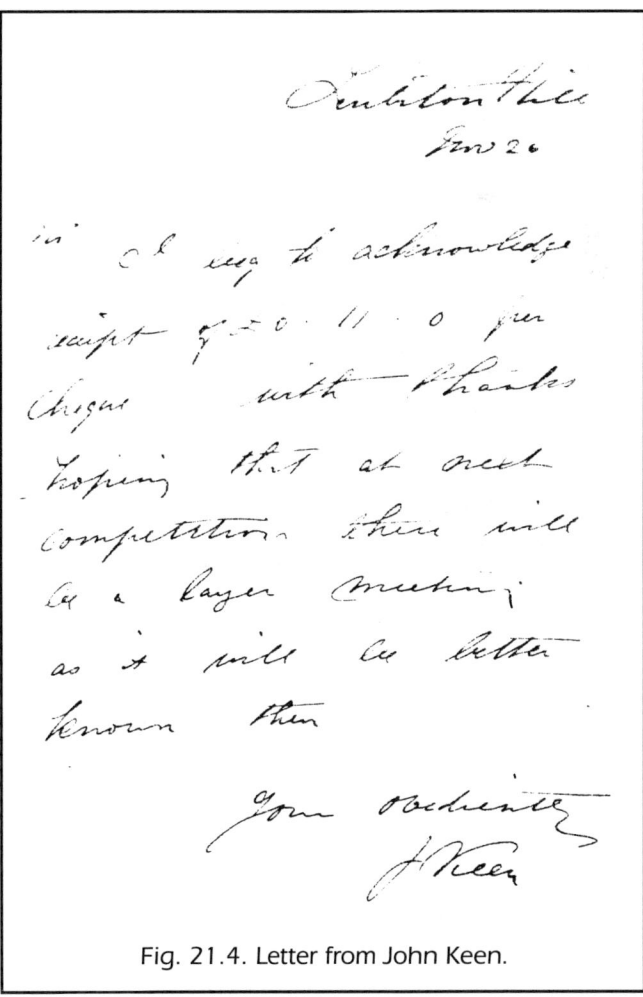

Fig. 21.4. Letter from John Keen.

produced the happy nostalgia apparent in the letters which passed during its final winding up. Certainly the last entries in the minute books read like pages from Scott's Antarctic diary.

30 March 1901: "Soon after dismounting at home the Hon. Sec. had an attack of vertigo which caused a fall onto the kerbstone and damage to his head and left ear which left him very deaf. His doctor on being called in ordered him immediate rest and no more riding until further order, also at least a three months cessation of all work."

3 November 1901: "Meet at White Hart, Roehampton. Present Henry N. Custance Esq. alone."

10 November 1901: "Meet at Coach & Horses, Kew Green. Present Henry N. Custance Esq. alone."

30 November 1901: Final entry. "Meet at Ealing Station 2:0 p.m. Present Henry N. Custance, Hon. Sec., alone. Having waited the usual 15 minutes the Club ran home again via Shepherd's Bush and the electric lines. The day was very fine and he supposes that the early meet prevented his being supported by other members."

Postscript

The following letter, undated and unsigned, was included in the hoard. Almost certainly it was written by the last captain of the club from 1897, Algernon H. M. Praed, to the Cyclist's Touring Club in 1926. It was Praed's nephew who sent the papers to Sothebys.

108, Gloucester Place W1

THE AMATEUR BICYCLE CLUB

Dear Sir,

In 1902, Mr. H. N. Custance handed over to me a tin box containing the Minute Books and other papers of the A.B.C., also a Gold Medal of the Club and a balance of some £13 as he wished to be relieved of the responsibility of the Secretaryship. He was much concerned—he was very ill at the time—about the Club being carried on and for a short time I issued cards of the meets as he had done, but as no members ever attended these meets I gave it up. He died in 1923. I am anxious now to wind up the Club and dispose of the property, medal, money and Minute Book of records, and have consulted the Rev. W. d'A. Crofton as to how to proceed in the matter. Having won the Challenge Medal himself many times, he is rather anxious to purchase the original medal at a fair valuation, and suggests that the proceeds, together with the money in hand, should be given to the Metropolitan Hospital Sunday Fund of which Mr. H. N. Custance was Secretary for so many years.

I think that this is quite the best use that can be made of the funds in question, but I wish to get in touch with any still surviving members of the Club to get their approval before coming to a decision. No subscriptions have been paid for 25 years now. Possibly the C.T.C. might like to preserve the archives of what is, I believe, one of the oldest, if not the oldest, bicycle clubs formed.

I enclose a list of the members in case you are in touch with any whose addresses are not as in the book, and I should be very glad if you would give me any help you can in the matter. Do not trouble to return the book.

Yours faithfully.

Rüdiger Rabenstein

22. T. H. S. Walker—English Cycling Pioneer in Germany

Research on any topic is a continuous process, and therefore I can only bring to your attention what I have discovered so far about an English sportsman who played such a vital role in importing cycle sport to my country, Germany. And there have been other English sportsmen who played a part in the transfer of sports from England to Germany.[1]

Youth

Thomas Henry Sumpter Walker was born on 29 June 1855 in Cambridge. From 1869 to 1872 he attended the famous Rugby School, where he played football and ran long distance. In 1868 he learned to ride a bicycle bought from a pawnshop, and he cycled with other schoolboys.[2]

In 1873 he moved to Godesberg, near Bonn in Germany, and went to school there, and during the summer of 1874 he worked for the Howe Machine Company in Glasgow, becoming its branch manager in Berlin in January 1877. Once there, in 1880 he ordered several bicycles from Britain for friends.[3]

Founder of a Bicycle Club

A first wave of the foundation of bicycle clubs began around 1869, with a second wave just before 1881, the long lapse because of the German-French war, 1870–71. In 1881 three clubs were founded in Berlin, the first one by Walker. On 18 February he founded the Berlin Bicycle Club (later: Erster Berliner Bicycle-Club), and was chairman until 1889.[4]

Translation by Katharina Nitz-Uliczka, Saeed Sheikh, and the author.

Fig. 22.1. Walker at the age of 28 (Allgemeine Sport-Zeitung, 1883).

Synopsis

T. H. S. Walker was born in Cambridge, England, in 1855. In 1877 he became the branch manager in Berlin, Germany, of the Howe Machine Company, based in Glasgow. In Germany, he founded the first bicycle club and published the first specialist paper for cyclists, and was a racing and touring cyclist. He organised the construction of a cycle track, where he cycled in important competitions. Walker introduced British amateur rules to Germany, and defended the ideal of the amateur. For many years he fought against restrictions on cyclists. In 1889 he ceased his activities in Germany and returned to London.

Racing and Touring Cyclist

On 31 July 1881 Walker competed for the first time in Munich, and unexpectedly won the 2,000 meters race.[5] When he joined his club races in Flora Park in Charlottenburg, Berlin, on 7 August and 28 September 1881, he was successful with one victory and a second place.[6] On Whitsun 1882 he beat all riders in the 10 km race during the Congress-Preis of the *Deutscher Velocipedisten-Bund* (DVB) in Munich.[7] But in Vienna he was unlucky in the "First Great Meeting of the Vienna B.C." on a trotting course.[8] In those years, Walker always went by bicycle whenever he participated in congresses or racing events, and he covered thousands of kilometers year by year.[9] In June 1883 in Hanover, he won the 5 miles Championship of Northern Germany organised by the *Norddeutscher Velocipedisten-Bund* (NVB).[10] In 1883 the *Allgemeine Sport-Zeitung* (ASZ) in Vienna called him "the best bicyclist in Germany."[11] Walker continued taking part in cycle races until the end of 1888, and rode in Leipzig, Frankfurt/Main, Bremen, Nürnberg, Berlin, Erfurt, London (1887, Alexandra Park), and Prague, among others.[12] However, by the mid-80s, he had taken up riding tricycles.

Fig. 22.2. "Track races" in Flora Park, Berlin, 1881 (Gronen & Lemke, 1978).

Editor and Publisher

In August 1881 Walker published the first German specialist paper for cyclists, *Das Velociped*, in Berlin.[13] After the foundation of the *Deutscher Radfahrer-Bund* (DRB) in 1884, his specialist paper was called *Der Radfahrer*, and it remained the official organ of the DRB until the end of 1887.[14] Walker was not only editor, but also a writer. He wrote perfect German, despite the fact that he was an Englishman, and dominated the paper. The *Velociped* published facts concerning clubs and related organisations, and reported races, international events, and problems with police.

In addition Walker published a few brochures, among them the *Radfahrer's Jahrbücher* (cyclists' yearbooks), which included a variety of facts and information about cycling.[15] He persuaded his English friend, George Lacy Hillier, to write a manuscript about the training of competitor cyclists, and Walker published it in 1888 in three languages—English, French, and German. The English title was *The Art of Training for Cycle Racing*.[16]

Participation in Clubs and Associations Activities

Walker was present when the first congress of German cyclists took place in Frankfurt on Main in June 1881, and a year later, when DVB was founded in Munich.[17] Walker's *Velociped* promoted the idea of German bicycle clubs growing and working together, but the delegates of Munich took advantage of their numerical superiority, and elected Munich as headquarters of the DVB with a complete Munich committee.[18] This motion angered the delegates from northern Germany so much that they founded a *Norddeutscher Verband* within the DVB, and asked the Munich delegates to call their organisation *Süddeutscher Verband* within the DVB. The result was predictable—the clubs split. On 13 November 1882, the clubs of northern Germany proclaimed the *Norddeutscher Velocipedisten-Bund* (NVB), while the southern clubs renamed their association *Deutscher und Deutsch-Oesterreichischer Velocipedisten-Bund* (DOeVB).[19] Officials from southern Germany accused Walker of having supported this separation, but he denied it.[20]

In Berlin, Walker energetically pushed ahead preparations for building a cycle racing track. For this purpose he founded the *Verein für Velociped-Wettfahren in Berlin* (VfW), a racing club, which aimed to organise races on its own account, independent of all velociped clubs. Walker became chairman. On 2 November 1884, his track at the Brücken-Allee was opened; it was 351.5 meters long.[21] In August 1886 Walker was the major initiator of the anniversary and congress of DRB in Berlin, and he had organised up till then a unique series of track races.[22] For the first time in Germany a Kaiserpreis (Imperial prize) was awarded, which was won by Joh. Pundt of Berlin, who was the DRB champion of 10,000 meters on the penny farthing. Walker went international by introducing "Championships of Europe" for bicycles and tricycles, which were won by E. Hall of London and E. Kiderlen of Rotterdam, respectively. From then on, he organised these championships each year in Berlin.[23] Hogenkamp reported that Walker initiated a road race Berlin–Hamburg in 1889, which was won by Pundt in nearly 23 hours.[24]

Walker was not only the driving force behind important cycle racing events, but also the whole cycle riding movement benefitted from his activities. To the English tourist, the association Cyclists' Touring Club (CTC), with its international flavour, meant that Walker became the "Chief Consul" in Germany for many years (and in Austria too), and a contact for international tourers.[25] The *Allgemeine Radfahrer-Union* (ARU), with similar aims to those of the CTC, joined it. Consequently Walker became an important figure in the two largest German cyclists' associations, as well as in the "racing association," DRB, and in the "tourist association," ARU.

The Amateur Question

It was Walker himself who redefined the concept of an amateur for the first German cycling association. Several months before the foundation of DVB, Walker published in his *Velociped* a draft version for the German Bicycle Union based on the rules of the *British Bicycle Union* (BU).[26] This definition of the amateur was adopted by the NVB in the same year, and published on 1 December 1882.[27] The difference between an amateur and a professional was dealt with as a main issue, and the amateur was defined as the opposite of the professional. These rules didn't include the general exclusion of social classes or of the occupational group of industrial or manual workers; however the distinction was based on the principles of business or hobby.[28]

It is remarkable that Walker could bring his English amateur rules to Germany, even though in 1882 there were no professional riders in Germany at all, though there were prizes awarded for events.[29] It seems that Walker was somewhat shrewd in formulating rules for the amateur. In fact he adopted the definition of the BU of 1878, but he omitted the following restriction: "who has engaged, taught, or assisted in bicycling or any other athletic exercise for money."[30] In accordance with this restriction Walker himself wouldn't have been able to start in England as an amateur, because he was an employee of a bicycle factory. In the absence of this restriction, Walker could qualify as an amateur in Germany. However some restrictions were enforced for a limited period of time on people involved with the bicycle trade.[31] NVB had an unclear restriction that amateurs could not earn money through bicycling.

Fig. 22.3. Track races during the DVB Congress, Munich, 1882 (Archiv Gronen, Binningen).

Fig. 22.4. Parade, during the DRB Congress, Berlin, 1886 (Archiv Gronen, Binningen).

The rule said: "Somebody who makes use of bicycle sport for his own profit" is a professional.[32] In May 1883, on the anniversary of NVB, Walker influenced this restriction. He added: "Manufacturers and bicycle dealers are not included," and the delegates agreed.[33] Certainly the credit is entirely his that there were no social restrictions introduced in German bicycling, in contrast, for example, to rowing in Germany.

In 1886 in Germany, the first cycle race of professionals was held, and at the end of the 90s, professionalism dominated the scene. Walker strongly defended the ideal of the amateur in his specialist paper *Radfahrer*, and the DRB followed these aims for many years. In 1901 Höfer wrote: "Walker wholly committed himself to the qualities of the amateur; he ended an article about this with some typical words: 'It's lucky that the acquisition of a bicycle isn't feasible for people without means, otherwise the days of cycling as a sport would be numbered.'"[34] Walker could only imagine his noble ideas of an amateur in an elitist society.

Freedom for Cyclists

In the 19th century, the Berlin metropol enforced serious and damaging restrictions for cyclists. In 1881, in his capacity as chairman of the Berlin B.C., Walker submitted several petitions to the Royal Police authorities, asking them to repeal or moderate harassments on bicyclists. For some years Walker's petitions were outright rejected.[35] In 1882, Walker's cyclist companion, a businessman, Paul Kurts, was charged but acquitted because there was no clear ban on cyclists, which encouraged other cyclists. In spite of this, the Berlin police kept harassing cyclists with various rules, until on 25 March 1883, the chief constable enacted a general cycle ban.[36]

Walker, in fact, did very well; he went to the court of justice several times, and started a press campaign. He was not interested in discussions with the police, but as an English democrat followed the line of resistance; in those days in Germany the authorities were of strict hierarchical Imperial order.

In 1884, the Berlin police passed a set of regulations which allowed cycling generally, but the list of forbidden streets and districts was very extensive.[37] In 1888, an obligatory bicycle license was introduced for registering and numbering cyclists. By 1896, cycling was allowed in the whole of Berlin.[38]

Hostilities and Resignation

In northern Germany when the activities and influence of English sportsmen were welcome in the early years, Walker stayed in Berlin. Regrettably, some officials of DOeVB blamed Walker as a foreigner, though he considered adopting German nationality, as the ASZ noted at the time.[39] The NVB was called "Anglo-Welfen-Bund" (Anglo-Guelph-Bond), and Walker's *Velociped* "a paper which is paid for by England."[40] Nationalistic remarks, such as these from Munich, were no rarity in Europe at the turn of the century. In fact, Walker endeavoured to be neutral and act as a mediator through *Velociped*, and he never strove for an important national position.

In 1887, at the anniversary of DRB in Frankfurt on Main, he faced hostility again. Though several

Fig. 22.5. Start of track race in Berlin, 1888. Walker is on the right with a white shawl (Gronen & Lemke, 1978).

Fig. 22.6. Walker at age 34 (Allgemeine Sport-Zeitung, 1980).

cyclists' associations and racing clubs had organised championships for several years as Walker's VfW in Berlin, DRB asserted that only its sports committee should be allowed to award championships, for sportive and political reasons. Walker pleaded for a sports committee filled by officials of all associations and racing clubs in parity.[41] So he found himself in bitter enmity with officials of the DRB. Some of his personal debates were even tested in legal courts, but Walker came through successfully.[42]

In spite of his successes, in 1889 Walker gave up his chairmanships of the Berlin B.C. and racing club VfW of Berlin, and his business and work as publisher of the *Radfahrer*. Disillusioned, at the age of only 34, he moved to London.[43] Höfer, the second chairman of ARU, commented on Walker's resignation: "T. H. S. Walker...retired from the cycle movement definitely, angry about the short-sightedness of the petty opinions and principles which became dominant in the German cycle movement."[44]

So far, I have not discovered anything else about Walker's life after 1889.

Appreciation

Contemporary opinions of Walker's work are definitely encouraging, except the ASZ criticism of "uncompromising independence" in 1890, which led to conflicts in the German Empire because of Walker's disagreement.[45]

Chronicler and *Stahlrad* editor Theophil Weber only reported appreciative facts about Walker.[46] Höfer concluded: "German cycle racing lost its best expert and honest patron."[47] The specialist paper *Radfahr-Humor* said in 1889: "Walker, who was one of the first pioneers of the modern bicycle sport in Germany, rendered outstanding services to our sport in many various ways."[48]

The ASZ (Vienna) clearly expresssed that: "Walker has to be called the precursor of bicycle sport in Germany, a courageous pioneer in words and actions."[49]

For further appreciations of Walker's contribution, I suggest you consult Schulze, Hogenkamp, Stockmann, Gronen/Lemke and Kaiser.[50] In light of my present knowledge about Walker, I do not hesitate to declare him as *the* pioneer of cycle movement in Germany.

Acknowledgement

Thanks to Walter Ulreich (Hinterbrühl, Austria) and Wolfgang Gronen (Binningen, Germany) for the use of their archives.

Notes

1. Autorenkollektiv. 1965, p. 246.
2. Weber. 1891, p. 11; MacLean. 1994.
3. Weber. 1891, p. 11.
4. *Allgemeine Sport-Zeitung* no. 8 (1881): 28; *Das Velociped* (1881–82): 91.
5. Höfer. 1901, p. 8.
6. *Allgemeine Sport-Zeitung* no. 37: 523 and no. 40: 573 (1881).
7. Weber. 1891, p. 12.
8. *Allgemeine Sport-Zeitung* no. 24 (1882): 452.
9. Weber. 1891, p. 12.
10. *Das Velociped* (1882–83): 188.
11. *Allgemeine Sport-Zeitung* no. 10 (1883): 186.
12. Weber. 1891, pp. 12–14; *Allgemeine Sport-Zeitung* (1881–89); *Das Velociped* (1881–82 and 1883–84).
13. Höfer. 1901, p. 9.
14. Weber. 1891, pp. 12–13.
15. Walker. 1886; *Allgemeine Sport-Zeitung* no. 50 (1883): 1077.
16. Hillier/Walker. 1888; Höfer. 1901, p. 17.
17. Weber. 1891, pp. 11–12.
18. *Das Velociped* (1881–82): 122ff.
19. *Das Velociped* (1882–83): 62ff; Rabenstein. 1991, p. 201.
20. *Das Velociped* (1882–83): 82; Weber. 1891, p. 12.
21. *Allgemeine Sport-Zeitung* no. 35 (1884): 765; Höfer. 1901, p. 11f.; Stockmann. 1936, p. 32.
22. Weber. 1891, p. 13; Hofer. 1901, p. 19.
23. Höfer. 1901, pp. 19ff; *Allgemeine Sport-Zeitung* (1890): 40.

24. Hogenkamp. 1916, p. 128.
25. *Das Velociped* (1882–83): 120; *Allgemeine Sport-Zeitung* no. 4 (1884): 73 and (1890): 40.
26. Bury/Hillier. 1891, p. 278; *Das Velociped* (1881–82): 51ff; Rabenstein. 1991, pp. 224–29.
27. *Das Velociped* (1882–83): 78ff.
28. Rabenstein. 1991, p. 227f.
29. Höfer. 1901, p. 18; *Das Velociped* no. 29 (1881–82): 403.
30. Bury/Hillier. 1891, p. 270; *Das Velociped* (1881–82): 51f.
31. Das Velociped (1881–82): 123.
32. Ibid., (1882–83): 186.
33. Ibid., (1882–83): 186.
34. Höfer. 1901, p. 18.
35. *Das Velociped* (1881–82): 20, 38f, 98; *Allgemeine Sport-Zeitung* no. 37 (1881).
36. *Das Velociped* (1882–83): 65f, 96, 149.
37. Ibid., (1883–84): 186.
38. *Berliner Illustrirte Zeitung* no. 19 (1896): 14; Gronen/Lemke. 1978, p. 73.
39. *Allgemeine Sport-Zeitung* (1890): 40. It is only the ASZ which wrote that Walker was a naturalized German. Perhaps he had to be German to become chairman of a club or to start a self-employed business.
40. *Das Velociped* (1882–83): 112, 147.
41. Höfer. 1901, p. 23f.
42. Weber. 1891, p. 15.
43. *Radfahr-Humor* no. 5: 101, and no. 7: 147 (1889–90); Höfer. 1901, p. 35; Weber. 1891, p. 15.
44. Höfer. 1901, p. 35.
45. *Allgemeine Sport-Zeitung* (1890): 40.
46. Weber. 1891, pp. 11–15.
47. Höfer. 1901, p. 35.
48. *Radfahr-Humor* no. 7 (1889–90): 147.
49. *Allgemeine Sport-Zeitung* (1890): 40.
50. Schulze. 1903, p. 7f; Hogenkamp. 1916, pp. 50–128; Stockmann. 1936, p. 31f; Gronen/Lemke. 1978, p. 65; Kaiser. 1984, p. 20ff.

Bibliography

Allgemeine Sport-Zeitung. Vienna (1881–90).

Autorenkollektiv. *Geschichte der Körperkultur in Deutschland 1789–1917.* Berlin: Sportverlag, 1965.

Berliner Illustrirte Zeitung. Berlin (1896).

Bury, Viscount, G. Lacy Hillier. *Cycling.* 3rd ed. London: Longmans Green and Co., 1891.

Gronen, Wolfgang, and Walter Lemke. *Geschichte des Radsports und des Fahrrads.* Eupen, Belgium: Doepgen Verlag, 1978.

Hillier, G. Lacy, and T. H. S. Walker. *Die Kunst des Trainirens für Radwettfahren.* Berlin: Verlag Walker, 1888.

Hofer, Robert. *Zwanzig Jahre Deutscher Rad-Rennsport.* Berlin: Verlag der Rad-Welt, 1901.

Hogenkamp, George J. M. *Een halve eeuw wielersport.* Amsterdam: Hogenkamp, 1916.

Kaiser, Uli. "...und es dreht sich das Rad!" Bund Deutscher Radfahrer (ed). *100 Jahre Bund Deutscher Radfahrer.* Frankfurt on Main: BDR, 1984, pp. 17–41.

McLean, R. (Librarian and Archivist of Rugby School). Letter about Walker, September 1994.

Rabenstein, Rüdiger. *Radsport und Gesellschaft.* Hildesheim, Germany: Weidmannsche Verlagsbuchhandlung, 1991.

Radfahr-Humor. Munich (1889–90).

Schulze, Adolph. "Geschichte des Radrennsports." *Sport-Album der Rad-Welt.* Berlin (1903): 5–16.

Stockmann, H. "Vom Parkweg in der 'Flora' zur Olympischen Radrennbahn am Funkturm." *Zeitschrift des Vereins für die Geschichte Berlins* no. 3 (1936): 31–35.

Das Velociped. Berlin (1881–82 and 1883–84).

Walker, T. H. S. *Radfahrers Jahr-Buch 1886.* Berlin: Verlag Walker, 1886.

Weber, Theophil (ed). *Sport-Album für Radfahrer.* Leipzig: Verlag L. Weber, 1891, part 2.

David V. Herlihy

23. The Michaux Memorial Campaign

The current edition of *The Encyclopedia Brittanica* credits Pierre and Ernest Michaux with the invention of the pedal-powered 2-wheeler, and further asserts that these Parisian artisans were the first to develop the bicycle. Specifically, we are told that this father and son team mechanized the kick-propelled draisine in 1861, and that they were soon making many hundreds of "pedal velocipedes" per year as a cycle industry quickly materialized.

Introduction: The Legacy of the Michaux Campaign (1890–1894)

This conventional account of the bicycle's invention and early development stems from a prolonged French campaign, launched about 1890, to memorialize Pierre Michaux as the original bicycle inventor. One century ago this fall, it culminated in the dedication of a national memorial in Pierre Michaux's native city of Bar-le-Duc. This paper will scrutinize that process, and challenge the long-held assumption that it produced reliable historical results.

The Michaux campaign was curious and complex indeed, offering all the intrigue of a modern-day soap opera. It began at the onset of the great "bicycle boom" with rousing patriotic appeals, as French cyclists reacted indignantly to German veneration of their compatriot Drais.[1] Yet it would be dogged throughout by historical ambiguity and bitter personal feuds. In particular, a surviving Michaux son, orchestrating a publicity campaign for his new cycle company, stirred the wrath of a former Michaux investor, Aimé Olivier. Consequently, the campaign dragged on for years, suffering multiple false starts. In the end, no fewer than 4 journals had wrestled with one another over its leadership.[2]

But perhaps the most important aspect from our vantage point is the fact that the historical premise was repeatedly revised. At first, Pierre Michaux alone was said to have simply invented a pedal machine in 1855—but no initial production theory convincingly linked this alleged achievement to the cycle craze erupting in Paris a dozen years later. By the time his memorial was dedicated on 29 September 1894, however, the date of invention had advanced to 1861, and he was declared the initial developer as well as inventor, sharing posthumous honors with his son Ernest.

To understand how the memorial campaign spawned such radical revisions in mid-course, we must first appreciate the historical obstacles it faced at the onset. For, as one journal cautioned another as the latter took over the project in early 1893: "Do you know why, dear colleague, you will have a difficult time succeeding in your project? Because the origins of the velocipede are unclear."[3] Let's examine this point in a historical context before moving on to study the campaign itself.

A Shaky Premise: A Survey of Pre–1890 Views on the Invention

The Boneshaker Period (1867–70)

The original pedal-powered 2-wheeler, now commonly called "the boneshaker," made its commercial debut in Paris toward the early part of 1867. The first trace of this machine entering the public domain may be a note in the January–February issue of the Moniteur de la

---

Synopsis

One hundred years ago, French cyclists dedicated a memorial hailing Pierre and Ernest Michaux as the original bicycle inventors and developers. The preceding campaign also produced a new account on the origins of the bicycle, one which has largely prevailed in the literature ever since. But did this involved process truly yield reliable historical revisions? The author presents strong evidence that it did not, and vouches instead for the original claim of the patentee, Pierre Lallement.

Carrosserie (Monitor of the Carriage Industry) which reported "we are seeing many velocipedes make their appearance on the Parisian macadam." Some months later, the 28 July issue of *Le Sport* marked the presence of the new pedal velocipede at the ongoing Universal Exhibition, identifying its maker as Michaux of Avenue Montaigne.

But the origins of this machine were unclear to the French public from the start. The article in *Le Sport* incorrectly asserted that Michaux, described as an *ouvrier-mécanicien* (worker-mechanic), had taken out a patent on the novel pedal device a few years before. Indeed, Michaux and his investors, the brothers René and Aimé Olivier, evidently sought to create this false impression, since they ran a concurrent advertisement implying that they owned a patent on the so-called vélocipède a pédales.[4] But the first Michaux cycle patent was not in fact granted until nearly a year later, and would cover only certain "improvements."[5]

Indeed, surprisingly, no blanket patent for this invention was ever granted in France. The only such claim ever sanctioned was that of Pierre Lallement, who had obtained an American patent the previous November, 1866.[6] Lallement had left France in July 1865,[7] some 2 years before Michaux advertised his first commercial cycle product, which was virtually identical in appearance to Lallement's patent drawing. Although by 1869 Lallement's claim to be the original inventor was widely known and accepted outside France, it was not disclosed by French sources until the advent of the Michaux campaign some 20 years later. And even then its historical significance was lightly dismissed.[8]

Hence it was the Michaux name which France first associated with the invention of the pedal machine. Yet although numerous articles in the press discussed the boneshaker in the ensuing years—many written in consultation with Michaux and his company—none appear to offer any specific claim on his behalf. Indeed, curiously, the Michaux company itself soon backed away from its initial claim to be the original inventors. Instead, it denied that the pedal system was in fact a new invention, insisting that it had merely perfected an ancient idea. Here are just a few examples of this recurring theme:

> 9 Nov. 1867—*The Field*: An English journalist recounts a visit with Michaux who "showed me a two-wheeled foot velocipede nearly a century old." The writer concludes "the two-wheeled velocipede is in fact a very old invention, and can be traced back more than 100 years." No mention is made of Michaux inventing the pedal system.
>
> 8 Nov. 1868—*L'Echo de l'Est*: A man who alludes to his contacts with the Michaux family writes: "I wanted to know the inventor, but I was told that he goes back to the dawn of time."
>
> 8 July 1869—*Vélocipède Illustré*: Richard Lesclide, a close associate of Michaux and the Olivier's, suggests that the bicycle dates from antiquity.

It is interesting to note that the foreign press did not generally share the thesis that the pedal velocipede was an ancient idea. In early 1869, a Boston paper compared the old with the new as follows: "The two are entirely dissimilar in principle, and should not be confounded by even a name in common."[9] A British review remarked in 1876: "Bicycling has no remote past….Everything about it is comparatively new, and a decade comprises its birth and growth."[10] Even contemporary French sources frequently stressed the bicycle's novel characteristics. Observed one: "…five or six years ago, you absolutely had to be an adult, well planted on your legs and, in sum, specially built for [pedal-less velocipedes]. But in 1868, any man, woman or child can play with this [new] instrument…"[11]

Highwheel Era (1870–88)

Thus when the boneshaker era ended about 1871, no clear theory of its invention had gained currency in France. Nevertheless, given Michaux's early prominence in the field, his vague reputation as bicycle inventor persisted. Eventually, a specific claim on his behalf crept into the literature. An 1874 publication, for example, reported that "Michaux's

Fig. 23.1. Michaux advertisment in La Vie Parisienne, 1868.

son" had invented the pedal velocipede from a tricycle—although no date was given.[12]

By 1880, the French cycle industry had revived to manufacture the English high-wheeler, and thus the unresolved historical question gained greater interest. In its June 1881 issue, the British publication *Wheel World* asked who in France had invented the original bicycle, and found no shortage of volunteers. In particular, Michaux himself—by then reduced to a pauper—was quoted as stating that in 1855 he had "invented the outside crank with direct action now applied to bicycles."

This appears to be the first reference directly linking Michaux with a bicycle invention in 1855. Previously, this year was not generally cited as a turning point in bicycle history, with one interesting exception: an item in the 18 November 1869 issue of *Vélocipède Illustré* which describes a retrospective cycle exhibition sponsored by the Compagnie Parisienne (formerly Michaux) of the Olivier brothers. It reported the presence of a transitional 2-wheeler from 1855, of an unspecified make, which had the boneshaker's original iron serpentine frame but apparently no pedals. Reflecting "another gap of ten years," the pedals were displayed on what was described as an original "true bicycle" from 1865 made entirely of wood "upon which long voyages were achieved."[13]

Although Michaux's belated claim for 1855 as the starting point of the bicycle was evidently vague and dubious, it was quickly embraced by the French cycling establishment. When Michaux died in early 1883, *Sport Vélocipédique* repeated it in his obituary, adding the detail that Michaux had modified a broken draisine. The author also made a feeble attempt to bridge the evident "production lag" by asserting that Michaux had made only a few wooden models at first, which he improved "little by little" until finally exhibiting a perfected iron version at the 1867 exhibition.[14]

Later that year, in the fall of 1883, the same journal once again alluded to the 1855 Michaux claim in response to an article by the Boston lawyer and cycle historian Charles Pratt published in *Wheelman* magazine. Disputing Pratt's depiction of Lallement as the original cycle inventor, the French review retorted: "In believing that M. Lallement first applied the pedal to the bicycle, the Americans are greatly mistaken. It was Mr. Michaux who made the draisine practical, well before 1863, the year in which Lallement built his first machine in Paris. Today it would still be easy to gather numerous testimonies to prove this."[15]

In point of fact, however, we have no record that such evidence proving Michaux's priority was ever collected. Indeed, 2 years earlier, the same journal had published the following advertisement: "Healthy reward to whomever can prove, by a newspaper article or any other serious document, that the pedal system was applied to velocipedes before the year 1866."[16] It was no doubt planted by American interests, eager to overthrow the Lallement patent still in effect. Yet extensive U.S. court records contain no appeals to Michaux's alleged priority.[17]

Despite its continuing lack of substantiation, the 1855 Michaux claim stuck in French literature for over a decade. It was repeated at a bicycle conference held in Tours in 1888,[18] and even reached *La Grande Encyclopedie*. Yet the details remained sketchy and inconsistent: some accounts gave the draisine as the inspiration, others a tricycle. Some described Michaux's son as an assistant, others did not mention him at all. And none offered any credible explanation why it took a dozen years to market the bicycle.

Still, the 1855 Michaux claim continued to circulate and even received international attention—if not total acceptance—in 1891 with the publication of Baudry de Saunier's *Histoire Général de la Vélocipédie*. Shortly thereafterwards, Baudry even pinpointed the exact date of Michaux's alleged brainchild: "the night of 5 or 6 February."[19]

Thus, at the advent of the Michaux campaign, the historical premise seemed reasonably secure—at least on the surface. Yet its fundamental weakness would nonetheless come exposed, as we shall now see.

A Troubled Project: The Memorial Campaign in Detail

The first call for a Michaux memorial was apparently sounded by *La Revue du Sport Vélocipédique* of Rouen. An article dated 8 August 1890 and signed with the pseudonym "V. Losman" called for "Glory to the Frenchman Michaux." The author noted with disdain that German cyclists were planning a tribute to Drais, whose mortal remains were to be re-buried that spring alongside a memorial in a new cemetery in Karlsruhe.

Although the article—which repeated 1855 as the year of invention—inspired some to contemplate a Michaux memorial,[20] no serious campaign materialized at first. Indeed, the idea might have been stillborn, had German cyclists not re-provoked their French counterparts the following year by announcing yet another scheme to glorify Drais. This time, the plan called for the dedication of his bust in a Karlsruhe square in the spring of 1893.

Though French cycle journals roundly condemned the growing "cult of Drais," *Vélocipéde Illustré* of Paris was the first to renew talk of a Michaux memorial. The idea appealed to its new director, Madame Richard Lesclide, since her late husband, who had only recently revived the review he originally founded in 1869, had once been a close Michaux ally. Moreover, the project offered an opportunity to undercut a rival journal, *Vélo-Sport* of Bordeaux, which had just opened a subscription to recognize the journalist Pierre Giffard for his work promoting cycling.[21] In its issue of 16 June 1892, *Vélocipéde Illustré* belittled the Giffard campaign and announced its intention to pursue a cause "one hundred thousand times more worthy": a memorial to Pierre Michaux.

Yet even this new initiative to honor Michaux might have fizzled, were it not for the timely intervention of Henry Michaux, a surviving son then living in London. In response to Madame Lesclide's editorial, he sent a warm letter of support published in the 4 August issue, noting his intention to visit Paris shortly. His prospective participation no doubt buoyed Madame Lesclide, for it promised to lend the historical legitimacy the project had been lacking to date.

Indeed, from the start, Henry demonstrated his ability to clarify historical ambiguities by recalling verbatim pointed conversations from his youth. In a blatant pitch to win Madame Lesclide's enduring affection, he offered the following anecdote to illustrate both his father's friendship with her late husband and the latter's legacy as "the only one deserving of the title 'Developer of the Bicycle'"[22]:

> I still remember hearing my father say, while extending his hand to his friend, *Le Grand Jacques* [Lesclide's pen name]:
>
> Michaux: "Hello dear master."
> Lesclide: "Why this title, papa Michaux?"
> Michaux: "It's simple, we are, my sons and myself, the builders, and you, my dear sir, are *Le Grand Jacques*, the great leader, for thanks to your journal, 10, 12, even 15 orders arrive to me regularly. Would you care to see my correspondence this morning and judge for yourself?"

Madame Lesclide's alliance with Henry and his younger brother Francisque also helped her secure the Michaux mantle against competing claims. Indeed, just as her campaign appeared ready to blossom, *Révue du Sport Vélocipèdique*—citing its original call for a memorial two years before—suddenly announced that it was finally opening its subscription.

Madame Lesclide denounced the rival campaign in her 8 September issue: "One of our colleagues from Rouen has dreamed of the edification of a statue to Michaux. We regret to inform them that the statue will come from *Vélocipède Illustré*, which has a right to the inventor's memory, whom it helped and directed from the start. Michaux's sons have given us the necessary authority and letters of credit and the project has been studied for over a month."

Under pressure from the Michaux sons, the Rouen journal soon canceled its campaign and refunded contributions. But their heavy-handed tactics fanned ill-will in the cycling community. The Touring Club de France, for one, characterized the Michaux opposition as "Strange, very strange."[23] To clear the air, Henry defended Lesclide's sole rights to the campaign in the 1 November issue of her review—once again drawing on his keen memory:

> An article in the *Revue du Sport Vélocipèdique*… seems to question your rights as the first journal to have had the idea of erecting a statue to my late father. Allow me to inform your readers that Mr. Lesclide himself…was the true instigator of this statue. I remember that in 1869, *Grand Jacques* said to my father, "[this street] will soon be called the Cité Pierre Michaux, and on that day your bust will be placed above the gateway until a statue is erected in your native city of Bar-le-Duc."[24]

Madame Lesclide also relied heavily on Henry's authority to refute persistent historical challenges. After a Lyon paper attacked Pierre Michaux's credentials, pointing out that he had not presented a bicycle until 1867, *Vélocipède Illustré* published a stern rebuttal.[25] Drawing on information supplied by Henry, the review made the following counter-assertions in its issue of October 6, 1892:

- ☐ On April 24, 1861, the Emperor stopped in the Place de la Concorde to admire young Ernest Michaux who was riding on the first pedal velocipede built by his father.

- ☐ 21 Michaux clients from 1862 are still living in Paris.

- ☐ Starting in 1863, Henry Michaux gave riding lessons to numerous royalty.

- ☐ The accounting books conserved by Michaux's sons reveal the following: In 1861, he sold 2 velocipedes; in 1862, he sold 142; and this figure progressively rose up to 1,100 before the exhibition of 1867.

[Author's Note: Contemporary accounts often cite the latter figures, even though no trace of this mini-industry has been found.]

A few weeks later in the same review, Henry echoed these prodigious pre-1867 production figures. In a letter dated 25 October he asserted that his father had sold over 100 velocipedes between 1861 and 20 May 1863.[26]

But just when it appeared that Madame Lesclide had mustered sufficient authority to dispel the persistent flaps, another foe surfaced: Baudry de Saunier. Although this recognized French expert on cycle history had been instrumental in perpetuating the original 1855 Michaux claim, he abruptly revised his view just as the Lesclide campaign was underway. His new book, *Cyclisme Théorique et Practique*, published in October 1892, reiterated the claim that the bicycle was born from a broken draisine in 1855, but credited Michaux's son Ernest with the achievement. Thus, he undercut the very basis for a memorial to Pierre Michaux.

On the surface, at least, Baudry's revision was curious. When Ernest died in 1882, one year before his father, no one had suggested that he was the inventor of the pedal velocipede. Indeed, although he earned a reputation as an inventor of steam engines, he had no bicycle patent to his credit, nor had he been a partner in the Michaux/Olivier cycle company.[27]

Baudry attributed his new account to the testimony of Gaston Biot, a former companion of Ernest. However, it appears likely that Aimé Olivier, the surviving brother of the investor pair, had a hand in engineering Ernest's sudden ascendancy. Indeed, as Baudry launched a counter-offensive to memorialize Ernest, he relied increasingly on the testimony of Olivier, whose relations with the elder Michaux had soured during a bitter lawsuit in 1870. Although Olivier stopped short of fully embracing the Ernest claim, he clearly relished the opportunity to belittle Pierre Michaux, while stressing instead his brother René's role in the invention.[28]

As this new twist increasingly threatened to derail the memorial campaign, *La France Cycliste*[29] called for patriotic unity:

> Several of our colleagues…have enthusiastically devoted themselves…to the erection of a statue to Michaux, the presumed inventor of the velocipede. I say "presumed" deliberately, because Michaux, like all inventors, has as many detractors as supporters, who affirm, on their part, without ever proving it, that their opinion is based on precise facts. At present, the Parisian locksmith seems to have the real rights to the honor of a pedestal and deserves our recognition, until established with supporting documents that the idea of adopting pedals to the velocipede was not his.

The author, however, evidently overlooked the fact that Pierre Michaux's claim lacked substance in its own right. Indeed, Baudry was rapidly making headway in persuading key industry figures to favor Ernest. But his efforts were vehemently opposed by Henry Michaux, who by this time had moved back to France to oversee Lesclide's memorial campaign and the launching of his new cycle company. Clearly, the Ernest revision did not fit the image he cultivated: i.e., that of a dutiful son carrying on the family destiny.

The growing prospect of a damaging and embarrassing show-down between the two Michaux camps dampened Madame Lesclide's enthusiasm. By late 1892, her journal dropped all mention of the memorial project.

But this peculiar silence irked a young journalist named Albert de Ricaudy, who lamented that German plans to honor Drais were flourishing while the Michaux cause floundered.[30] Using his forum as a cycling columnist for the Parisian daily *L'Evenement*, de Ricaudy clamored for action. On 28 November he burst out: "And Michaux? Whatever happened to Michaux? Is he the inventor of the pedal velocipede or not? If yes, why has the project to build him a statue broken down? If no, how is it that no one has demonstrated in a positive fashion the falsity of [his] claim?…Let's get on with it, for heavens sakes! Let's probe, investigate, research his patents—if he has any.[31] Let's go to Bar-le-Duc, if we must—but let's at least clear our conscience!"

By early 1893, de Ricaudy's patience was at an end. On 4 January he wrote: "For the one hundredth time, I demand to know from my colleague why the Michaux statue has been abandoned….It's only fair that the public know the reasons behind a silence altogether at odds with the previous commotion….If *Vélocipède Illustré* plans to renounce this work of justice….I demand they at least say so! Others more enterprising and disinterested can thus lead this movement!"

Finally, in early February 1893, de Ricaudy took matters into his own hands. Ignoring his own call for immediate historical investigation, he plunged headlong into the stalled project. First, he found a sculptor willing to produce a bust of Michaux for just 2,500 francs. Then, on 10 February, he announced the opening of a public subscription. Ten days later, he persuaded a syndicate comprising about a dozen cycle journalists including Pierre Giffard and himself, to spearhead the project.[32] With their letter of intent in hand, he quickly departed for Bar-le-Duc to enlist the support of the mayor, Charles Busselot.[33]

De Ricaudy's impudence finally broke Madame Lesclide's silence. Denouncing his economic bust scheme as "grotesque," she insisted that Henry Michaux was patiently assembling a "blue ribbon" committee which would ultimately render far more homage to the Michaux name.[34] On 18 February she published another letter of support from Henry in which he vowed: "I do not recognize ever having authorized anyone but *Vélocipède Illustré* to pursue the erection of a statue to my father, least of all Mr. de Ricaudy. I am in perfect agreement that the subscription recently launched should be stopped."

But just as Madame Lesclide's interest appeared to rekindle, her relations with Henry suddenly deteriorated. In her issue of 23 February, she printed a letter from two of his disgruntled ex-business partners, at their request, announcing that they were breaking off all relations with the Michaux brothers, due to breach of contract. And in the same issue, the journal finally acknowledged that "the Michaux file is still lacking critical information."

Madame Lesclide sent a confidential letter to the mayor of Bar-le-Duc the following week,[35] which appears to clarify her disenchantment with the memorial campaign. Dated 3 March 1893, it reads:

> I just this moment left a former investor of Pierre Michaux who declared to me that the crank (and not the pedal, which had already been known for some time) was adapted to the velocipede in the shop of Pierre Michaux, but not by him. I was given names, and I will continue my investigation, and will keep you informed.[36]

Evidently, even Lesclide herself did not believe the historical declarations emanating from Henry, whom she characterized as "very intelligent—that is, in a commercial sense." She also revealed that he would have been arrested some days before for an unspecified "grievous misstep"—had she not paid his bail. She warned the mayor to keep the matter hushed, lest Henry's "projects" (which she intimated were of interest to the city) be jeopardized.

Lesclide's enthusiasm for the project evidently spent, Henry wasted no time in jumping aboard de Ricaudy's ship—despite his previous condemnation of the latter's independent efforts. Indeed, de Ricaudy's hand had strengthened considerably in the interim. His visit to Bar-le-Duc in late February had won the enthusiastic support of the mayor, who agreed in turn to meet with his patronage committee in Paris to finalize plans for a grand Michaux inauguration that spring.

As the mayor left Paris on 1 March, the committee—headed by Pierre Giffard—presented him with a warm thank-you note from Henry.[37] Alluding to the lingering historical doubts, he wrote: "I attest in the name of all the members of my family that the invention and application of pedals to velocipedes is indeed the work of my dear late father."[38] "There now!", gloated Giffard's new cycle daily, *Le Vélo*. "That should end the sordid rumor that the Michaux family does not want a monument to the memory of its chief!"

But just as the project finally seemed to break free from turmoil, the explosive Ernest dilemma—which until then had been largely suppressed—burst into full view. In the 3 March issue of *Revue des Sports*, Baudry charged in a scathing editorial that "Pierre Michaux, with his poor brain, never invented anything in his life." Demanding a halt to "an historical gaffe of the first degree," he insisted that all the honor should go instead to Ernest.

At this point, a discouraged de Ricaudy officially turned the troubled project over to Giffard's *Le Vélo*, which explained to its readers that it alone had the necessary space to handle the crisis.[39] Giffard proceeded to blast Baudry's meddling—pointing out how only a year before he himself had credited the elder Michaux with the pedal invention.[40] A pragmatist at heart, however, Giffard scrambled behind the scenes to defuse the issue. He hastily drew up plans for a compromise solution to credit both Michaux for the invention in "about 186-," and to include both their images.[41]

The patronage committee approved the scheme in an emergency session held 6 March, along with the following clarification:

> Following certain recently published articles, which have tended to establish that Pierre Michaux, whose bust we had at first intended to erect, did not invent, but simply built and propagated the pedal, whereas his son Ernest alone had the idea, the committee unanimously adopts the proposition of its honorary president, Pierre Giffard.[42]

Although the new, more expensive design meant the inauguration would be postponed at least until the fall, the committee clearly hoped that its concession would at least safeguard against any further embarrassment. At first, its strategy appeared to work: Baudry promptly accepted the compromise, and even announced that he was contributing to the cause.[43] *Le Vélo* reader response was also favorable. "Bravo!" commended one, "you have maneuvered brilliantly. What do we cyclists care if father Michaux built the first pedal velocipede or his son did?"[44]

But despite Giffard's deft diplomacy, the project did not in fact escape further humiliation. On 7 March, four days after Baudry's initial attack, *L'Eclair*, a Parisian paper, reported the embarrassing rift in the cycling community. Revealing a distinct partiality toward the Ernest claim, it ridiculed the memorial campaign organizers for not having studied the case beforehand. The article was especially embarrassing to Henry, who had insisted all along that his father was the sole inventor. Moreover, it put Mayor Busselot in a bind just as he was about to ask the city council's permission to erect a bust of Pierre Michaux.

Still, the *L'Eclair* affair might have blown over had Henry immediately accepted Giffard's compromise solution. But Henry continued at first to resist the inclusion of his brother Ernest. During a meeting with Busselot in the aftermath of Baudry's attack, Henry evidently prevailed upon the mayor to stick with the original plan to erect a bust of Pierre Michaux. Indeed, after *L'Eclair* renewed the attacks, Busselot fired off a spirited rebuttal which the paper published on 9 March. "I do indeed plan to ask the town council for the necessary approval to erect the Pierre Michaux memorial, but I did not make this decision without consulting the two surviving sons on the origins of the pedal. In two separate letters in my possession, these men declare that their father is alone the inventor of the pedal. Let me add that I just received the older son (Henry) in Bar-le-Duc, and he confirmed to me one more time that his brother Ernest had absolutely nothing to do with the invention."

Henry perhaps gambled that if the city approved the original plan to honor his father alone, the patronage committee would be forced to follow suit and drop its compromise proposal. Indeed, on 11 March, Busselot went before the city council requesting approval for the original Michaux bust and 500 francs towards its erection. He spoke of a "patriotic duty" to remember this native son in light of the German veneration of Drais. Curiously, he gave the date of invention as 1855—even though Henry had previously suggested a much later date. Perhaps its inclusion was meant to appease Baudry—since it was the one detail he had consistently given.

But any hope that a Pierre Michaux memorial could be bulldozed through the city council was soon dashed. Neither Baudry nor Giffard showed any willingness to stray from their fragile compromise. Giffard, however, offered an olive branch to Henry by paying him token homage. He reprinted the mayor's letter to *L'Eclair* and sang its praises: "Now there's an excellent and worthy letter, which sums up the Michaux question in just a few lines, in a categorical manner, and the son's testimony reveals exactly what I had suspected all along."[45] But despite the flattery, Giffard refused to budge on the joint memorial, noting that it would be unwise to reopen the harmful debate. Shared homage, he insisted, was still the best solution since "it is also indisputable that Ernest Michaux was the first and best jockey of the wooden beast which left his paternal workshop."[46]

So the committee stood by the compromise, but one problem obviously remained: it had proclaimed Ernest the inventor in "186-," whereas the city had approved a bust of his father for an alleged invention in 1855. Something had to give. On 18 March, de Ricaudy departed for another visit to Bar-le-Duc, ostensibly to help select a memorial site.[47] But there seems little doubt that his true mission was to resolve the historical impasse. Indeed, shortly after de Ricaudy's visit, the mayor summoned Henry Michaux to discuss the discrepancies once more.[48]

This time, however, Busselot evidently leaned heavily on Henry to accept the committee's compromise. On 21 March 1893, Henry at last complied, sending a conciliatory clarification to *L'Eclair*. For the first time, he revealed that his brother Ernest had built the first bicycle, after all. In March 1861, he purportedly modified a broken draisine belonging to a Mr. Brunel—but Henry was quick to point out that Ernest was merely following his father's instructions (this belated and suspect account, of course, has been a staple of cycle histories ever since).

Giffard again expressed his appreciation to Henry for "a dialog whose authenticity is most enlightening."[49] Clearly pleased that his compromise plan finally had a historical foundation, he mused: "This categorical letter has the double advantage of refuting certain absurd tales and specifying, historically, the exact way in which the pedal was adopted by Michaux and his son." At last, the way appeared clear for the inauguration of the joint Michaux memorial in late 1893.

But new hurdles lay ahead. Indeed, Henry still had not actually endorsed the committee's historical premise. For whereas the official account had Ernest conceiving the idea and Pierre executing it, Henry coyly switched their roles. Thus, while conceding a role for Ernest, he nonetheless salvaged the greater glory for his father.

The gambit failed, however, to placate Baudry. Infuriated that Pierre Michaux had crept back in as the inventor, he withdrew his support for the compromise memorial. In April 1893 he wrote another inflammatory diatribe assailing Pierre Michaux, again drawing on Olivier's support. He also reverted to his position at the start of the dispute; i.e., that Ernest alone had been the true inventor in 1855.[50]

Baudry's renewed offensive drew yet another defensive letter from Henry published in *Vélocipède Illustré* on 30 April 1893. This time, he explicitly refuted the traditional 1855 date (although he failed to explain why the mayor had also given that year after consulting with him about the invention). Henry instead reiterated his recent clarification that the actual year was 1861, and that his father was the one, true inventor. He even offered as proof yet another revelation: Mr. Brunel, whose velocipede had prompted the breakthrough, still owned the historic front wheel.[51]

But the renewed wrangling had taken its toll. The patronage committee, dispirited and short on funds, announced that the dedication would be suspended until the following year.[52] That delay, however, actually helped matters, for it allowed Henry's revisions to sink in while the objections faded. By early 1894, Henry's new account had become standard fare in the French press, and the nation's major cycle manufacturers finally felt comfortable embracing the Michaux memorial cause.[53] One by one they rallied, and the memorial was finally prepared. The lavish inaugural ceremonies on the final September weekend of 1894, which included a race from Paris to Bar-le-Duc, proved an unqualified success.

Not everyone, however, was satisfied with the historical outcome. Aimé Olivier fired off a booklet entitled *Les Inventeurs du Vélocipède: René Olivier (1863–1870)*. He reasserted that his deceased brother had been the true developer and lobbed a cryptic parting shot at Henry, intimating that neither Pierre nor Ernest Michaux was in fact the original inventor.

Another discontented figure was Fr. Louis Lallement, the son of the original patentee, who had died a pauper in Boston, U.S.A. in 1891, just as the Michaux campaign percolated. Although as a young cleric he had kept a low profile during the campaign, he let his objections be known in later years. In 1909, for example, he responded to an article from the children's magazine *Pêle Mêle* on the origins of the cycle.[54] It gave the then standard account casting Michaux as the original inventor, and Lallement as the opportunist who had tried in vain to usurp the former's idea. Louis sent a letter of protest to the editor, along with supporting materials.

The author of the article, André Savignon, responded with a formal retraction which noted in part: "In America, the opinion of knowledgeable persons is unanimous in recognizing Lallement as the inventor of the velocipede. Due to an irony of circumstances which is altogether too frequent in the history of inventors, Lallement did not find his compatriots so disposed to render him justice."[55] And in a private letter to Father Lallement, dated 14 June 1911, he apologized for having offended the priest's "legitimate filial instincts," adding: "as a publicist, I

Fig. 23.2. The Michaux memorial as finally erected.

am astonished that the 'Michaux error' has gained such broad circulation in France and is held so tenaciously."[56]

Conclusion: A Flawed Outcome

The early French cycle press failed to produce a clear account of the bicycle's origins, an omission which would hamper the patriotic push years later to crown a French inventor. In particular, although Michaux had initially billed himself as the original inventor when introducing his first commercial machine in 1867, he had never detailed his claim, despite his close contacts with the press. Nor did he or his investors, the Olivier brothers, ever directly challenge the well-known Lallement counter-claim.

Instead, they were evasive about the origins of their new product, even denying that it contained any fundamental "core" invention. To be sure, the 2-wheeler had been tried before—and the new machine did resemble the old draisine, at least superficially. Yet if Michaux himself had indeed applied the pedal, as later claimed, why would he, of all people, downplay—even deny—the originality of his own invention?

Indeed, the actions of Michaux and Olivier belied their own "company line." Clearly, they themselves had well anticipated the potential of the bicycle's novelty, carefully planning their cycle operation over several years before finally commercializing their product.[57] Moreover, the fact that they falsely claimed in 1867 to have secured a patent covering the pedal system clearly shows that they were fully aware of its basic originality and value.

True, a direct Michaux claim was ostensibly supplied in 1893 with the testimony of a surviving son who claimed to have witnessed the invention as a 7-year-old in his father's shop. And Henry did recast the murky 1855 claim, which had been popular in French literature for at least a decade, into a somewhat more plausible account involving 1861. Yet a close examination reveals that he waffled repeatedly on the details, and that his unsubstantiated assertions lack basic credibility. Evidently, his true ambition was to manipulate the process for material gain.

Indeed, barring the unlikely discovery of new, independent support, his century-old account of the bicycle's invention and initial development should now be discounted. Rather, our attention should shift to the as-yet viable Lallement claim for 1863.[58] With continued and persistent inquiry, we may yet acquire a fuller understanding of the bicycle's debut so thoroughly obscured a century ago.

Notes

1. Karl Drais von Sauerbronn, the German-born inventor of the kick-propelled Draisine, which he patented in France in 1818.
2. *La Révue du Sport Vélocipèdique*, *Vélocipède Illustré*, *L'Evenement* and *Le Vélo*.
3. *Le Vélo*. 4 February 1892.
4. The same advertisement, which read "Michaux inventeur" also ran in the *Courrier de la Drôme* on 7 December 1867.
5. French patent 80637, dated 24 April 1868.
6. U.S. Patent 59915, dated 22 November 1866.
7. Confirmed by the City of London passenger list of 25 July 1865.
8. Baudry de Saunier acknowledged the Lallement patent in his 1891 work *Histoire Générale de la Vélocipèdie*, but professed not to know whether Lallement or Michaux was the original inventor.
9. *Boston Daily Advertiser*. 4 February 1869.
10. *Bicycling News*. 18 August 1876.
11. *Paris Caprice*. 28 April 1868.
12. Duharme, Ernest. *Les Merveilles de la Locomotion*. Paris, 1874.
13. Conceivably, Michaux could have built this 1855 transitional machine, although we have no evidence that he was involved in velocipede production at that time. The well-used 1865 wooden bicycle was presumably an Olivier original. Aimé Olivier alludes to a bicycle trip across France in the summer of 1865 (*La Nature*, 1892, p. 155), and Keizo Kobayshi has found corresponding references in the diary of Olivier's father, Jules (Kobayashi, Keizo. *Histoire du Vélocipède de Drais à Michaux*. Paris, 1993. p. 92).
14. *Le Sport Vélocipèdique*. 20 January 1883.
15. Ibid., 6 October 1883.
16. Ibid., 17 September 1881.
17. Author's own research.

18. Conference held 31 March 1888 organized by M. Garsonnin.
19. *L'Industrie Vélocipèdique.* September 1892 (p. 242).
20. Notably, Pierre Giffard, then editor of *Le Petit Journal.*
21. Ironically, it was Giffard who ultimately steered the project to a successful conclusion.
22. Henry also stated that Lesclide deserved a memorial himself for his role as the first developer. This title was ultimately consigned, however, to the Michaux memorial.
23. Révue Mensuelle du Touring Club de France, October 1892.
24. I have found no record of Richard Lesclide supporting the calls for a Michaux memorial.
25. *L'Echo de Lyon.* 30 September 1892.
26. *Vélocipède Illustré. 27 October 1892.*
27. Ernest Michaux patented a miniature steam engine on 11 February 1864 (French patent 61858).
28. René Olivier died in a carriage accident in 1875.
29. *La France Cycliste.* 10 November 1892.
30. De Ricaudy published his own account of the invention in *L'Evenement* of 26 September 1892. After interviewing Francisque Michaux and Aimé Olivier, among others, he concluded that Pierre Michaux had invented the bicycle in 1863.
31. Michaux did have a patent before 1867: French patent 23576 covering a set of shears, dated 19 May 1855.
32. *Le Vélo.* 21 February 1893.
33. *Le Vélo.* 22 February 1893.
34. *Vélocipède Illustré.* 27 October 1892.
35. I recently found Lesclide's letter to Busselot in the departmental archives in Bar-le-Duc.
36. Unfortunately, the Michaux file did not contain any additional correspondence from Lesclide.
37. *Le Vélo.* 2 March 1893.
38. Henry Michaux's original letter is in the memorial file at the departmental archives of Bar-le-Duc.
39. On 5 March 1893 *Le Vélo* announced that it was taking over the project.
40. *Le Vélo.* 4 March 1893.
41. Ibid., 4 March 1893.
42. Ibid., 7 March 1893.
43. Ibid., 8 March 1893.
44. Ibid., 5 March 1893.
45. Ibid., 9 March 1893.
46. We have, in fact, no substantiated accounts of Ernest riding a bicycle.
47. *Le Vélo.* 19 March 1893.
48. In his 21 March letter to *L'Eclair*, Henry mentioned having been summoned by Busselot.
49. *Le Vélo.* 28 March 1893.
50. *Journal des Vélocipédistes.* 29 April 1893.
51. Brunel's wheel was apparently never presented to the public, however.
52. *Le Vélo.* 25 April 1893.
53. Michelin, for example, contributed 200 francs as announced in *Le Vélo* on 15 November 1893.
54. *Le Pêle-Mêle.* 11 June 1911 (pp. 11–12)
55. *Le Pêle-Mêle.* 16 July 1911 (p. 10).
56. Copy of this letter furnished by Pierre Durand of Pont-à-Mousson.
57. *Vélocipède Illustré* noted in its issue of 10 June 1869 that the Olivier's had devoted "long years" of preparation before finally introducing their product in 1867.
58. As stated in his testimony given in May 1882 in *Pope Manufacturing vs. McKee & Harrington*, discovered in 1992 by the author.

John McVey

24. The Hoopdriver Recycle

Some twenty years ago the BBC serialised *The Wheels of Chance*[1] with an actor reading an edited version of H. G. Wells' story. It tells the story of Mr. Hoopdriver, a draper's assistant, disparagingly described as a counter jumper in a large establishment in Putney in 1896. Hoopdriver is fully aware of his lowly position in life. He spends most of his waking hours in the shop, and lives in the dormitory above. He is also expected to make an appearance in church on Sundays. In his own words: "No other kind of men stand such hours. A drunken bricklayer's a king to it."

Hoopdriver has ambition. He wishes to escape, but as the story begins, his vision is limited to a two week touring holiday in the New Forest, an approved and temporary release from slavery. He purchases an elderly cross-frame safety cycle: "An old fashioned affair with a fork instead of a diamond frame, a cushioned tyre, well worn at the hind wheel, and a gross weight all on of perhaps three and forty pounds."

Hilarious descriptions follow of Hoopdriver's attempts to master the machine, and he sets off on his adventures still a barely competent rider.

A chance remark by an early rising nanny he passes sets the scene for his impending adventure: "Look at the gentleman on his bicycle."

Gentleman, not a counter jumper, but gentleman!

Hoopdriver sees young drapers in a shop window preparing for the days toil: "Even so had Hoopdriver been on the previous day. But now, was he not a bloomin' dook, palpably in the sight of common men."

Hoopdriver's lack of riding skills coupled with his new self image of "bloomin' dook" enables him to fall off at the feet of a very upper-class young lady, who kindly bandages his injured hand. Truth gradually penetrates Hoopdriver's limited experience of life and he realises that the girl, "the lady in grey," is being lured to a fate worse than death by another cyclist, a bounder. Hoopdriver rescues the girl, steals the bounder's (superior) bicycle, and is himself rescued and eventually caught by the girl's family and friends, all on bicycles.

There were many references to towns and villages as the characters made their journey, and even pubs and coffee houses were mentioned, often by name. The romantic atmosphere of the book was skilfully adapted to the radio and enhanced by the artistry of the narrator. The result was a welcome daily escape from the misery of a Coventry student slum in wintertime, and from the tedium of endless set books, essays, seminars, and, worst of all, examinations.

An idea was born

Wells seemed to be inviting the reader to follow in his wheel tracks, and the New Forest in August sounded attractive. I promised myself that, one day, one day, I'd buy an old bike, like Hoopdriver's, and retrace the route. How many of the pubs would still be there? Could I stay in the same hotels? The story ended, the

Fig. 24.1. Illustration from The Wheels of Chance.

essays continued, and for nearly 15 years the idea was almost forgotten.

At the 1993 Banbury Run Autojumble I looked for and found a cheap cycle motor to restore. It was a Trojan mini motor of about 1950. There was, unusually for a motorcycle event, a derelict but complete Penny Farthing "for restoration." I looked, went away, came back, decided against it, but the bug had bitten.

Realising that I would need a suitable bicycle on which to hang the mini motor, I bought a very rusty Gents sit-up-and-beg from a barn loft in Newport Pagnell. This was carried down some near vertical steps and thrown into the rear of the family hatchback. Only when wheeling it towards my workshop did the truth dawn. This was a very large bicycle. The mini motor was forgotten, and Hoopdriver, or at least the vestiges of Hoopdriver, remembered. This seemed to be the machine for the trip, a 28-in. double cross bar Gents with 28-in. wheels. It was in fact early 30s, had seen Army service, and was just too big for me to ride comfortably. My wife named it "Sir Walter," assuming it to be a Raleigh. I renamed it "Desperate Dan" as it seemed the sort of machine my childhood hero might have owned. It was used for training runs in Northamptonshire until a more suitable machine could be found.

Research—Planning the Recycle

The logical first step was to find a copy of the book and read it. This proved extremely difficult. While I retained a basic memory of the story, I had never actually read the book and could not remember the title. My local library and secondhand bookshops were unable to help, as were the BBC. Finally my local bicycle shop proprietor told me about the Veteran Cycle Club. I joined, and received some helpful booklets on the subject, and a yearbook[2] which contained a list of the club's library books, and there it was, as expected, *The Wheels of Chance* by H. G. Wells (1896).

Finding a suitable bicycle did not prove difficult. A club member sold me a circa 1900 "Gamages" diamond-frame safety. This appears to be virtually identical to the rovers used by John Foster Fraser and his colleagues, as described in *Round the World on a Wheel*, 1897[3] and by Bechamel and later by Hoopdriver in *The Wheels of Chance*. A cross-frame safety would have been the perfect choice, but I was unable to obtain one in time for the run.

The bicycle used was a circa 1900 "Gamages" 26-in. diamond-framed safety cycle, with 28-in. wheels—probably made by Hobarts of Coventry. As bought, the cycle was rideable but poorly restored, having had paint sloshed over it while it was still rusty. Parts which should have been nickel plated were similarly daubed, and it looked pretty awful.

The frame was very pitted, so it was shot blasted to remove all the paint and rust, and polished with a smooth aluminium hydroxide (like emery paper) disc in an angle grinder. It was then treated with phosphoric acid, a rust killer, and then powder coated black, and baked. All other metal parts were ground back to good metal, cupro-nickel plated, and polished. The assembled frame looked very nice.

The brakes were a problem. The front is of an archaic type known as a "plunger." As the name suggests, when the brake is applied, a rubber block is "plunged" down on the front tyre with no discernible retardation whatsoever. The rear brake didn't suffer from the same problem, however. There wasn't one. Road conditions in the 1890s meant that the cyclist was most unlikely to meet much traffic and he or she was supposed to stop by using the aforementioned plunger, and by "back-pedalling," there being no freewheel device. The pedals go round all the time, and the theory is that by pedalling backwards the bike slows down. I have never mastered this technique, so decided to use a coaster hub. This looks like an ordinary wheel hub, but incorporates a freewheel and a back-pedal brake that actually works.

The Route

A first reading of *The Wheels of Chance* revealed that there was considerably more detail about the first half of the journey than the second. The hundred or so miles between Putney and Chichester are liberally strewn with inviting pubs and coffee houses, while for the next hundred there are very few landmarks.

This led to some speculation. Did Wells actually make the trip? He claims to have been one of the participants in the adventure: "We sat on incredibly hard horsehair things having anti-macassars tied to their backs by means of lemon coloured bows."

This is, however, Wells' only reference to himself in the story. It seems as if he was more familiar with the London to Chichester part of the journey than the rest. My father-in-law, Derek Hallifax, has suggested a possible explanation: "Opposite Chichester Cathedral is the Dolphin and Anchor hotel. Apparently they were once two separate inns, both dating from about 1662. The

'Independent Post Coach' company ran a service from the Anchor to London on Tuesday, Thursday, and Saturday leaving at 8 a.m. and passing through (note this route) Midhurst, Haslemere, Godalming, Guildford, Cobham and Kingston, over Putney Bridge, to Ludgate Hill in London; returning on Monday and Wednesday and Friday. The driver, who was also one of the proprietors of the coach firm, was George Neal, who was buried at St. Pancras Church in Chichester in 1832. H. G. Wells' mother was Sarah Neal, 'descended from innkeepers and coach masters.' So perhaps Wells made this journey by coach a few times, while doing some family visiting."

Derek Hallifax, on hearing of my plans to recycle Wells' route, suggested the idea of sponsorship for the charity Tools for Self Reliance. TFSR recycles obsolete hand tools and sends them to Africa. Derek volunteered to research the route and to drive a support vehicle during the actual event. He found that a surprising number of landmarks still exist: the "Marquis of Granby" in Esher, where Hoopdriver consumed "Burton and biscuit and cheese," the "Angel" at Midhurst, where the young lady in grey and her companion stayed. The "tea, toy and tobacco shop" is now probably the coffee shop next door to the Angel and still has "the cheerful sign of a teapot" both above the door and giant size, in the window. This cafe, recently redecorated, boasts a mediaeval wall painting and a vague legend that Wells once stayed there.

The Run

On my last training run, a week before Hoopdriver proper, I did about 50 miles in temperatures in the 80s. I developed food poisoning from a pub lunch en route, and it was doubtful I would be fit to ride on 9 July. However, by the day before the run strength had returned sufficiently to make an attempt. I unloaded the bicycle in Putney and set off to push up Putney Hill, as it says in the book.

The Marquis of Granby was my first stop for a quick lemonade. This hotel still looks very 19th-century and is surrounded by trees and golf greens—a very pleasant spot. Pressed on for lunch at the Talbot, Ripley (The Golden Dragon) where the landlord welcomed us. Guildford High Street was easily recognisable from the illustration in the book. Pausing to cool off became more and more frequent as the temperatures soared. I found my (lost) support team watching cricket on Milford Heath. Had my photograph taken by the railway arch, where Bechamel argues with the lady in grey. I was aiming for Haslemere but the heat was unrelenting and we stayed at the Wheatsheaf just outside Haslemere, but ate a terrific meal at an ancient inn, the Swan, in Haslemere itself. I cannot recommend it enough. Hoopdriver, as we now refer to the bicycle, was given a place of honour for the night—leaning against the bar in the "Functions Room."

After breakfast in a beautiful Italianate dining room, I followed Hoopdriver's winding route beyond Haslemere. By far the most memorable part of the route for me is the long winding climb through warm, damp, dense forest, which kept off the blistering heat. Arriving at the top of a very large "down," I set off for the descent. I don't remember pedalling for the next two or three miles. I cannot better Wells' description of this experience: "A sudden wonderful gratitude possessed him. The glory of the holidays had resumed its sway with a sudden accession of splendour. At the crest of the hill he put his feet upon the footrests, and went down that excellent descent. A new delight was in his eyes, quite over and above the pleasure of rushing through the keen sweet morning air. He reached out and twanged his bell in sheer happiness."

At Midhurst we peered into the Angel, and lunched in the cafe next door. I was photographed standing under the hanging teapot.

On to Goodwood, a high and treeless down with fabulous views from the top. This was probably the hottest part of a record-breaking weekend. If the long push up had me near fainting, the second long fast descent of the day into Chichester made it worth the effort, but the coaster hub was never quite the same.

Monday

An early start from Chichester had me in Bognor before 9 a.m. I spent one minute on the beach and set off west again. Finding the road disappeared into the sea at Itchenor, I paid the ferryman to take me, and Hoopdriver, to Bosham (burial place of King Canute's daughter). This is a delightful part of the world, and well worth a visit by the cyclist—it's all dead flat.

Wednesday

Set off on a dreary sticky day to "do the Portsmouth bit." As the weather was poor, and the route frankly tedious, I decided to go for a longer run than usual. Hayling, Havant, Portsmouth, Fareham, Wicken, Bishops Waltham, Twyford, Winchester, Stockbridge, Idmiston.

Friday

After a day at home I set off for Salisbury and Sixpenny Handley. The hill outside Salisbury is something special, but the constant whizzing past of big diesels as you trudge toward the top cannot be recommended. "Trudge" because with no gears one would be inclined to wobble, and one wobble in modern traffic could be one too many. I was repeatedly appalled by the standard of some drivers throughout the trip.

On this road was a pub. I hesitate to name it. I had a first class pint and a first class English breakfast at 1 p.m. and was severely bitten by fleas! This 17th-century building is the first pub after that awful Salisbury hill, and I feel Hoopdriver and Jessie (the lady in grey) must have stopped there. It does not seem to have been decorated (or cleaned?) since new brewers took it on in 1897. I suspect it to be the site of Hoopdriver's fight. It is about two miles (all uphill) outside Salisbury, not Winchester as it is in the book, where we were quite unable to find a pub, or even a building, on both ancient and modern Stockbridge roads, or a place called Wallenstock.

Saturday

The section past Blandford was far more pleasant. As I left the town I watched a peregrine falcon soaring. It seemed a good omen. A beautiful tree-lined avenue runs past Badbury Rings.

On approaching Ringwood, the previously fine cycle track disappeared in a dreadful roadworks. I pushed and carried the bicycle some two miles into Ringwood on the central reservation, unable to get off through the traffic. The westerly flow finally stopped and let me cross. A mile outside Ringwood I saw another falcon.

Sunday

The last day dawned, in fact the only part of the route that really goes through the New Forest. It was another beautiful day with only a few miles to ride. Just short of the Rufus Stone, I changed into my Hoopdriver outfit—Norfolk jacket, brogues—and whizzed down the hill to the "Stone." There were numbers of cyclists there waiting for me. We were duly photgraphed, and set off to the Sir Walter Tyrell, the "Rufus Stone Hotel" of the story. There is a new building now, but the old pub lives on as a house next door.

Festivities followed, but the ride was over. The old bike had done well and the rider was well pleased with his performance, exactly a year after early retirement due to illness.

Conclusion

Clearly we amateurs have only scratched the surface. There is far more information to be found, I am quite sure. There is a great deal of Wells in Hoopdriver, but also in Bechamel. The book is unsatisfactory in that it leaves the reader wondering what happens next. Does Hoopdriver study as he promises Jessie, and escape from drapery? As Wells himself did? We do not know.

Anyone who has enjoyed a book and regretted the end of a story will understand the attraction of attempting a "recycle." Much has changed since Hoopdriver's holiday. Two years later came the first motorised bicycles and the first successful attempts to glide and then fly. Twenty years later WWI brought an end to the rigid class structure described by Wells. But much of his route is still there, some parts virtually unchanged, and still capable of giving pleasure.

Notes

1. H. G. Wells, *The Wheels of Chance: A Holiday Adventure* (J. M. Dent and Sons, 1896).
2. Veteran Cycle Club *Yearbook 1993-94* (Quorum Technical Services Ltd.).
3. John Foster Fraser, *Round the World on a Wheel* (Futura, 1899).

Other Titles Available from Bicycle Books

Title	Author	US Price
All Terrain Biking	Jim Zarka	$7.95
The Backroads of Holland	Helen Colijn	$12.95
The Bicycle Commuting Book	Rob van der Plas	$7.95
The Bicycle Fitness Book	Rob van der Plas	$7.95
The Bicycle Repair Book	Rob van der Plas	$9.95
Bicycle Repair Step by Step (color)*	Rob van der Plas	$14.95
Bicycle Technology	Rob van der Plas	$16.95
Bicycle Touring International	Kameel Nasr	$18.95
The Bicycle Touring Manual	Rob van der Plas	$16.95
Bicycling Fuel	Richard Rafoth, M.D.	$9.95
Cycling Europe	Nadine Slavinski	$12.95
Cycling France	Jerry Simpson	$12.95
Cycling Kenya	Kathleen Bennett	$12.95
Cycling the San Francisco Bay Area	Carol O'Hare	$12.95
Cycling the U.S. Parks	Jim Clark	$12.95
In High Gear (hardcover)	Samuel Abt	$21.95
The High Performance Heart	Maffetone & Mantell	$10.95
Major Taylor (hardcover)	Andrew Ritchie	$19.95
The Mountain Bike Book	Rob van der Plas	$10.95
Mountain Bike Magic (color)	Rob van der Plas	$14.95
Mountain Bike Maintenance (color)	Rob van der Plas	$10.95
Mountain Bikes: Maint. & Repair*	Stevenson & Richards	$22.50
Mountain Bike Racing (hardcover)*	Burney & Gould	$22.50
The New Bike Book	Jim Langley	$4.95
Roadside Bicycle Repairs (color)	Rob van der Plas	$7.95
Tour of the Forest Bike Race (color)	H. E. Thomson	$9.95
Bicycle History, 4th. Conference Proceedings		$45.00
Bicycle History, 5th. Conference Proceedigns		$45.00

Buy our books at your local book store or bike shop.

Book stores can obtain these titles for you from our book trade distributor (National Book Network for the USA), bike shops directly from us. If you have difficulty obtaining our books elsewhere, we will be pleased to supply them by mail, but we must add $2.50 postage and handling (and California Sales Tax if mailed to a California address). For Priority Mail, add $1.00 per book. Prepayment by check (or credit card information) must be included with your order. Actual postage incurred will be charged on orders from outside the U.S (all such orders will be sent surface mail unless Air Mail specified when ordering).

Bicycle Books, Inc.
PO Box 2038
Mill Valley CA 94941
Tel.: (415) 665-8214
Fax (415) 753-8572

In Britain: Bicycle Books
463 Ashley Road
Poole, Dorset BH14 0AX
Tel.: (0202) 715349
Fax: (0202) 736191

* Books marked thus not available from Bicycle Books in the U.K.